17660

942.86

Stockton - Billi
LIBRARY
Technical Col

Stockton & Billingham College

T021295

19. APR
13.
-6.
-8.
-7.
22.

D1625912

DURHAM

THE KING'S ENGLAND

Edited by Arthur Mee

In 41 Volumes

THE KING'S ENGLAND

DURHAM

By
ARTHUR MEE

fully revised and edited by
B. BERRYMAN

Illustrated with new photographs by
A. F. KERSTING

HODDER AND STOUGHTON

COPYRIGHT © 1969 BY HODDER AND STOUGHTON LTD
AND THE EXECUTORS OF THE LATE ARTHUR MEE

ILLUSTRATIONS © 1969 BY A. F. KERSTING

FIRST PUBLISHED 1953
NEW EDITION REVISED AND RESET 1969

SBN 340 00080 5

Stockton - Billingham
LIBRARY
Technical College

17660
942.8

Printed in Great Britain
for Hodder and Stoughton Ltd.,
St. Paul's House, Warwick Lane, London, E.C.4,
by Richard Clay (The Chaucer Press), Ltd.,
Bungay, Suffolk

INTRODUCTION TO REVISED EDITION

IN preparing the new edition of THE KING'S ENGLAND care has been taken to bring the books up to date as far as possible within the changes which have taken place since the series was originally planned. In addition the editor has made his revisions both in text and illustrations with a view to keeping the price of the books within reasonable limits, in spite of greatly increased production costs. But throughout the book, it has been the editor's special care to preserve Mr Arthur Mee's original intention of providing something more than just another guide book giving archaeological, ecclesiastical, and topographical information.

In the case of every town and village mentioned in the King's England Series, it has been the intention not only to indicate its position on the map, but to convey something of its atmosphere. And the biographical selections about people who are ever associated with that part of the country in which they lived, or who are commemorated in the parish church—which was such a popular feature of the former edition—have been retained and in some cases supplemented.

The present editor of *Durham* is indebted to Mr T. E. C. Walker and Mr S. Warner, who compiled the first edition.

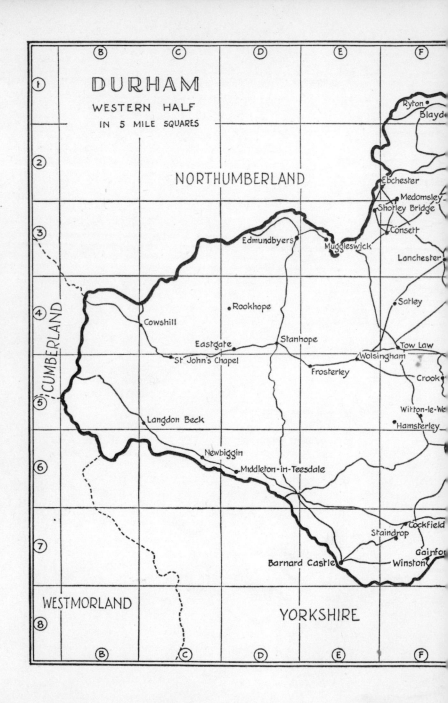

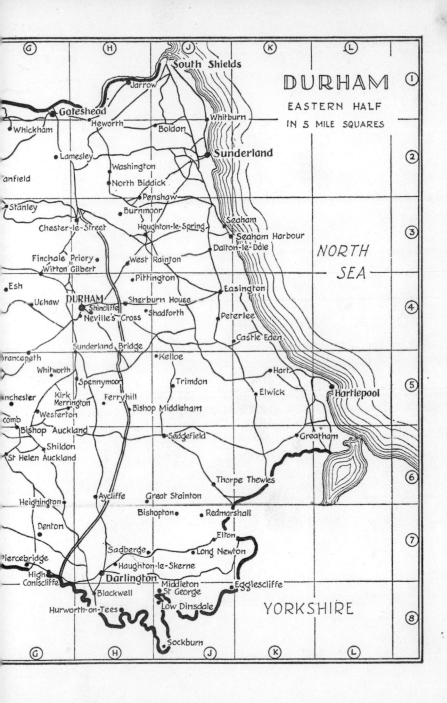

DURHAM
EASTERN HALF
IN 5 MILE SQUARES

NORTH SEA

YORKSHIRE

South Shields
Jarrow
Gateshead
Whickham
Heworth
Boldon
Whitburn
Lamesley
Washington
Sunderland
Stanley
North Biddick
Penshaw
Burnmoor
Chester-le-Street
Houghton-le-Spring
Seaham
Seaham Harbour
Dalton-le-Dale
Finchale Priory
Witton Gilbert
West Rainton
Esh
Pittington
Easington
Uchaw
DURHAM
Sherburn House
Shincliffe
Shadforth
Peterlee
Neville's Cross
Castle Eden
Sunderland Bridge
Kelloe
Brancepeth
Hart
Whitworth
Spennymoor
Trimdon
Kirk Merrington
Ferryhill
Elwick
Hartlepool
Wolsingham
Westerton
Bishop Middleham
Bishop Auckland
Sedgefield
Greatham
Shildon
St Helen Auckland
Thorpe Thewles
Aycliffe
Great Stainton
Heighington
Bishopton
Redmarshall
Denton
Elton
Sadberge
Long Newton
Piercebridge
Haughton-le-Skerne
High Coniscliffe
Darlington
Middleton St George
Egglescliffe
Blackwell
Low Dinsdale
Hurworth-on-Tees
Sockburn

LIST OF ILLUSTRATIONS

DURHAM

INTRODUCTION

FEW English counties have a more remarkable history than has County Durham, yet few are less generally known and appreciated. Durham is not a large county, but within its confines it has landscape of surprising contrasts, natural and man-made; it is a landscape which reflects an eventful story, as the persistent explorer will soon discover.

Least changed by the hand of man, and far away from the ancient cathedral and the vast coalfield which have been the mainsprings of Durham's development, are the northern Pennines, where the boundaries of five counties meet. Cumberland, Westmorland, Northumberland, Yorkshire, and Durham all have a share in these bleak fells; and it is on Burnhope Seat, a little less than two and a half thousand feet above sea level, that Durham carves itself out from its neighbours. This, in a sense, is mid-Britain, for here Cape Wrath is as close as Beachy Head, the Solway Firth as near as the North Sea.

From this westerly height the boundaries of County Durham diverge eastward until they are identified with the River Tees to the south, and with the Derwent, and then the Tyne, to the north. The land slopes to the east, towards the North Sea which it meets some 40 miles away with a coastline of much variety.

In the wild and barren Pennine fells Durham's chief rivers have their source. The Tees springs into life, a mere trickle, on the slopes of Cross Fell in Cumberland; the Derwent rises inconspicuously in Northumberland; but the Wear is born a river, at Wearhead, where the Burnhope and Killhope burns, swollen with the waters of innumerable moorland streams, tumble down their deep-cut valleys to meet and mingle. Durham can lay no claim to the upper reaches of the Tyne, for its tributaries belong entirely to Northumberland.

The Wear is Durham's own river, and to follow its course from Wearhead to the sea at Sunderland is to discover the Durham landscape in all its variety. The fells which surround the head of the river still bear the marks of lead-mining which flourished in these parts a century ago; now, only abandoned railway tracks, and the deserted ruins of cottages, mines, and smelting mills remain, and the scene has an air of desolation.

I

In Weardale itself the landscape becomes more genial. Grey stone walls enclose the green pastures, trees shade the river as it broadens out and ripples over a stony bed, and the road which threads the valley passes through a succession of small stone-built villages. On either side the fields rise to meet the high heather moors which stretch for miles, south to Teesdale and north to the Derwent Valley. The dale has its industries—modern cement works at Eastgate, limestone quarries around Stanhope, and steelworks at Wolsingham —but the rural aspect prevails.

The small towns of Stanhope, Frosterley, and Wolsingham all stand on the north bank of the river, their grey ruggedness softened by the surrounding fields and woodland. Beyond Wolsingham the river, now wide and shallow, bears south-east. Still the hills rise on either side, but more modestly than the fells and moors of the west. To the south is a delightful land of forest, field and common, watered by rushing streams, and with quiet cross-country roads meandering towards Teesdale. Raby Castle, in its fine park, lies on the lower slopes looking across to Yorkshire.

North of the Wear we reach the western edge of the coalfield, where colliery villages mushroomed little more than a century ago. Despite the scars of mining around Crook and Tow Law, it is a pleasant district. From the gorse-lined roads which cross northwards to Lanchester and the industrial north-west beyond, and eastward to the city of Durham, there are attractive views over wooded hills and the little valleys of the Browney and Deerness rivers.

As the Wear flows on past the picturesque village of Witton-le-Wear the hills recede and the valley broadens. This is south-west Durham, and at last industry begins to mar the scene. All around Bishop Auckland coal was intensively mined until recent years, and the area has its share of drab pit villages and derelict mine-workings. Yet here, as in other parts of the coalfield, a revolution is taking place. Spoil heaps are being cleared or grassed over, derelict land is being reclaimed, modern houses are replacing the ill-planned and hurriedly built cottages of the 19th century mining boom, and the working towns—Shildon, Bishop Auckland, Newton Aycliffe, and Spennymoor—are busy with new industries.

Here too there are compensations. North and south of the ridge which rises eastward from Bishop Auckland the land is spread out like a living map, with all the contrasting features of the Durham landscape. Town and country, farm and factory, industrial waste and scattered woodland share the scene, with Durham Cathedral visible to the north, and, on a clear day, the sea to the east. The

Wear, twisting and turning, follows its course past the incomparable Saxon church at Escomb and Auckland Castle, the bishop's palace, and meanders on through quiet country, surprisingly rural with industry so close at hand.

Then, in its most dramatic gesture, almost encircling the rock on which Durham Cathedral and Castle stand, it asserts its importance as the county's principal river and flows on between richly wooded banks past the beautiful ruins of Finchale Priory, past proud Lumley Castle, and through the glorious parkland of Lambton Castle.

And now, quite suddenly, the Wear changes in character and becomes an important industrial waterway, its banks crowded with docks and shipyards. So to Sunderland and, within sight of the Saxon monastery church of Monkwearmouth, majestically to the open North Sea.

The course of the Tees is less varied but not less interesting. Rising on Cross Fell, it has many miles of Pennine heights to traverse before it becomes Durham's southern boundary, and Yorkshire's northern. With this increased significance it flows on purposefully to the new reservoir at Cow Green, then launches itself dramatically over the volcanic rocks of the Whin Sill in the waterfalls of Caldron Snout and High Force. The river banks between the falls are in season gay with wild flowers; the wildness of the upper reaches recedes, but still the moorlands beckon, and roads struggle over the heights of Langdon and Bollihope Commons to drop steeply into Weardale.

Downstream the valley is green and beautifully wooded; mediacval stone bridges span the river at Eggleston and Barnard Castle, where the castle ruins on their rock dominate the scene. Now the hills are left behind, and the Tees flows through quiet farming lowlands which rise gradually to the hills around Bishop Auckland. The north bank of the river is graced by the charming villages of Gainford, Winston, and Piercebridge, less rugged, more snug than the villages of the western dales.

As if reluctant to reach the industrial east, our river now takes an involved course, avoiding Darlington, and meandering through secluded low-lying country with more delightful villages—Hurworth, Neasham, Dinsdale, and Middleton One Row. At Yarm (the Yorkshire town which looks across to the Durham village of Egglescliffe) the Tees is wide and deep enough to be navigable, and after two or three more rural miles it succumbs to the vast industrial complex of Teesside.

The Tees was formerly Durham's southern boundary right to the sea at Teesmouth, but administrative changes in 1968 severed Stockton, Norton, and Billingham from the county and transferred these towns, whose history is part of the Durham story, to the new County Borough of Teesside in the North Riding of Yorkshire. Consequently the county boundary now skirts the northern edge of Teesside to rejoin the river as it opens out to the North Sea.

Durham's northern boundary zigzags across moorland heights to join the Beldon burn shortly before it mingles with the Nookton burn to become the River Derwent. For the next 16 miles or so the Derwent separates Durham from Northumberland, at first cutting a deep and narrow valley through delightfully unspoiled country, with stretches of pretty woodland along its banks. So to the beautiful Derwent Reservoir, and there on the eastern skyline are the stark chimneys of Consett's ironworks. The river, however, pursues a rural course below the northern edge of the elevated table-land of north-west Durham, pocked and scarred by two centuries of coal-mining, but with some pleasant countryside nevertheless. Below Ebchester the boundary strikes north to the Tyne, which the Derwent joins downstream at Blaydon, and from here to the coast at South Shields this great waterway is Durham's northern limit.

Tyneside is Durham's most intensely industrialised area. For some 12 miles the river bank is encrusted with shipyards, docks, quays, warehouses, and factories, and the working towns of Gateshead, Felling, Hebburn, Jarrow, and South Shields have almost merged into one. Southwards to the Wear the land, comparatively flat, is densely populated and occupied by large coal-mines and industrial plant, with stretches of open country and farmland to relieve the eye.

The sandy beaches of South Shields and the sight of the open sea offer a welcome escape to the soul weary of the industrial scene. But the real fascination of the northern part of the Durham coast lies in the low limestone cliffs, curiously weathered, and thronged with colonies of sea-birds; they are quite unrivalled anywhere in Britain. Indeed the whole of the Durham shore must once have been very beautiful; now much of it is sadly spoiled by the refuse of coal-mining.

South of Sunderland the cliffs are cut through by steep-sided ravines, or "denes", as they are called locally, with streams running down between wooded banks to meet the sea. The best are Crimdon Dene and Castle Eden Dene, part of which is a nature reserve; for the rest, Nature has had to yield to industry, and the once golden beach is black with coal dust. The future of the Durham coal trade depends on the huge collieries which border the sea, and indeed stretch for several miles beneath it.

Inland from the coast is the east Durham plateau, its grassy uplands extensively quarried and mined, and overlaid with sprawling colliery towns and straggling villages, yet retaining unexpected pockets of unspoiled country. Here too is the new town of Peterlee. South of the plateau and inland from Hartlepool a broad tract of quiet, flat, fertile farmland stretches towards the Tees, with small, ancient villages presided over by the dignified little town of Sedgefield.

In the flat marshes and sands of Teesmouth, south of Hartlepool, the Durham coast ends, a far cry from the western heights with which we began.

With such variety and interest, it is surprising that County Durham is so little visited for its own sake. Perhaps an answer is to be found in the fact that the main routes through the county offer little hint of the attractions to east and west. The Great North Road, the Durham Motorway, and the London–Edinburgh railway line pass through the relatively flat, monotonous, and at times unsightly area of mid-Durham. The traveller by road is even denied the unrivalled view of Durham City which the railway affords, and almost everywhere from Darlington to Gateshead are reminders that Durham is one of the nation's workshops.

Yet there is rich reward to be had in exploration—panoramic views from undulating roads, the freedom of the open fells, the delights of woodland and river scenery, the sights and sounds of industry at work, the sense of history in castle and church, and the contrast of modern town and ancient village. This is the County Durham of today.

The County Durham of prehistoric times was a wild land of forest and heath, unattractive to early man, who left little evidence of settlement. Even the very fine Bronze Age collection from the Heathery Burn cave near Stanhope is an isolated find.

Roman Durham is far better represented. The organisation of Roman military rule depended upon communication with York, and for this purpose a road, which the Saxons called Dere Street, was driven through the county to Corbridge and Hadrian's Wall. Every 10 miles or so along its length there was a fort, and remains of these can be seen at Piercebridge, Binchester, Lanchester, and Ebchester. A branch road called the Wrekendike led from Lanchester to the supply garrison at South Shields. We know little of the native population of Brigantes at this time; they were probably little disturbed by the Roman presence.

After the withdrawal of the Romans, Durham suffered centuries of disquiet. The Scots raided repeatedly from the north, and from the continent of Europe came invading hordes of Angles and Saxons, driving out the Britons. In the 7th century, however, Celtic Christianity was established on the banks of the Wear and the Tyne in the monasteries of Monkwearmouth and Jarrow, and literature and the arts flourished until, a hundred years later, Danish raiders again began to harass the coast of Northumbria, and under their attacks the Anglian kingdom declined. The monasteries were sacked and looted, and the monks of Lindisfarne left Holy Island with the sacred remains of St Cuthbert on the journey which was to end at Durham in 995.

The formation of the present county of Durham had its origin in a royal grant of land by a king of Northumbria in the 9th century, when a vast area between Tyne and Wear was given to the Congregation of St Cuthbert. Later endowments added land between Wear and Tees. After the Norman Conquest the "Patrimony of St Cuthbert" came almost entirely under the sway of the bishops of Durham. The king was the nominal ruler, but the bishop was invested with supreme power. He had his own parliament, his own mint, his own law courts. His territory was a Church State, a palatinate, and he was a Prince Palatine, ruling from his Durham castle with all the autocracy of mediaeval monarchs. Durham Cathedral stands in all its magnificence as a symbol of the power of the Prince Bishops, which was not finally vested in the Crown until 1836.

The early years of the palatinate saw the building, or rebuilding, of most of Durham's ancient parish churches, although there are also important survivals from pre-Conquest times in the monastery churches of Monkwearmouth and Jarrow, and in the unique 7th century church at Escomb. Many other churches can show Saxon crosses and carved stones as evidence of early foundation. Beautiful 13th century work is to be seen at Hartlepool, Darlington, Staindrop, Sedgefield, and Chester-le-Street.

As a buffer state against Scots invasion, Durham was frequently subjected to warfare and devastation; outbreaks of plague added to the miseries of the people. The castles of Raby, Lumley, Witton, and Brancepeth stand today as stern reminders of those war-like days. Not until after the Civil War did Durham begin to enjoy a more settled and prosperous existence, when the fortresses could be adapted for peaceful occupation.

In the 18th century the expansion of the coal trade, which had already existed for 400 years, was made possible by laying wooden wagonways from the pits of north Durham to the Tyne and Wear; the demand for ships increased; and vast tracts of uncultivated land were enclosed for agricultural development. In the west of the county lead-mining flourished. All this activity stimulated the growth of the market towns, such as Bishop Auckland, Stanhope, Darlington, and Stockton (now in Yorkshire).

In the 19th century public railways were born in the county, and soon cuttings, embankments, inclines, and viaducts began to change the face of Durham as a network of lines grew. But the effect of railways on the landscape was as nothing compared with the upheaval which transformed much of rural Durham during the great rush for coal which began about 1830. All over the coalfield the earth was ravaged for its mineral riches, ugly villages of pitmen's cottages spread like a rash over the land, and the countryside was blackened with smoke and dust. Ironworks at Consett, Spennymoor, and Tow Law created towns where scarcely a single dwelling had formerly stood. At Hartlepool, Sunderland, and along the Tyne shipbuilding and other heavy industries flourished as never before. Between 1820 and 1900 the population of the county increased sixfold.

The present century has seen many changes in County Durham. Depression followed the industrial boom, and once more the people knew the miseries of want, and of war. Today another industrial revolution is in progress. Many coal-mines have closed, but many new industries are being established. The explorer in modern Durham will find clean and well-planned trading estates, new roads, new homes, new towns. He will find that the ugliness of the coalfield is being slowly eradicated. And, when he has tired of the industrial scene, he will turn with pleasure to the many natural delights of the Durham countryside.

B. BERRYMAN

Aycliffe. Five miles north of Darlington it lies, between the Great North Road and the main Edinburgh–London railway line, its buildings loosely grouped around a spacious village green above the little river Skerne.

The church stands to the south of the village. It has been here for 1000 years or more, evidence of this being the Saxon masonry at the west end of the nave. The north arcade is Norman work, and the north aisle and the porch were rebuilt in 1882; with these exceptions the building dates from the 13th century, a notable feature of this period being the pointed doorway which is flanked by stone heads of a young man and a woman in a wimple.

The most important old possessions of the church are the remains of richly-carved Saxon crosses set up as gravestones about the year 1000. They are a link with the time when Bishop Ealdhun gave his daughter Ecgfrida in marriage to Waltheof, Earl of Northumberland, and Aycliffe was part of her dowry.

In the south aisle is a cross with carvings of monsters writhing in an elaborate interlacing pattern, and at the base of it lies the head of another cross carved with interlacing work. In the north aisle stands a Saxon cross with a Crucifixion scene, groups of standing figures, and a rare carving of St Peter being crucified, head downwards. Let into the wall of the chancel are two more Saxon carvings and three fragments of later grave-covers with floriated crosses.

Other ancient relics are the font, which is probably Norman, and two early 14th century monuments in the north aisle—a worn stone figure of a cross-legged knight, and a priest's gravestone with high relief carving of a floriated cross and a chalice between two birds. The church can also boast some fine 17th century woodwork—a little square pulpit, organ screen, richly carved armchair, and splendid series of pews.

To the north-west of the village, adjoining the Aycliffe Trading Estate, is the expanding new town of Newton Aycliffe. Building started here in 1948 to provide a planned modern environment for a new community drawn from many parts of Britain.

A pleasant feature is the naming of streets after famous people in Durham's story—Elizabeth Barrett Walk, Havelock Close, St Cuthbert's Way and so on.

Barnard Castle. This is a delightful, breezy old town on a bank above the Tees, set in a quiet countryside enlivened here and there by military camps.

In early times the Roman road from Bowes to Binchester crossed the river here, at a ford where the gasworks now stands. The ford was supplanted by the 16th century bridge a little further down-stream—a handsome structure of mellow brown stone with two ribbed and pointed arches.

On the steep rocky bank rising 100 feet above the bridge are the imposing ruins of Barnard Castle, the Norman stronghold from which the little town derived its name. The first castle here was built before 1100 by Guy de Baliol, lord of Bailleul in Picardy, to whom the site was given by William Rufus; but soon after 1150 this was rebuilt in stone by his nephew or great-nephew, Bernard. Around the castle of Bernard, or Barnard, the town grew up; there seems to have been no settlement here earlier, and the first townsmen must have been those who supplied the garrison or sought its protection.

Bernard Baliol was succeeded here by John Baliol, founder of the Oxford college, whose wife founded Sweetheart Abbey, near Dumfries, in his memory; and here was born their son, the second John Baliol, who became King of Scotland in 1292 and ruled for four uneasy years. A later owner was Richard Neville, "Warwick the King-maker". His daughter Anne married Richard III and is said to have made several improvements to the fortress. Thus did Barnard Castle once more come into royal possession.

During the Rising in the North in 1569 Barnard Castle was garrisoned for Queen Elizabeth I and gallantly defended against the rebel peers by Sir George Bowes of Streatlam. After 11 days he surrendered, but his resistance here had effectively curbed the rising. In 1629 the castle was dismantled by Sir Henry Vane.

The ruins of Barnard Castle, covering about six and a half acres, are reached from the open space called Scar Top, overlooking the Tees at the bottom of Galgate. A round-headed gateway, dating from about 1300, leads through the outer wall into the Town Ward. Inside are the remains of a gatehouse, and round the corner towards the town are the ruins of Brackenbury's Tower, with an opening in its vault for lowering provisions to the dungeon.

From the Town Ward we cross the dry moat and pass into the Middle Ward through a gateway formerly guarded by a drawbridge. Bridging the moat again we find ourselves in the area of the Inner Ward, the highest point of the castle rock. Beyond the wall which surrounds the Inner Ward—except on the river side—projects the massive round Keep, 50 feet high, which was built about 1300 with stone from Cat Castle in Deep Dale. The inner side of the base is square and is probably a relic of the original stone keep built by Bernard Baliol. The walls are 10 feet thick and the ground floor, 20 feet across, has a curious roof in the shape of a flattened dome. A flight of stone stairs winds round in the thickness of the wall to the upper storeys, and from the windows there are views of the glorious river scenery which Sir Walter Scott described in *Rokeby*.

Between the Keep and the river were the Great Chamber, the Great Hall, and the tower called Mortham's Tower. The graceful oriel window projecting on corbels from the outer wall of the Great Chamber was probably inserted in the 15th century, and given its Tudor mullions later. Of the Great Hall two traceried 14th century windows remain. Much of Mortham's Tower collapsed in the 19th century, but the 13th century lower part remains, and the spiral stair which led to the upper floor can easily be traced. On the north side of the Inner Ward are the ruins of two more towers.

About one and a half miles east of Barnard Castle the Tees flows past Egglestone Abbey, on the Yorkshire bank, and it is at this point that the battlemented single-arched Abbey Bridge of 1772 crosses the river high above the brown peaty water, now turning into torrents of foam as it rushes wildly over the rocks. The glorious wooded gorge forms a lovely vista, with the tower of Barnard Castle Church at the end.

This spacious and dignified church stands at the corner of the marketplace. Like the castle, it has its roots in Norman England, and in spite of drastic restoration in the 19th century, when the tower was built, still displays evidence of its antiquity. It has a fine Norman south doorway with two rows of zigzag moulding, two deeply-splayed Norman windows in the chancel, and a Norman north arcade with pillars resting on high bases inserted in 1870 when the floor was lowered.

The south arcade with eight-sided pillars and pointed arches is 14th century work, and so is the north transept. The wide chancel arch, displaying embattled capitals and square rosettes, dates from the 15th century. A serene-looking head of Edward IV is carved on the left pillar; on the right is one of Richard III.

In the chancel, which is raised six steps above the nave and has a 15th century roof with finely moulded beams, is an Elizabethan communion table resting on the mediaeval stone altar. At the other end of the church is an octagonal 15th century font made of black marble from the Tees near Abbey Bridge.

In an arched recess in the north transept lies the massive and dignified stone figure of a 14th century vicar, Robert de Mortham, wearing robes embroidered with flowers; his head is on a cushion and he holds a chalice.

Beside this monument is another arched recess containing a collection of mediaeval gravestones with carved crosses, swords, and shears. A stone built into the wall nearby has a worn carving of St Anthony, flanked by two little pigs on their hind legs. At one time this stone was in the wall of a neighbouring house, and like much other carved stonework in the town may originally have come from the castle.

This transept also has two windows worthy of note: one shows St Hilda reading the Bible to a party of women below Whitby Abbey, and the other portrays St Aidan preaching on the shore below Bamburgh Castle.

Several other monuments are in the basement of the tower. One of the oldest commemorates the son of a vicar who ministered here in Cromwell's time—an infant who

> . . . peeped into the world where he could see
> Nought but confusion, sin, and misery.
> Thence 'scaped into his Saviour's arms. Thus he
> Got Heaven for fourteen days mortality.

In a canopied niche nearby stands a stone figure of a calm-faced figure of Justice with a sword; it commemorates Sir John Hullock, Baron of the Exchequer, who was born at Barnard Castle in 1767, and died suddenly at Abingdon in 1829 while on circuit. Here also is an inscription to Captain Augustus Webb who was fatally wounded during the charge of the gallant "six hundred" at Balaclava.

In the churchyard, near the Norman doorway, is the curious table tomb of George Hopper, who died in 1725 aged 23. Round the top of the tomb are the words *Here stands my statue graved in stone*, and on one side is a niche with a relief of the young man in a long coat and three-cornered hat, his hair falling over his shoulders, and a flower in his right hand; on the opposite side is carved a skeleton with a scythe.

The bitterest period in the town's history is commemorated by a low stone cross beside an avenue of lofty lime trees in the churchyard; it was set up *in memory of 143 inhabitants of Barnard Castle who died of Asiatic Cholera from August 18th to October 18th 1849.*

Quite close to the church is the octagonal market cross, which is capped by a turret containing the fire bell. Built in 1747 by Thomas

Breaks, a native of the town, it supplanted the tolbooth which stood at the other end of the marketplace. Dairy produce was formerly sold between the classical columns on the ground floor, and in the middle was a lock-up. Upstairs is the hall where the administrative work of the town used to be done, and where courts were held. The two holes in the weathervane were made in 1804 by two Teesdale Volunteers, firing from the door of the Turk's Head Inn 100 yards away.

In 1838 Charles Dickens, in search of material for Dotheboys Hall in *Nicholas Nickleby*, stayed at the King's Head Inn, and every morning used to cross the road to get the time from a grandfather clock in Thomas Humphrey's shop at Amen Corner, on the north side of Barnard Castle Church.

There he saw a timepiece of remarkably original design, with a pendulum designed to counteract the effect of changes of temperature upon its length, and one day he asked Thomas Humphrey who made it. "My son there," said Thomas, and Dickens thereupon christened it Master Humphrey's Clock. The shop has gone—it was pulled down in 1933—and the clock is now at Lartington in the North Riding of Yorkshire.

Just below the market cross is the 16th century Blagraves House, once an inn and now a café. It has a striking projecting gabled wing and leaded windows, and on the wall are four little figures of men playing musical instruments. This may well have been the house where, on October 24, 1648, the principal townspeople entertained Oliver Cromwell to mulled wine and shortcake when he was on his way to Richmond.

Below Blagraves House, in the quiet, tree-lined street called Thorngate, is a fine 18th century stone house with a pedimented door approached by a double flight of steps. It was once the home of Sir John Hullock, the prominent lawyer whose monument is in the church.

At the top of the marketplace is Galgate, a broad sloping road with a central line of trees. This follows the route of the Roman road to Binchester, near Bishop Auckland. The name Galgate refers to the gallows where the lords of Barnard Castle executed malefactors.

In this road is the 18th century house (now a garage) where Roderick Murchison began his geological studies as a result of a chance meeting with Sir Humphry Davy at Rokeby, across the Tees. He became the great authority on the rock formation which he named the Silurian. Another eminent man who lived here was William Hutchinson, the 18th century solicitor who wrote a famous history of the county of Durham. He built the group of houses called the Grove; his initials, and those of his wife, are on the weather-vane.

From the market cross, Newgate runs eastward to the most magnificent building in Barnard Castle—the enormous Bowes Museum in the sumptuous Renaissance style of a French château, and a truly astonishing spectacle to come upon in a small country town. It was founded by John Bowes, son of the tenth Earl of Strathmore and Mary Miller of Stainton.

John Bowes inherited the neighbouring Streatlam Castle and other English estates of his father, but he spent much of his time at his home in Paris and it was there that he met his wife, a French actress named Josephine Benoite, who was later granted the title of Countess Montalbo. Herself a talented artist, she wholeheartedly encouraged her husband in his hobby of collecting works of art, and he always maintained that the founding of a gallery and museum was her idea. Calais was the site first chosen for it, but because of the unsettled state of France they finally decided on Barnard Castle, near the Bowes's ancestral home. Mrs Bowes laid the foundation stone in November 1869, but neither she nor her husband was destined to see complete fulfilment of their long-cherished wish. Mrs Bowes died in 1874 at the early age of 44, and her husband died in 1885; not until June 1892 was their museum opened. In 1956 it was taken over by the Durham County Council.

Built of local stone—from Streatlam and Stainton—the Bowes Museum is 300 feet long and covers nearly an acre. Round it is a public park of 21 acres. In it are many thousands of beautiful things—paintings, tapestries, porcelain, ivories, exquisite embroideries and lace, furniture and many relics of the past.

Portraits of John and Josephine Bowes hang in the spacious entrance hall, from which a stone staircase with a magnificent wrought-iron balustrade leads to the upper galleries.

Several rooms on the first floor are devoted to French art of the 18th and 19th centuries; some are lavishly furnished as bedrooms and salons, others contain superb collections of porcelain and objets d'art, and an attractive display of French costume.

English furnishings of the 18th century adorn the Gilling Castle Room, a pine-panelled gallery decorated in green and gold.

The remaining rooms on this floor contain displays of 19th century English art, mediaeval European painting and carved wooden altar-pieces, and tapestry, embroidery, and costume spanning eight centuries.

On the second floor are splendid displays of pottery and porcelain from France, Germany, Italy, and England, and in the picture galleries important collections of Spanish, Italian, and French painting are exhibited.

No visitor to the Bowes Museum should miss the delightful Children's Room, with its collection of dolls' houses and dolls dressed in various national costumes, or the Teesdale Rooms on the ground floor, which contain many kitchen utensils and farming implements used by the dales folk of the 18th and 19th centuries.

To the west of Barnard Castle there are many delightful walks in the woods, and on the Yorkshire bank is Towler Hill, where J. S. Cotman painted a famous picture of Barnard Castle. The view has changed since his time, but much of the old charm of the town still remains.

Binchester. A quiet little neighbour of Bishop Auckland, it now consists of little more than a few farmhouses. But long centuries ago the Romans built a fort here. They called it Vinovia, "pleasant spot", and indeed it is the finest Roman site in County Durham—a little flat-topped hill with a steep side overlooking a beautiful bend of the Wear and a fine view of Bishop Auckland to the south. About 200 yards north-west, Dere Street crossed the river on its way from York to Hadrian's Wall, and a branch led from it to one of the gates of Vinovia.

The fort occupied some seven acres, and although the site is now covered with grass, parts of the ramparts can still be traced. Water was supplied from a well outside the east corner, and under the prominent northern corner was found an arched culvert through which water was brought in from an aqueduct.

A flight of modern stone steps leads down to the hypocaust, where hot air circulated beneath a Roman bath. The most perfect hypocaust in the North of England, it was found about the year 1815, when a plough struck a ruined wall of the room which stood above.

The steps lead to a passage which has three openings in the left wall. The centre one was enlarged by breaking away the wall when the hypocaust was found, but the side openings, arched with red tiles, are still perfect.

It is possible to investigate the whole chamber by creeping among the pillars, each composed of 16 tiles. When the hypocaust was first found it had its original number of pillars—11 rows with eight in a row; but one whole column was later removed by a visitor, and a few of the 87 still standing have had to be restored. The room above, now filled in again, measures 22 feet by 16.

Coins, pottery, and other relics have been unearthed on this site at various times; but the most important discovery was made in 1891 when men were laying a water-pipe in the field south of the fort. This was a large and perfect Roman altar dedicated by Pomponius Donatus, probably the commander of the fort, to Jupiter and the Overseas Mothers. It is now in the Museum of Antiquities at Newcastle University.

Bishop Auckland. Market town and centre of a busy industrial area, Bishop Auckland can fairly claim to be the "capital" of South-West Durham. It is set on the edge of a steep bank above the Wear, and from the marketplace, with its Victorian town hall and church of St Anne, a narrow "chare" leads precipitously to the riverside. To the west a 15th century bridge of two arches and a 19th century railway viaduct span the river, side by side.

Since the 12th century the bishops of Durham have had a residence here, but the town's history doubtless began much earlier, for the main thoroughfare, Newgate Street, is part of the Roman road from York to Hadrian's Wall.

Auckland Park, the bishop's demesne, covers some 800 acres to the north-east of the town, and here there is always rich reward in wandering up and down tree-clad slopes and beside the river Gaunless and the Coundon Burn that wind across the park to join the Wear.

A battlemented and pinnacled gateway with a clock turret, built by Bishop Trevor in 1760, leads into the park from the marketplace. Beside this imposing structure stands the 17th century Lodge, a stone house with a battlemented front and big mullioned windows, at one time a woollen factory.

From the gateway runs a drive separating the castle and its garden from the park. The garden is bounded by a stone screen with open pointed arches, erected by James Wyatt for Bishop Barrington about the year 1800; beyond this stands the bold and rugged pile of Auckland Castle, the last of 14 country seats formerly attached to the See of Durham.

Starting as a Norman manor house in the days of Bishop Pudsey, the building was converted into a castle by Bishop Bek about 1300 and improved by his successors. During the Commonwealth it was confiscated by Parliament and sold to Sir Arthur Haselrigg, who pulled down the old chapel and other parts of the castle and with the materials built himself a new mansion in the courtyard.

After the Restoration Bishop John Cosin spent an enormous sum of money in restoring the castle to its former dignity. He formed a great new chapel out of the ancient hall, and later bishops in their turn carried out further alterations and improvements.

The austere south side of the building, with a gay flower-decked lawn in front of it, is barely 200 years old. The east side, which has a lofty battlemented bay window enriched with ornamental carving and heraldry, is early 16th century work; and so is the projecting wing at the back, known as Scotland because Scottish prisoners or hostages are said to have been housed here.

The oldest work within the castle (apart from the chapel) is in the kitchen, which has stone shafts dating from the early 14th century. Another room, once a library, has some 16th century oak panelling adorned with painted arms of Queen Elizabeth I and foreign potentates of her time.

The most impressive apartments are the dining-room and the drawing-room, each 20 yards long and adorned with sacred paintings and portraits of the bishops—Shute Barrington and Van Mildert by Sir Thomas Lawrence, Edward Maltby by Beechey, Lightfoot and Wescott by Sir W. B. Richmond, and many others.

One apartment with a handsome ceiling is known as King Charles's Room, a reminder that the unhappy king was here on three occasions. The earliest was when he was Prince of Wales; the second as a guest of Bishop Morton on May 31, 1633, while on his way to Scotland; the third was as a prisoner on February 4, 1647, after Bishop Thomas Morton had been expelled from the castle.

The magnificent chapel, the finest feature of Auckland Castle, is attached to the main block at its extreme north-east angle. This was the Norman hall converted into a house of prayer by Bishop John Cosin after the Restoration, and within it are the original pillars of the Norman arcades, each with four clustered marble shafts adorned with round or foliated capitals. In the spandrels of the massive moulded arches, too, can be seen the shafts which supported the roof before Cosin's lofty pinnacled clerestory was added and now support angels with outstretched wings dating from Bishop Lightfoot's time. The 17th century roof of the chapel, with panels displaying heraldic arms and eagles on garlands, is one of the best of its period in England.

At the west end of the building is an ante-chapel formed by the lofty open screen, which together with the 24 stalls and the richly carved pulpit and lectern, was the gift of Bishop Cosin. He had a penchant for adorning churches in a lavish way; indeed, his work at Durham Cathedral led to a preacher referring to him as "Our young Apollo who repaireth the Choir and sets it out gaily with strange

Babylonish ornaments". The organ and loft, delicately carved, were set up in 1688 by his successor, Bishop Crewe.

The lively and flamboyant Bishop Cosin died in 1672 and was buried, as he wished, in this chapel which he had so richly decorated. A huge memorial stone covers his grave in the middle of the nave.

In front of the altar-steps another black marble slab (engraved with a beautiful cross) marks the grave of a 19th century bishop who also did much to enrich this chapel: Joseph Barber Lightfoot, the distinguished theological scholar and writer, who was buried here on December 27, 1889.

The chapel, restored and redecorated by him, was rededicated on August 1, 1888, in the presence of a large number of colonial and American bishops who were in England for the third Lambeth Conference, a gathering portrayed in one of the nine new windows which Lightfoot inserted. The windows as a whole illustrate the history of Northumbria from the time of St Aidan and St Cuthbert; the faces in them are portraits of Lightfoot's friends.

Among other bishops buried in this chapel were Henry Montague Villiers, a noted preacher, who died in 1861, and Brooke Foss Westcott, the Bible commentator, who died 60 years later. Another bishop, Richard Trevor, who was buried at Glynde in Sussex in 1771, is commemorated here by a remarkable sculpture which portrays him reading a book; it was the work of Joseph Nollekens.

Bishop Auckland's ancient parish church is St Andrew's, perched on a little eminence above the Gaunless on the southern edge of the town. On this dominating site once stood a Saxon house of prayer which in Norman times was enlarged and converted by Bishop de St Carileph into a collegiate church for secular canons expelled by him from Durham.

In the 13th century this building was replaced by the present handsome church, which in turn underwent considerable alterations and enlargements at the instigation of Anthony Bek, Bishop of Durham from 1283 to 1311. Other alterations were made through the centuries, particularly in Victorian times, but the church remains substantially a beautiful example of 13th century or Early English architecture.

The biggest parish church in the county—it is 157 feet long—St Andrew's boasts a tall west tower with an upper stage added in 1417, and a beautiful 13th century porch with an upper chamber. One of the two richly moulded arches of this porch is flanked by worn carved heads of an armoured knight and his lady.

A graceful feature of the spacious interior are the Early English nave arcades with richly moulded pointed arches resting on pillars alternately clustered and eight-sided. From an arch of the north arcade a stone head of Edward I faces the aisle. The dark oak roof and the clerestory with its pairs of trefoil-headed windows both date from the 15th century.

In the chancel are 28 finely-carved choir-stalls which were installed in 1416 by Cardinal Langley. The fronts of the desks and the massive bench-ends are adorned with tracery, and the misericord seats with carved flowers and foliage.

In the middle of a big blue stone in the chancel floor is an inscribed brass plate engraved with sprays of foliage. The Latin epitaph begins "Farewell, Fridesmond" and refers to the first wife of Richard Barnes, Bishop of Durham in Elizabethan times.

Near the lectern is a holy-water stoup of more than usual interest; found in the churchyard in 1850, it was hollowed out of a Roman altar probably brought from Binchester about 1450 by Bishop Neville, whose arms it bears.

At the other end of the church, well-framed in the graceful pointed tower arch, is a fine relic of Saxon times—an 8th century churchyard cross reconstructed from five fragments found when the south transept was rebuilt in 1881. The best-preserved fragment is a panel at the base which displays three robed figures with haloes; above it is a carving of the Crucifixion, and amid beautiful scroll ornament on the shaft an archer is taking aim at beasts devouring the fruit on encircling branches.

At the west end of the north aisle are various carvings found with the cross—fragments of Saxon and Norman work—and also some later mediaeval grave-covers. Near them lie two figures. One, a fine black oak effigy dating from about 1320, is of a cross-legged knight in chain armour, with a big boar at his feet; the other, a stone figure of about 1400, is of a woman in a tightly-buttoned dress, with a fat hound crouched uncomfortably at her little feet. Mounted on a piece of oak on the wall above is a big mutilated brass of a priest of her day.

In the churchyard is the grave of Thomas Wright, the 18th century astronomer whose story we tell at Westerton.

Bishop Middleham. This attractive village, two miles north-west of Sedgefield, has a few grass-grown mounds testifying to its former importance; they mark the site of a manor house which until the end of the 14th century was the chief home of the bishops of Durham, two of whom died here. By that time the house had fallen into ruin, and the castle at Bishop Auckland had become their favourite residence.

On three sides of the site the ground drops steeply to marshy land, and to the north-east stands the church, with a modern bell turret. The ancient porch shows the worn stone head of a bishop (probably the builder) on one side of its pointed doorway, and built into the interior of the porch are fragments of mediaeval coffin-covers with carved crosses.

The nave arcades have pointed arches on round columns, and below the spandrels are grotesque heads of men and animals carved by mediaeval masons. The original altar stone with four consecration crosses lies under the communion table, and another 13th century relic is the dignified font of grey Frosterley marble, with round bowl and massive shaft.

St Michael, to whom the church is dedicated, is strikingly portrayed by L. C. Evetts in the modern glass which fills the lancet in the west wall.

Over the north doorway is a hatchment with the arms of a 17th century vicar, Thomas Bedford, together with a long inscription recording his death and that of his wife, Alice, *mother, grandmother and great-grandmother to 74 children.*

Inscriptions on the north wall of the chancel commemorate two distinguished members of the Surtees family who lived at Mainsforth Hall. This house, which stood about a mile west of the church, was demolished in 1962.

One inscription pays tribute to Brigadier General Sir Herbert Conyers Surtees, DSO (1858–1933), author of several parish histories and of the records of the family of Surtees. The other honours Robert Surtees (1779–1834), eminent author of the *History and Antiquities of the County Palatine of Durham.*

Robert Surtees, who was born at Durham on April 1, 1779, was a lonely child with a love of collecting coins and items of classical and mediaeval lore. He was sent to the Kepier Grammar School at Houghton-le-Spring, and afterwards took his MA degree at Christ Church, Oxford.

After a short period in London, reading for the Bar, Surtees returned to Mainsforth, and there lived for the rest of his life, busily compiling the great work on his native county for which he is chiefly remembered. Every summer he would drive round the county in a gig, and every winter pore over ancient records. His first volume was published in 1818; the fourth and last was brought out in 1840, six years after his death, by the Rev James Raine.

Surtees kept up a continuous correspondence with Walter Scott, and the great writer and his wife visited Mainsforth for a night or two

The Bowes Museum, Barnard Castle

The Market Cross and Marketplace, Barnard Castle

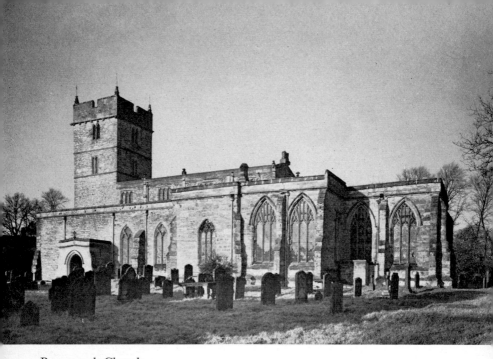

Brancepeth Church

Brancepeth Castle

when on their way to London in April 1809. It was a habit of Surtees to write stirring ballads in the ancient style, and to send them to Scott as original records collected from local people. They appear in all good faith in Scott's printed works, and it seems that Scott was never let into the secret.

There are many pleasant tales of the kindly Robert Surtees—of his dining-table surrounded by his favourite dogs, of the old ponies he would not have destroyed, and of the rock plants he grew on the garden wall so that passers-by might have the pleasure of seeing them.

In January 1834 Surtees caught cold while travelling on a coach from Sunderland, and on February 11 he died. His grave is here, in the shade of a yew on the south side of the churchyard. Robert Southey was at his funeral and wrote a description of it. The Surtees Society for the publication of historical manuscripts relating to the North of England was founded in Robert Surtees's memory a few months later.

Bishopton. Standing on high ground above the tiny Bishopton Beck, this quiet village has an impressive relic in Castle Hill, a striking 40-foot mound now covered with grass and elder trees. On this artificial hill once stood a castle keep, with elaborate double entrenchments which covered an area of seven acres.

This fortress is believed to be the one held in 1143 by Roger de Conyers, Constable of Durham, who was fighting against a usurping bishop, William Cumin, Chancellor of the King of Scotland. Cumin had salted the body of the previous bishop, Galfrid Rufus, and this procedure enabled him to keep the death a secret until with the help of some rebellious barons he had captured Durham Castle and arranged for a monk to bring forged letters from the Pope confirming his own election as bishop.

When the plot was discovered, Cumin immediately began a reign of terror; but some monks succeeded in escaping from Durham to York, and there elected as their bishop William de St Barbara, who took refuge at Bishopton.

Bishopton's neat church has some 13th century walls, and part of an original trefoil-headed window can be seen on the north side of the chancel arch. It also has a Norman font with an eight-sided bowl, protected by an oak cover in the form of a crocketed spire.

The font-cover is 17th century work, and so are two oak chairs notable for their richly-carved backs, with little dragons writhing at the top corners. Another notable piece of woodwork is a long oak chest bound with iron straps; it is probably 700 years old.

C

The churchyard still has the base of its old stone cross, and let into the south wall of the nave is a mediaeval gravestone with a floriated cross; close by is a painted sundial of 1776 with the latitude marked.

Blackwell. Though a residential suburb of Darlington, south-west of the town, it still retains its village aspect, and with its abundance of trees presents a pleasing picture to travellers entering the county from Yorkshire. Curiously, the highway here takes a turn to the south-east as it is carried across the Tees by the plain but dignified bridge built in 1832 by John Green of Newcastle, and considerably widened in 1963.

About a mile to the south of Blackwell are the so-called bottomless ponds known as Hell's Kettles, traditionally formed during Christmas of 1179. It is thought that they were caused by underground erosion of limestone and sandstone, the thin roof of clay and gravel suddenly falling in "with an horrible noise".

In a well-wooded park stands Blackwell Grange, a fine old house which in 1736 was the birthplace of George Allan. He entered into partnership with his solicitor father, but was enabled through his marriage to a rich Yorkshire heiress to devote much of his time to genealogy, heraldry, and natural history.

In this house he set up a printing press so that the results of his researches might be available to his correspondents and friends, and here also he established a remarkable museum and library which he generously opened to other scholars, and, indeed, to the general public; in three and a half years it was visited by over 7000 people.

George Allan died in 1800, and some years later his valuable collection was bought by the Newcastle Philosophical Society and formed the nucleus of the famous Hancock Museum in that city. It includes ethnographical specimens brought to Yorkshire from the Pacific Isles by Captain Cook, and many stuffed birds which Thomas Bewick used for his engravings.

Blaydon. A song has made it famous—Tynesiders the world over sing of *Gannin' alang the Scotswood Road to see the Blaydon Races*, although the last meeting was held in 1916 and a power station now occupies the site of the race-course. Situated at the junction of the Derwent and the Tyne, and linked to Newcastle by the new Scotswood Bridge which in 1967 replaced the old Chain Bridge (mentioned in the song), Blaydon is a working town, with a wide range of engineering and manufacturing industries.

A reminder of the area's former dependence on coal-mining is the memorial to Tommy Ramsay, one of the founders of the Durham Miners' Association. He died in 1873, and was buried in the town cemetery, where a statue portrays him with a roll of handbills and the rattle with which he used to call the miners to meetings. The inscription pays tribute to his long and self-sacrificing labours in the cause of human progress.

Boldon. There are wide views over the flat north-east corner of the county from this village, for it stands on a prominent little hill above the Don. It has its place in history, too, for it was on Boldon Hill, on March 24, 1644, that a Scottish force was routed by the Royalists led by William Cavendish, Marquess of Newcastle.

But its chief title to fame is the Boldon Book, a Durham Domesday record which Bishop Hugh Pudsey made of his 141 estates in 1183. After setting out the services due to him at Boldon, most of the other entries repeat that they are "in all respects like Boldon". The original manuscript is lost, but two early copies are preserved at Durham, and another is in the Bodleian Library at Oxford.

The little River Don, which winds round the hill on its way to the Tyne at Jarrow Slake, may in Bishop Pudsey's day have been navigable as far as Brockley Whins, close to Boldon Colliery station; when the railway viaduct was built over the river in 1894 the framework of a ship was discovered on the shingle bed.

Boldon's most prominent landmark is the 13th century church, crowned by a stumpy stone spire supported by gabled buttresses.

In a recess in the north wall of the sanctuary lies a stone figure of a 14th century priest, his tonsured head on a cushion, and his feet on a branch of foliage. In a recess in the south aisle is another 14th century figure in priestly vestments, but the head is modern work; carved at the feet are two beavers sharing a single head.

In the sanctuary are two fine 17th century oak armchairs with richly carved backs; another notable feature is the east window with modern glass portraying the Holy Lamb surrounded by saints and angels.

Brancepeth. Perhaps the neatest village in all Durham, it has a single street crossing the main road from Crook to Durham, with a row of pretty creeper-covered cottages leading to the park in which the church and castle stand.

Brancepeth Castle has a history dating from Saxon times; indeed, before the drastic restoration and rebuilding in the early 19th century it was thought to have been one of the oldest fortified castles in the country.

The earliest owners of Brancepeth were the Bulmer family; they had property here before 1100. In 1174 it passed by marriage to the all-powerful Nevilles, who preferred it to Raby as a residence, probably because it was nearer Durham; and most of the ancient building still remaining is credited to Ralph Neville, first Earl of Westmorland, grandfather of Warwick the King-maker, and himself a man of great power and influence. He was Marshal of England from 1399 until his death in 1425.

The Nevilles forfeited the castle as a result of the Rising in the North, which is said to have started here in 1569. Wordsworth, in *The White Doe of Rylstone*, tells us that

> *From every side came noisy swarms*
> *Of peasants in their homely gear;*
> *And, mixed with these, to Brancepeth came*
> *Grave gentry of estate and name,*
> *And captains known for worth in arms,*
> *And prayed the earls in self-defence*
> *To rise, and prove their innocence.*

In 1613 James I granted the Brancepeth estate to the notorious Robert Carr, or Ker, Earl of Somerset, who held it until 1615, when he was accused of poisoning Sir Thomas Overbury and sent to prison. The property was forfeited and in 1636 was bought by Ralph Cole, grandson of a Gateshead blacksmith; but in 1701 the fourth Cole of Brancepeth died in poverty and it was bought by Sir Henry Belasyse, father of the lovesick girl associated in song with Bonnie Bobby Shafto, who lived at Whitworth Hall across the Wear.

In 1796 the estate was sold to William Russell, a Sunderland banker who had made a fortune from coal. He and his son Matthew, who was called the richest commoner in England, rebuilt the castle, spending more than £120,000 in operations which practically destroyed the ancient fabric. In 1828 the transformed Brancepeth passed by marriage to the family of Viscount Boyne who held it until 1922, when it became the headquarters of the Durham Light Infantry. Now it houses a research laboratory for a firm of glass-makers.

The broad drive leads to a great gateway (at the north-east of the castle) flanked by two round towers in Norman style and leading to a spacious courtyard enclosed by lofty walls and towers.

To the south and west the castle rises abruptly from the steep wooded banks of the Stockley Beck, here crossed by a battlemented bridge. The trees along the beck are all that remains of the great West Wood, which in 1635 had the distinction of supplying the timber for the British Navy's first three-decker, *Sovereign of the Seas*. Some 1400 trees were felled here and then sent to Woolwich for the making of those old wooden walls of England.

A dignified gateway with two stone pillars flanked by a little stile leads from the castle grounds to Brancepeth Church, which, unlike the castle, has suffered little at the hands of the restorer and retains a wealth of fine 17th century woodwork. It has an imposing tower dating from about 1240, and a lofty 13th century nave with 14th century eastern bay and clerestory and roof added about 1500. The aisles, transepts, and beautiful chancel are all 14th century work, done under the benevolent patronage of the Nevilles. The north porch is one of many splendid additions made to the church through the generosity of John Cosin, rector here from 1625 to 1644, who became Bishop of Durham after the Restoration.

The outstanding feature of the interior is the wealth of fine woodwork. Particularly handsome is the chancel screen given by Cosin; it has five bays with richly carved tabernacle work, the three finials rising to the pointed arch from a mass of crocketing and clustered pinnacles.

Over the chancel arch are two more fine specimens of carving. The upper one, probably part of the original roodloft, consists of oak panelling with rows of heraldic shields. Below is a smaller oak screen consisting of 27 square oak panels filled with intricate tracery, and painted white; it is thought to have been brought from the Jesus altar at Durham Cathedral by George Cliffe, a monk of Durham who became rector of Brancepeth after the Dissolution.

Round the walls of the sanctuary is some 16th century panelling, and high on the north wall is an enormous oak panel flanked by Corinthian columns which was intended to bear an epitaph to Cosin. It is strange that this should not have been provided, for the church undoubtedly owes much to his munificence. In addition to the chancel screen, he presented the massive altar table, the graceful stalls, the complete set of panelled pews in the nave, the pulpit, and the cover of the marble font. Cosin's pulpit, richly carved oak, has a lower seat and desk, and a sounding-board elaborately carved with fruit and cherub heads. His font-cover, a tall, six-sided structure of black oak, has open Gothic arches forming a kind of cage for a wooden dove, and then an elaborate spire crowned by a reclining angel.

Another fine piece of woodwork here is the 14th century Flanders chest in the organ chapel; little figures of men and monsters are included in its rich carving. From Flanders, too, came the three roundels of bible scenes in one of the 14th century windows of the north aisle.

The finest monuments are in the chancel, the most impressive being the big stone effigy of Robert Neville, the Peacock of the North, who died in 1318 during a Border skirmish and was brought here for burial. Wearing a surcoat over his chain armour, and with a sword and shield at his side, he gazes up at the roof. Near his head are the remains of two priests, four angels, and six lions; curled up at his feet is a little dog.

On the other side of the chancel are fine oak figures of Ralph Neville, second Earl of Westmorland, and one of his two wives. (He was a peaceful member of a family constantly engaged in bitter strife, and he died peacefully in 1484.) His head lies on the Neville badge—the bull's head with outstretched tongue which is said to be a link with the Saxon family of Bulmer whom they succeeded at Brancepeth. His feet rest on a crouching dog, and two little dogs peep out from the folds of his lady's long dress. At their heads are fragments of six guardian angels.

The memorial of yet another of these proud Nevilles is on the floor of the tower. This is the huge marble altar tomb of Ralph Neville, third Earl of Westmorland, who in 1523 died of grief at the loss of his only son.

Among many other memorials in Brancepeth church are two brasses. One, in the floor at the east end of the south aisle, portrays a 14th century knight armed with sword and dagger, his feet resting on a hound. (This brass was once stolen, and years later was found in a London shop.) The other, in the chancel floor, is a half-length brass of a 15th century priest, Richard Drax, in the robes of a Bachelor of Law; symbols of the four Evangelists are set in the corners of the huge blue marble slab.

Similar symbols appear in the four corners of a worn and mutilated carved stone built into the south-east buttress of the chancel; this dates from about 1300, and has as its main subject a figure of Christ.

Two other ancient external features of interest are a sundial on the south-west buttress (to mark the hours of service) and the sanctuary bellcot on the eastern gable of the nave.

Burnmoor. This village at a corner of Lambton Park has for centuries belonged to the Lambton family. Their old hall in the park was replaced early in the 19th century by a magnificent castle designed by Joseph Bonomi for John George Lambton, first Earl of Durham, a distinguished statesman; but in 1854 this was nearly destroyed by falling into a long-forgotten coal-mine underneath, and masses of brickwork had to be built into the cavity in order to save it. Today the castle is in use as a college of adult education.

A fine 14th century bridge with four sharply pointed arches spans the Wear to give access to the 1200-acre park from Chester-le-Street; the river flows across the park between gloriously wooded banks.

Burnmoor Church, built by the second Earl of Durham and dedicated in 1868, contains many memorials of the Lambton family. The most notable is the huge marble Angel of Victory in the north aisle; it was carved at Rome in 1894 by Waldo Story, and commemorates the third Earl of Durham and his twin brother who for a brief span was the fourth Earl. The third Earl is also commemorated by the east window, where he is portrayed as an armoured knight kneeling at the foot of the Cross.

In the churchyard, above the family vault of the Lambtons, is a reproduction in Irish limestone of the famous cross at Monasterboice in Ireland. Richly carved with floral and scrollwork patterns, adorned by little birds and beasts, the cross commemorates Beatrix Frances, Countess of Durham, who died in 1871.

Castle Eden. It is indeed an Eden, a tiny village with two rows of neat houses shaded by fine trees near the entrance of a beautifully wooded park, and near them a small church with slender embattled tower and lead-covered spire. Built in 1764 on the site of the little church pictured in the vestry, this house of prayer was enlarged in 1896, when the tall round pillars with elaborate gilded capitals were set up to form aisles.

Relics of the earlier church are the worn 13th century stone figure of a priest and the little 17th century font of white marble which has an oval bowl.

The loveliest sight here is the window by L. C. Evetts of Newcastle. A splendid composition framed in lovely leadwork and glowing with warm colour, it shows a pilgrim casting down his burden, while a young armoured man grasps a sword to defend himself against a fiery dragon. The window is dedicated to the memory of

Rowland Burdon, 1857–1944, sixth and last surviving of his name, and of other members of the Burdon family who were also lords of the manor of Castle Eden from 1758. My sword I give to him that shall succeed me in my pilgrimage, and my courage and skill to him that can get it.

On the north wall of the chancel is a marble inscription to Rowland Burdon, MP for Durham, who rebuilt this church. He designed the cast-iron bridge which crossed the Wear at Sunderland.

In the churchyard are two eight-sided stones said to have come from one of the city gates of Durham.

Castle Eden Castle, an 18th century Gothic building with battlements and mullioned windows, stands in the park. From the park the Castle Eden Burn runs down a delightful wooded dene to the sea, two and a half miles away. The mouth of the Burn is crossed by a fine railway viaduct of eight lofty brick arches, and beyond this the black waves deposit their load of coal dust on the beach.

At the upper end of the dene a famous discovery was made in the year 1776. Workmen uprooting a hedge about 100 yards from the Castle Lodge came upon a skeleton buried with a beautiful Saxon drinking-vessel of decorated bluish-green glass in perfect pristine condition. One of the last productions of the Syrian workmen in Gaul before they were driven out of business by the invading anti-Semitic Germans, it is now in the British Museum. Cologne Museum has an identical glass which was found in the Rhineland.

Chester-le-Street. No place in the county can boast a history longer than that of this small but busy town, situated where the Con Burn meets the River Wear, six miles north of Durham.

In Roman times there was a fortress here, occupying some six or seven acres beside the road built by their engineers from Binchester to Newcastle. Many Roman relics unearthed on the site from time to time can be seen in the old church.

In the story of Saxon England Chester-le-Street has a prominent and hallowed place as one of the resting-places of the beloved St Cuthbert's remains. In the year 875 the monks of Lindisfarne, fearing a record onslaught by the Viking invaders, fled from their island sanctuary, carrying with them the coffin of St Cuthbert containing his body, relics of St Aidan and other priests, the head of the martyred King Oswald, and the lovely Lindisfarne Gospels, that masterpiece of 7th century art now preserved in the British Museum.

For seven long years the monks bore the coffin through the north of England; from town to town, from village to village, it was carried on the shoulders of the faithful until at last, in 882, they came to Chester-le-Street, and here built themselves a little wooden church. In that little church, standing on the site of a Roman camp, the saintly relics were enshrined for the next 113 years; then, in 995, with Northumbria again under threat of invasion, the monks set forth once more with the coffin of St Cuthbert, finding sanctuary for a month at Ripon, and then, as the legend has it, at a place revealed to one of them in a dream—at Dunholm, where Durham Cathedral now stands.

While the body of St Cuthbert lay within its walls, the little wooden church of Chester-le-Street was a cathedral, the centre of a vast diocese extending from North Sea to Irish Sea, from River Tees to Forth. During those 113 years the town was the seat of nine Saxon bishops, but following the transfer to Durham it declined in importance and its church, now no more than a parish church, gradually became ruinous.

So it remained until about 20 years before the Norman Conquest, when Bishop Egelric gave orders for a new and more imposing church in stone to be built. While his workmen were digging foundations they unearthed the treasury of the Roman garrison, with a hoard of gold which the Bishop promptly appropriated and took off to Peterborough, whence he had recently come. It is only fair to state that he used it in a worthy manner, building roads across the Fens and raising the noble abbey church; nevertheless, William the Conqueror threw him into the Tower of London for his misdeeds.

Egelric's church was largely rebuilt in the second half of the 13th century, when it was raised to the status of a collegiate church, with a dean, six prebendaries, and five vicars. It was considerably altered again early in the 14th century, and it has been restored in more recent times.

The dominating external feature is the 13th century tower, capped by an eight-sided belfry containing a fine peal of nine bells; one of them, bearing the name of Cuthbert, was given to the church soon after 1400, when the beautiful stone spire was added.

Built against the north wall of the tower is a little stone building erected about the same time; originally the cell, or anchorage, of a hermit, and one of the best preserved anchorages in England, it contains two rooms on the ground floor and two more above. A narrow slit in the wall of the upper floor enabled the anchorite dwelling there to see the altar in the south aisle; another opening enabled food to be handed to him from the tower.

After the Reformation this anchorage became an almshouse for poor widows, and in 1626 a curate with an eye to making it his own residence tried to eject them; he even obtained a warrant from Durham to give them a ducking. However, with the help of three strong men, and "a barr to the inner doore", the ladies held their own and in the end were allowed to stay.

Within the church the most impressive features are the lofty nave arcades, fine 13th century work with pointed arches on round pillars. The tall chancel arch dates from the same period, and so does the narrow chancel, though some of its masonry may belong to the Saxon building of Bishop Egelric. In the south wall are beautiful 13th century sedilia with trefoil-headed arches, but the fittings—the carved altar, the panelled oak reredos with its gilded figures of the Madonna and St Cuthbert, the tall traceried screen, and the choir-stalls—are all modern work; so is the bishop's throne, a reminder that this church was a seat of bishops for over a century—from Eardulph in 883 to Aldhun in 996. Mounted on the wall is a small brass of a lady in simple 15th century dress; it represents Alice Lambton, who died in 1434.

Three big paintings in the chancel graphically portray early incidents in the long story of Chester-le-Street. The pictures show the flight of the monks from Lindisfarne with the coffin of Cuthbert; King Alfred granting the Saxon Bishop Eardulph all the land between Tyne and Tees; and the building of the little wooden cathedral in 883.

More early history is illustrated in a north aisle window which depicts the writing of the Lindisfarne Gospels and the Saxon translation which was made in this church, written between the lines of the Latin text by a monk named Aldred. In the middle of the window St John is shown writing his original Gospel, and to the left Bishop Eadfrith is seen writing the Lindisfarne Gospels on Holy Island. Two bishops illuminate the manuscript, and a monk recovers it from the waves. Then Aldred is shown writing his translation with a quill pen, and lastly, Bishop Aldhun fleeing from Chester-le-Street with the Gospels in 995, when the body of St Cuthbert was carried to Durham.

On a stone bench along the wall of the north aisle rest 14 effigies of members of the Lumley family. Known locally as Lumley's Warriors, they were placed here in 1594 by pedigree-proud John, Lord Lumley, and judging from the costume 11 of them must have been made to his orders.

On the wall above each figure in this Aisle of Tombs is a worn tablet bearing the name and heraldic arms. The first is Liulph, the founder of the family, an Anglo-Saxon nobleman who was murdered in 1080 by the Bishop of Durham's chaplain; the second is Liulph's elder son, Uchtred, and the third is William de Lumley, a cross-legged mediaeval figure which has probably been here since his burial in this church; his feet are on a lion which is trampling a dragon, and under his right hand is a headless parroquet. Next in order came William Lumley the Second; the curly head of William Lumley the Third resting on a helmet; Roger, with his legs broken below the knee; bearded Robert with his feet resting on a shield; and Sir Marmaduke, with head resting on his gauntlets.

Two mediaeval figures of Frosterley marble follow, both brought from Durham Cathedral. They are intended to represent Sir John Lumley, and Ralph, first Baron Lumley, who was killed at Cirencester while fighting for Richard II. At the east end, wearing capes and gowns, are Richard, Lord Lumley, and George, Lord Lumley, who won renown in the Scottish wars and added to the family fortunes by marrying the daughter of a rich Newcastle man.

The sculptured pageant ends, in chronological order, with two figures at the west end (near Liulph). They represent Sir Thomas Lumley, who married a daughter of Edward IV; and, in ermine cape and long gown, the originator of this proud display—John, Lord Lumley, who died in 1609, and was buried, not here, as might be expected, but at Cheam in Surrey.

At the end of this aisle is a gallery called the Lambton Pew; its panelling and arcaded wooden front date from 1829. In the crypt here lies John George, first Earl of Durham, who was known locally as Radical Jack and has a measure of fame as the first Governor-General of Canada. Near him lies his son, the "Master Lambton" or "Red Boy" painted by Sir Thomas Lawrence.

Many ancient relics are also preserved at the west end of the church, near the massive 15th century font. Here are several fragments of Saxon crosses, including two of particular interest; one has a relief carving of a woman holding a child, the other a mounted warrior and a double-headed dragon, with the name Eadmund written partly in runes and partly in Roman characters.

Also preserved here is a fine collection of relics from the Roman fort, the most important being the bust of an emperor wearing a crown of laurel. An inscription commemorates a prefect of cavalry who brought water into the fort and rebuilt a bath, and a 2nd century tombstone has a recut inscription to Silvinus, who died at the age of 25. Among the other exhibits are a small stone vase carved with garlands, a massive pine-cone of stone, and a large Roman handmill made of black lava from the Rhine.

In a park beside the River Wear, a mile to the east of Chester-le-Street, is Lumley Castle. Ancestral home of the family whose monuments make such a brave array in the church, it is now a hall of residence attached to Durham University. It is an impressive sight, especially from the east, where its battlemented walls of yellow stone, mellowed by many centuries, soar nobly above the steep and thickly wooded banks of the Lumley Beck.

From the time of Edward the Confessor, Lumley succeeded Lumley as overlord of these domains, but the greater part of the castle now standing dates from the closing years of the 14th century. That was when Ralph Lumley, created first Baron Lumley by Richard I, received permission from the king and the Bishop of Durham to build himself a fortified house.

Considerable alterations were made to the castle in Elizabethan times by John, Lord Lumley. Other changes were wrought early in the 18th century by the great John Vanbrugh, who was commissioned by Richard Lumley, first Earl of Scarbrough, one of the leading Royalist officers at the Battle of Sedgemoor.

Lumley Castle stands four-square, with a battlemented tower at each corner. In the centre is a quadrangle, and on the north side is a courtyard surrounded by old stone gabling. The stately east front, overlooking the Lumley Beck, has a noble gatehouse with two square flanking turrets and a low entrance arch surmounted by carved shields and helmets. Under the guardroom on the south side of this gateway is a dungeon, 10 feet square and 16 feet deep.

The gatehouse leads to the quadrangle which retains its original windows on three sides. On the west side of the quadrangle is the original entrance to the Great Hall, flanked by eight-sided turrets capped by little heraldic beasts holding shields. Over the entrance arch are two long rows of heraldic shields which were placed there in the 16th century to the order of the ancestor-proud John, Lord Lumley.

The finest feature of the castle interior is the Great Hall. Little altered by Vanbrugh, apart from the windows, it has a handsome stone fireplace of about 1600, flanked by a tall pair of fluted pillars and decorated with a frieze of ox-heads and round flowers. At one end of the hall is an equestrian statue of the Saxon Liulph, first of the Lumleys; it is a hollow wooden figure, some 300 years old. Adorning the walls are 16 enormous pictures in black frames (mostly imaginary portraits of ancestors painted for Lord John), and 16th century marble busts of Henry VIII, Edward VI, Mary, Elizabeth I and James I, who once stayed at the castle.

There are splendid views of Lumley Castle from the public path across the park.

Cockfield. This wind-swept village with its long sloping street used to be famed for the geese which were reared on Holy Moor, the common on the top of the hill.

At the foot of the main street is the church, a 13th century building which was so enlarged and altered in 1911 that little of its antiquity is evident. Relics of its earliest days are a font with huge eight-sided bowl, some mediaeval stones with carved swords and crosses which are built into the wall of the porch, and memorials of a priest, a knight, and a girl in the sanctuary floor.

The priest's memorial is a long narrow grave-cover with carved cross and chalice. The knight's memorial is a grave-cover with a raised cross; a shield forms part of its stem, and his name, Roger Vavasour, can still be seen. Close to this is a worn stone figure of a 14th century girl who, as the legend runs, was drowned in the moat of Cockfield Hall.

Cockfield's most famous son was Jeremiah Dixon, an 18th century Quaker. A man of many parts, he is said to have invented several machines which were used in the neighbouring collieries. The Royal Society sent him to St Helena to observe the transit of Venus, and between 1763 and 1767 he was employed with Charles Mason, to survey the disputed boundaries of Maryland and Pennsylvania. The line they defined became famous as the Mason–Dixon line, separating free America from the southern slave states.

Consett. This busy industrial town is spread out over a hillside sloping towards the River Derwent, and its tall chimneys, rising from a long grey mountain of slag, form a feature of the skyline visible for miles. The great steelworks have had a great reputation for more than a century; much less well known is the fact that the town's Salvation Army band, formed in 1879, was the first in the world.

Consett's most interesting modern building is St Patrick's Roman Catholic Church, which dates from 1959. It is brickbuilt in basilican form, with a broad nave, a clerestory with pairs of small windows, and aisles formed by round arcades supported on round pillars. Over the altar is an ornate canopy.

In their midst, the townspeople have two attractive parks; close at hand they have all the beauty of the Derwent Valley.

Cowshill. It is just a cluster of houses at a corner of the road through Weardale. There is splendid scenery all around, and at the bridge below the brown waters of the Wear rush over a waterfall into a pool beneath. Four miles beyond the village the road enters Cumberland; this is at Killhope Cross, 2056 feet above the sea, and it is the highest stretch of main road in England.

The snowfall is sometimes particularly heavy here, and in the middle of the 19th century the lead-miners went to work on skis in the winter. Skiing was then, as now, a popular sport in upper Weardale, and barrels of beer were awarded for proficiency.

The most impressive sight in the neighbourhood is the Burnhope Reservoir, at the head of Weardale. It is a magnificent stretch of water in a high hollow of the hills, with the lower side of the dam descending steeply in great grassy terraces. This dam is 600 yards long, 267 yards wide at the base, and 43 yards wide at the top, along which runs a public motor road. The dam was built of local stone hewn beside the site, but also contains the remains of 15 houses of Burnhope hamlet which were pulled down when the work was started. The old packhorse bridge was spared, but is now under 100 feet of water. A 1000 men were employed on the whole undertaking, which began in 1930 and was finished in 1937.

Water from 10,000 acres of moorland is gathered into these 100 acres of reservoir, 1300 feet above the sea. Its capacity is about 1400 million gallons, and a pipe 44 miles long carries five million gallons a day to Sunderland, South Shields, and Jarrow.

On the wall by the dam is this inscription in grey granite:

In commemoration of Peter Lee, chairman Durham County Water Board, 1920 to 1935 who by his able guidance contributed in no small measure to the satisfactory construction of Burnhope Reservoir. This memorial is the workers' tribute to his great ability and constant endeavour to promote their welfare.

Crook. It is a small industrial town near the western edge of the coalfield, sheltering below the steep slopes of Mount Pleasant and Dowfold Hill. From these heights there are far-reaching views embracing Durham Cathedral to the east, the Cleveland Hills to the south, and Weardale to the west. Crook probably takes its name from a bend in the Beechburn Beck, which flows through the town to join the Wear.

The town centre is a broad open green, and at its lower end is the 19th century parish church of St Catherine. It has some attractive modern windows by S. M. Scott of Newcastle; one at the west end depicts craftsmen at work on the building of the Temple of Jerusalem.

Dalton-le-Dale. This is a small village at the upper end of a wooded valley running down to Seaham Harbour. Its little church has a Norman north doorway with worn zigzag carving, a 13th century south doorway sheltered by a porch dating from about 1450, and 13th century lancet windows. One of the lancets in the south wall is filled with splendid modern glass by L. C. Evetts, depicting the Parable of the Sower.

In an arched recess on the south side of the chancel is a panelled altar tomb surmounted by a worn figure of a man in armour, with his head on a helm and his feet on a lion; it is thought to represent Sir William Bowes of Streatlam, who died about 1420. In a low recess in the north wall of the nave is a damaged stone figure of an unknown 15th century woman, locally known as the Good Nun.

The most remarkable feature in the church is a row of raised numerals set about five feet apart on the north wall, to record the hours from seven in the morning to one in the afternoon. A ray of sunshine once passed through a slit in the roof above the middle window in the south wall, to mark the time on this extraordinary sundial.

Darlington. "George, thou must think of Darlington; remember it was Darlington sent for thee." Those words were addressed to George Stephenson by a far-seeing Quaker business man named Edward Pease when the great locomotive pioneer was suggesting an alternative route for the line from the coalfield to Stockton; and in them lies the key to Darlington's fame as the cradle of public railways and its subsequent rise to industrial eminence.

The town has a long history. Set in a pleasant countryside, it was originally a Saxon settlement beside the little River Skerne, which flows into the Tees about three miles to the South. It grew into a township of considerable importance in Norman times, and thenceforth prospered as a market town. When John Leland carried out his ecclesiastic survey of the district for Henry VIII he described Darlington as "the best market town in the Bishoprick after Durham".

Daniel Defoe, it is true, in his *Tour through Great Britain* two centuries later, dismissed it as having "nothing remarkable in it but dirt, and a high bridge over little or no water". But a man who could ignore its beautiful church need not be taken too seriously, and we can still picture it as being a pleasant market town (as, indeed, at its heart it still is) with flourishing textile industries when the Stockton and Darlington line was built, early in the 19th century. That momentous event transformed Darlington into one of the biggest and busiest towns in the county of Durham. The man primarily responsible for the transformation was a Quaker mill-owner named Edward Pease (1787–1858), one of the most distinguished members of a Darlington family of industrialists long noted for their great public spirit and their devotion to good causes.

Many were interested in the railway project, but it was Edward Pease's vision, wealth, enterprise, and influence which enabled the great George Stephenson to carry out the work; and it was Edward Pease who shared chief honours with Stephenson when on September 27, 1825, a train of 34 vehicles was drawn from Shildon to Darlington and then on to Stockton by an engine driven by George Stephenson himself. It was preceded by a signalman on horseback, and drew a gross load of nearly 90 tons at an average speed of between 10 and 12 miles an hour. Such was the first journey made by the first train on the first public railway in the world.

For over a century railway locomotives were built and repaired in Darlington, until, in 1966, the workshops were finally closed. Today the town has many engineering industries, and a worldwide reputation for its steel bridges.

There are many ways into Darlington, for it is the meeting-place of many roads. The traveller by train will alight at the big Bank Top station, on the main line from London to Edinburgh. Here, standing on a platform, are two clumsy and grotesque locomotives which played their part in the development of the town as a great engineering centre. One is the historic *Locomotion No 1* (originally called *Active*) which was built by Robert Stephenson & Company at Newcastle-upon-Tyne, and was in use on the Stockton to Darlington line until 1841. With its tender it weighs eight tons.

Beside it stands the locomotive *Derwent*, which was built in Darlington in 1845 for the Stockton and Darlington Railway Company, and subsequently purchased by Messrs Pease for use on their private lines.

Locomotion No 1 stands on two original rails of the Stockton and Darlington Railway, and on the London side of the station is a relaid length of the track with the original stone sleepers. A little to the north of the station is a notice marking the spot where the route of the original Stockton and Darlington Railway crosses the present main line.

The centre of Darlington is the broad marketplace, with the spire of St Cuthbert's Church soaring on one side of it, and on the other the Town Hall clock-tower given by Edward Pease.

At a busy corner close by is a bronze statue of Joseph Pease (1799–

Durham Cathedral, seen across the River Wear

Durham: Elvet Bridge, with the cathedral and castle beyond

The west towers of Durham Cathedral and the further bank of the River Wear

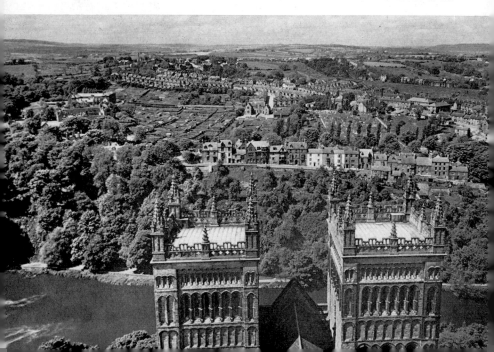

1872), second son of the railway pioneer, which was unveiled by the Duke of Connaught in 1875 on the occasion of the jubilee of public railways. Round the base are various bronze reliefs—Pease among his friends, the early railway, a charity school, a group symbolising freedom. Joseph Pease, who helped his father to establish the Stockton and Darlington Railway, was the first Quaker MP. He frequently spoke in the House on social and political reform, always wearing his Quaker dress.

In Tubwell Row, on the north side of the marketplace, is Darlington's Public Museum. It presents an attractive shop window to the passers-by and in rather cramped quarters displays a great deal to make them linger—railway relics, models of locomotives, silver pennies from the Durham mint, early playbills, big-game trophies, stuffed birds, oriental arms and armour.

In Crown Street, near the Museum, is the Public Library. It contains a fine reading-room adorned with many photographs and prints of old Darlington and paintings of the surrounding countryside. An art gallery in the same building displays many works by local artists, including John Dobbin's painting of the opening of the Stockton and Darlington Railway.

Outside the library is a memorial to the indomitable journalist W. T. Stead, who went down with the *Titanic* in 1912; it is a piece of granite, about two feet high, with an iron ring let into it. An inscription on the wall above states that it was the stone to which he tethered his dogs and pony when he was resident at Grainey Hill.

For nine years Stead edited Darlington's famous newspaper, *The Northern Echo*, the first halfpenny daily in England. The paper made its bow in 1869, and two years later, on the strength of some outstanding articles he had contributed to its columns, W. T. Stead became editor. He was only 22, and it is a remarkable fact that never before had he been in a newspaper office; but he was a born editor and he served the paper with great success until 1880, when he moved south, to win fame in Fleet Street. Grainey Hill, two miles out of Darlington, was his first home after his marriage, and he used to ride on a pony to his office after dark, returning about two or three in the morning.

None of Darlington's public buildings can compare with the nobly-proportioned Church of St Cuthbert, which stands in its beautiful churchyard, between the busy marketplace and the River Skerne. Successor of a Saxon church on the same site, it was designed by Bishop Hugh Pudsey in the last quarter of the 12th century, and despite various changes it remains to this day a splendid example of

D

a cruciform church built at a time when Norman architecture was giving way to the Early English style.

The arcaded belfry and graceful ribbed spire, which soars to a height of 180 feet, are late 14th century additions, but they enhance the symmetry of the whole building.

Outstanding architectural features of the interior are the 13th century roofs of transepts and nave (the oldest in the county), and the four noble arches of the tower, each 36 feet high; below the eastern arch is a low, pointed arch which is really a stone roodloft dating from about AD 1400 and now supporting an organ gallery.

The chancel has undergone considerable alteration, but it still has its beautiful 14th century sedilia and 15th century Easter sepulchre. It has also retained 18 stalls of black oak given to the church by Bishop Langley early in the 15th century. Their traceried bench-ends have poppyheads with carved seraphim and human faces, and buttresses of lions, birds, and prim little angels. The seats are misericords, with carved animals, eagles, monsters, and little scenes—a man striding along holding bunches of flowers, another grasping an ogre with a chain round its neck, a king guarded by two griffins.

There are also two finely carved Jacobean armchairs in the chancel, and in the adjoining vestry, which has a 15th century roof, is a Jacobean altar table. A modern feature of interest is the mosaic reredos picturing the Last Supper. It was originally designed for Westminster Abbey by the Darlington artist John Dobbin, but was rejected by the Dean.

In the south transept stands the old eight-sided font, with a Restoration canopy which rises nearly halfway to the roof, and is, in fact, the tallest in the county. Fastened to the wall close by is a worn 13th century figure of a woman with a purse hanging from her girdle.

On a wall of the north transept is an inscription to Brigadier General Roland Boys Bradford VC, MC, *who at the age of 25, the youngest brigadier general in the British army, was killed in the Great War at the Battle of Cambrai 30 November 1917.*

At the base of one of the nave pillars is a red stone Norman sun-dial, and, on the pillar opposite, is the head of a Saxon cross.

Darlington is fortunate in possessing many parks and recreation grounds, the oldest and biggest being South Park, through which the little River Skerne flows on its way to the Tees. Here, on a hill overlooking a little lake, is a memorial to John Fowler (1826–64) the inventor of the steam plough, who married a daughter of Joseph Pease, MP. It is a big block of red granite surmounted by a model of his invention, surrounded by sheaves of corn.

Denton. It lies in a quiet hollow below hills that look down upon the Tees—a pretty cluster of whitewashed farm buildings with a little church which was originally Norman but was rebuilt in late Victorian times and retains only one witness to its antiquity. This is a 12th century gravestone of blue marble, let into the wall of the vestry and now screened by a cupboard door. Nearly six feet long, it bears a much-worn relief of a woman with her hands clasped in prayer. Round the margin is an inscription in Lombardic letters saying that *Hici gist Aubrey de Coynners sa compayn.*

The east window of the church, portraying the Crucifixion, commemorates John Birkbeck, who was parson here for 60 years.

Durham. *This city is celebrated in the whole Empire of the Britons;* so begins an Anglo-Saxon poem. Today Durham's fame is worldwide. Tourists in their thousands, following in the steps of the mediaeval pilgrim, journey to the shrine of St Cuthbert, and millions more are, through painting and photograph, familiar with the noble spectacle of cathedral and castle soaring high above the River Wear. County town, cathedral city, and seat of a university, Durham has much to interest the visitor, but to appreciate fully all the sights it offers it is necessary to have some knowledge of its long history.

The early story of Durham is obscure, although the remains of the fort called Maiden Castle on the promontory to the east of the city are evidence that men have lived in the neighbourhood since prehistoric days. Less shadowy beginnings of community life here date back no further than Anglo-Saxon times.

The Anglo-Saxon Chronicle records the consecration of a bishop in 762 at a place called Aelfet ee (Swan Island) in the district still called Elvet which lies in the loop of the river to the east of the cathedral. Here arose an Anglian village served by St Oswald's, the mother church of Durham.

Nothing more is known of the history of this settlement until the year 995, when monks were bearing St Cuthbert's body, after its brief stay at Ripon, towards Chester-le-Street, where it had previously been enshrined for 113 years. Northumbria was then being harried by Danes as well as Scots, and the holy men were anxious to find a new and more secure headquarters. When the party arrived in the neighbourhood of Elvet, the island hill (Dunholm, which we now call Durham) must have struck them as an ideal spot, and after a pause for discussion it was decided to settle there.

Legend tells of the coffin suddenly becoming immovable at a neighbouring hill until the saint announced his intention of resting at Dunholm; and of how, not knowing the place, the travellers were fortunate enough to overhear a milkmaid tell another that her lost cow was in Dunholm, and by this means found the spot.

For three days the body lay in a small wattled church built for the purpose, perhaps on the site of the present church of St Mary-le-Bow, and then for three years rested in another building called the White Church. During this time Aldhun, Bishop of Chester-le-Street, induced his son-in-law, Uchtred, later Earl of Northumbria, to make a forced levy on the people between Coquet and Tees in order to build a more fitting shrine.

By September 998 they had built the first part of their Saxon cathedral, and it was dedicated in the presence of the thankful gathering of workmen. Cuthbert's coffin was duly transferred to the new building, and Durham soon became a place of pilgrimage.

Shortly after the year 1000 the city had to be fortified against the Danes and Scots, and twenty years passed before the cathedral was finished. It had a central tower, and another with brass-covered pinnacles at the west end. To this cathedral came the converted Canute on barefoot pilgrimage from Garmondsway, near Trimdon, bringing with him deeds concerning gifts of land. Great stores of valuables also found their way here when it was proved that the city was able to withstand siege, and also sacred relics collected from other shrines, including the bones of the Venerable Bede, stolen from Jarrow.

A stormy period followed the Norman Conquest. When the northern rebellion broke out in 1068, Robert Cumin, Earl of Northumberland, was sent to the city with 700 soldiers, and the routed remnant of insurgents took refuge in a strong tower they had hurriedly built—the earliest Durham Castle. The Earl and his retinue settled for the night in the bishop's palace at the west end of the cathedral, but by morning all but one had been burnt with the building in which they lay. This massacre was the work of the men of the surrounding countryside, and when William the Conqueror came north to avenge it he spared the city but laid waste the district around. The monks had once again fled with the sacred relics, this time to Lindisfarne, and none were left to attend to the wounded and dying who crowded to the cathedral for sanctuary.

In 1072 the Conqueror came to Durham to confirm the privileges granted by Canute, and there is a story of him being smitten with a fever when about to inspect the body of St Cuthbert at High Mass. He is said to have rushed from the cathedral, and to have ridden down Dun Cow Lane, fording the Wear and not stopping until he reached the Tees.

The Conqueror had outlawed the Saxon Bishop Ethelwin, and in his place had appointed Walcher of Lorraine, a canon of Liege, described as an amiable, honourable man with pleasant manners. Walcher was friendly with Waltheof, the new Earl of Northumbria, and in the year of William's visit had persuaded the Earl to build a stronger castle of stone. This work, with the aid of a forced levy, he had begun.

When Waltheof died Walcher succeeded him as Earl—he is said to have paid £400 for the title—and the bishopric was thus endowed with political sovereignty over a vast domain; for centuries the bishop was the representative of the sovereign (though not always with the sovereign's goodwill) and as such he was called Count Palatine, or Prince Palatine, overlord of a county palatine.

It was Walcher who laid the foundations of a reformed monastery at Durham, and part of the permanent home which he started to build for these monks can be seen at the undercroft, near the south-east corner of the cathedral cloister.

In 1080 Walcher was killed by a Gateshead mob for condoning the murder of Liulph, Saxon ancestor of the Lumleys of Lumley Castle; and he was succeeded by William de St Carileph, a priest from Bayeux, who with Duke Robert conspired to overthrow William Rufus and was banished for three years to Normandy.

While in Normandy the bishop made plans for building a nobler cathedral, and on his return in 1091 he proceeded to put them into effect. Five years later he died at Old Windsor, where he had been commanded to appear at court to suffer the king's displeasure, but he had the satisfaction of seeing the new cathedral take shape, and he is still honoured as one of our greatest mediaeval builders. Simeon, the Durham chronicler, describes him as a learned man, industrious, wise, and eloquent.

William Rufus kept the See vacant for three years before appointing his favourite, Ralph Flambard, a great builder and a man of vision, who did more for the city than any other bishop, making it stronger and far more imposing. He constructed a stouter and higher city wall of stone in place of earth, built a wall from the choir of the cathedral to the castle keep, and dug a moat. He also cleared Palace Green of dwellings, probably moving the inhabitants to the new suburb of Framwellgate which lay west of the city, adjoining Crossgate, the original trading centre of Durham. Certainly Framwellgate Bridge was built by him.

In 1104 the translation of St Cuthbert's body to its new shrine gave rise to the important annual Fair of St Cuthbert. In 1112

41

Flambard founded Kepier Hospital and built the church of St Giles around which the north-east suburb grew. In 1128 he died, but by then he had built the nave and aisles of the cathedral—work made possible by contributions from the increased flow of pilgrims.

The next bishop, the learned Galfrid Rufus, was appointed in 1133 and two years later set up his mint at the north-east corner of Palace Green, where it continued for 400 years.

In 1136 King Stephen occupied the castle, and while there arranged with David of Scotland the withdrawal of the Scottish troops who were supporting the Empress Maud and had been threatening to take the city. Three years later the Treaty of Durham was signed in the castle, and the bishopric became for a time an oasis in a Scottish Northumbria.

Bishop Rufus died in the castle in 1140 and was buried in the chapter house he had built. William Cumin, the Scottish Chancellor, made an immediate bid for the See. With the aid of the barons he took possession of the castle, and although the monks would have none of him it was two years before a band of them could slip away to York to elect a lawful bishop, William de St Barbara. The new bishop then proceeded to occupy Bishopton Castle with the help of Roger Conyers, ex-Constable of Durham.

All this so enraged Cumin that he ejected the monks who would not support him, tortured the citizens, and filled the castle with plunder from the surrounding countryside. He then forged letters from Rome substantiating his claims to the bishopric.

After fleeing to Jarrow and then to Lindisfarne, Bishop de St Barbara managed to collect an army and marched to Durham, setting up a fortification at the church of St Giles. Cumin thereupon wreaked his vengeance on the remaining monks by bursting into the locked cathedral while they were at prayer and enforcing the closing of the building for over a year. Not until 1144 was the usurper driven out, and then not before he had razed the suburbs of Elvet and St Giles.

Nine years later Bishop de St Barbara was succeeded by the 25 year old Hugh Pudsey, a relative of King Stephen. The Archbishop of York objected violently to the appointment, so Pudsey proceeded to Rome with a magnificent escort and was consecrated by the Pope.

When Richard Coeur de Lion set off on his Crusade he left Pudsey as regent over all the country north of the Humber, but he incurred the displeasure of the other regent—William Longchamp, Bishop of Ely—and was lured south and held prisoner at Southwell.

Pudsey was released under promise of giving up his earldom of

Northumberland, but was fully restored to power when the Bishop of Ely in turn fell into disgrace. On the return of King Richard he was in possession of a large sum which he had ostensibly collected for the king's ransom, and this he spent lavishly on the cathedral and castle and other buildings in the diocese, notably St Cuthbert's Church at Darlington.

In 1179 or 1180 Pudsey granted Durham its first charter (still treasured in the city) giving his borough of St Nicholas with Framwellgate "all the free privileges as the burgesses of Newcastle possess". He practically rebuilt the castle after a disastrous fire of which traces still remain on the buttresses of the North Terrace. He renewed the city wall along the river—the foundations of it can still be discerned. He rebuilt the destroyed borough of Elvet, and united this suburb with the city by building Elvet Bridge. He also refounded Kepier Hospital and rebuilt the church of St Giles; but his crowning work was the completion of the Galilee Chapel at Durham Cathedral.

Pudsey's efforts undoubtedly increased the attractions of the city to pilgrims, and when the annual festivals of St Cuthbert took place, on March 20 and September 4, there were devotional attractions inside the cathedral and sports and games outside. In the intervals between the festivals the relics were sent on tour through England and Scotland to make the shrine even better known.

Hugh Pudsey died at Howden in Yorkshire in 1195 while on his way to London, having been bishop for 42 years; he was succeeded by Philip de Pictavia, who was for ever at odds with his clergy. On supporting King John against the Pope, Philip was duly excommunicated, and on his death, in 1208, he was buried in unconsecrated ground.

For nearly 10 years the See of Durham was vacant, and then it fell to the proud and extravagant Richard Marisco, Chancellor and favourite of King John. He, too, was bitterly opposed to the monks, threatening them with death should they show themselves outside the cloister, encouraging his servants to assault them, and swearing that the Church of Durham should have no peace during his lifetime. He ruled for nine years, dying at Peterborough in 1226 while on his way to London to meet charges of simony and sacrilege.

His successor, the excellent Richard Poore, was translated from Salisbury, where he had started to build a new cathedral. He was elected in opposition to the king, who occupied Durham Castle for a time. It was Poore who decided to pull down Carileph's Norman apse and to replace it with the Chapel of the Nine Altars, though not until after his death was the work begun.

43

In 1229 he drew up the famous compromise, called Le Convenit, which settled the long dispute between the bishop and the monks and defined the rights which each party was to enjoy. Thereafter the city developed vigorously, though not without occasional scenes of strife.

Richard Poore died in 1237 and was succeeded four years later by Nicholas de Farnham, who resigned in 1248. Walter de Kirkham, Dean of York, was the next bishop, and then Robert de Stitchill, Prior of Finchale, who in 1273 was followed by Robert de Insula, a native of Lindisfarne who had become a monk at Durham.

In the time of Bishop de Insula the reforming Archbishop Wickwane refused to institute a nominee of the monks to a living in Yorkshire, and illegally demanded to inspect Durham Priory during the temporary absence of the bishop. Finding Sadlergate blocked by the barons of the bishopric he proceeded to excommunicate the bishop, the prior, and the entire body of monks.

In 1283 Bishop de Insula died, and Wickwane returned. Again refused admission to the cathedral, he proceeded to the church of St Nicholas and from the pulpit began to rebuke the prior and monks. Some of the youths of the borough thereupon became so threatening that the bishop had to slip out through a side door and make his way down the steps at the back of the church. He reached Kepier Hospital in safety, though his horse lost an ear.

Two years later the popular Prior Hugh of Darlington settled the dispute but scarcely had he done so than another difference arose. Since the days of Canute the lords of Raby had been accustomed to present a stag at Durham on the feast of St Cuthbert; but in 1290 Ralph, third Lord Neville, announced to the prior that when he presented the stag he would like to be entertained to dinner, with all his retinue. Having been informed that this would be impossible at such a busy time he nevertheless arrived with the stag, and instead of taking it to the prior's hall marched to the shrine of St Cuthbert. The monks immediately caught up heavy candlesticks and attacked the servants of Neville, causing them to carry off the stag to the kitchen. Neville sued for assault and the prior complained to the Pope, but the dispute was settled by the intervention of friends.

This disagreement occurred in the days of Bishop Anthony Bek, a nobleman who succeeded Robert de Insula without opposition in 1284 and at once started to regain for the bishopric the importance which his predecessors had to a degree lost. He was a great builder, and constructed the magnificent hall in the castle; it had two thrones in which he sat as both temporal and spiritual ruler of the palatinate.

In 1296 he took part with Edward I in an expedition to Scotland with 26 standard-bearers, 140 knights, 1000 foot-soldiers and 500 cavalry. Some of the men complained that they had no obligation of service outside the palatinate, and in 1298 returned without permission. The bishop thereupon imprisoned them at Durham, making himself as unpopular with his barons as he was soon to be with the prior and monks.

In 1300 Bek seized the lands of the prior, Robert Hotoun, besieged the monastic buildings, cut off the water supply, and installed a rival prior. Prior Hotoun was thrown into prison, but managed to escape and take his appeal to Rome. The famous Pope Boniface VIII gave a decision in his favour, but Hotoun died before he could be reinstated.

Bek travelled to Rome to answer the charges against him; but he did so without a licence from Edward I, and in his absence the king seized all the temporal powers of the See. He was afterwards restored to favour, however, and received the title of King of the Isle of Man as well as his former one of Prince Palatine. He died in 1311 in the manor house he had built at Eltham, Kent, and was buried in Durham Cathedral.

His successor, another monk of Durham named Richard Kellaw, founded a chapel on Elvet Bridge, and granted the citizens the right of free fishing between the two bridges. A wise and kindly man, he held office for only five years, dying in 1316, the year when the city was overwhelmed by a disastrous flood which broke down the weirs and drowned many people in their homes.

The next bishop, Louis de Beaumont, was appointed through the influence of his cousin Isabella, Edward II's queen. He had the misfortune to be waylaid at Rushyford while on his way to consecration, and was imprisoned at Mitford Castle in Northumberland until a ransom was paid. A man who knew no Latin, and had great difficulty with his installation ceremony, he tyrannised the monks.

In 1334 the scholarly Richard de Bury was enthroned as Bishop of Durham. He had been tutor to Edward III, and the King attended his magnificent banquet in the castle in company with Queen Philippa, the two archbishops, five bishops, and seven earls, together with abbots and priors, knights and squires innumerable. He was a generous man, and the parishioners of St Margaret's had special cause to be grateful to him, for he allowed them to have a font in their church when the prior had disputed it, as well as obtaining funds for them to finish their south aisle.

Thomas Hatfield, tutor to the Black Prince, succeeded Richard de

Bury in 1345. He was a warrior bishop and had a considerable share in the victory over the Scots at Neville's Cross in the year following his enthronement. This made Durham a safer place to live in, but was followed three years later by the Black Death.

Hatfield rebuilt the roof of the castle and in 1379 granted tolls for the purpose of paving the town. Two years later he was buried under the splendid throne in the cathedral.

More famed for his public works was Bishop Walter de Skirlaw, who came here from Bath and Wells in 1388 to take over from Hatfield's successor, John Fordham, secretary to Richard II. He built the monks' great dormitory and part of the cloister, as well as bridges at Shincliffe, Bishop Auckland, and Yarm.

The next bishop, Thomas Langley, who was enthroned in 1406, also made his mark on the city. Chancellor of England, Dean of York, a cardinal, and Henry V's ambassador in France, he restored the Galilee Chapel, completed the cloisters, and in 1414 founded two schools on the east side of Palace Green.

Two years later a terrible plague afflicted the city, and in 1429, on Corpus Christi Day when the city was crowded with visitors, a terrific thunderstorm destroyed the central tower of the cathedral. (It was the Guild of Corpus Christi which in 1437 first conducted a piped water supply from a well near Framwellgate to the market-place for the use of citizens.)

Langley was followed in 1437 by Robert Neville, nephew of Henry IV, grandson of John of Gaunt and uncle of Warwick the King-maker. In 1448 he entertained the young Henry VI on his pilgrimage to St Cuthbert's shrine. In 1451 the local weavers became the first trade fraternity of Durham to receive a charter.

In 1457 Neville was laid to rest near his ancestors in the south aisle of the cathedral, and Laurence Booth, a canon of York, was appointed in his place. He was a Lancastrian, receiving the post through the influence of Queen Margaret, and after the Yorkist victory of Towton he was astute enough to submit, thus saving the city from reprisals. In 1476 Booth became the first Bishop of Durham to be made Archbishop of York.

The next bishop, William Dudley, Dean of Windsor, held office for seven years and was followed by the learned John Sherwood, collector of Greek manuscripts. He was suspected of causing a rising against the oppressive commissioners of Henry VII, and found it expedient to retire to Rome, where he died in 1494.

His successor, Richard Fox, who was translated from Bath and Wells, was particularly active in defending the border against the

Scots and in checking the raiding activities of his own countrymen in Redesdale and Tynedale. After a truce had been signed he went to Melrose Abbey to arrange the marriage between James IV of Scotland and Princess Margaret, the alliance which ultimately led to the accession of James VI of Scotland to the throne of England. He made important alterations to the hall of Durham Castle, and entertained Princess Margaret there when she was on her way to Scotland for her wedding.

Fox was translated to Winchester in 1501, and was succeeded by William Sever (Sinews), Bishop of Carlisle, who is said to have been the son of a sieve-maker of nearby Shincliffe.

Sever's successor, Christopher Bainbridge, Dean of York, came to Durham in 1507, and gave the prior and monks the control of the bank of the river below the cathedral. This enabled the monks to police and safeguard the area, and, late in the 18th century, the prebendaries to carry out the tree-planting on the banks which is still so much admired. Bainbridge later went as ambassador to Rome and was made a cardinal. He was poisoned in 1508 by a servant he had struck in anger.

The rich Thomas Ruthall, Dean of Salisbury, was the next bishop. When he was with Henry VIII in France the Scots invaded the See, and he hurried back to Durham Castle to superintend the musters. His forces were in the forefront of the English army at the resulting battle of Flodden, and the defeated king's banner, armour, and sword were later hung in the cathedral. The much-harassed people of the city attributed their triumph to the intercession of St Cuthbert.

Cardinal Wolsey held the bishopric for six years following Ruthall's death in 1522, but in all that time never even bothered to visit the city. He resigned in 1528 and was succeeded two years later by the able Cuthbert Tunstall. His term was one of vast change.

In 1535 came the visitation of the monastery, when little could be found to the detriment of the monks. In 1536 the Durham insurgents bore away the banner of St Cuthbert on the Pilgrimage of Grace. Two years later came the legalised looting of the shrine of St Cuthbert, and with it the destruction of the source of much of the city's trade. The valuable offerings of generations of pilgrims disappeared at one blow, and the saint's coffin was forced open and carried into the vestry.

On the last day of 1539 the prior surrendered the whole monastery to the king, but in May 1541 its revenues were restored and the cathedral was endowed with a dean, 12 prebendaries, and 80 or so minor officials. The last prior became the first dean, and 12 monks

47

were appointed prebendaries. One of them, a former prior of Finchale, even married.

In 1542 St Cuthbert's body was buried behind the high altar in a vault made of stone from the base of his shrine which had stood on the spot.

In 1547, the first year of Edward VI's brief reign, came the dissolution of Kepier Hospital and the suppression of the Corpus Christi Guild whose plays and pageants had attracted so much trade to the city. A year or two later Bishop Tunstall was sent to the Tower of London on a charge of treason, and it was proposed to carve out of his diocese a new See of Newcastle. The Duke of Northumberland planned to rule the original palatinate from Durham Castle, and his son Guilford Dudley was to be consort to Lady Jane Grey ruling in London.

The accession of Mary put a stop to all these schemes; Tunstall was released, papal jurisdiction was revived with a great festival in the cathedral, and St Cuthbert's shrine was re-established much as we see it today. But Bishop Tunstall never returned to Durham; on Queen Elizabeth I's accession he refused to take the oath, and was committed to the custody of the Archbishop of Canterbury for the rest of his life. He died at Lambeth Palace on November 18, 1559, and was buried in the chapel there.

James Pilkington was the first Protestant bishop, and in 1565 he granted the city an important charter which must have gone some way towards compensating it for the loss of trade caused by the Reformation. The first alderman was Christopher Surtees, probably of the same family as the great historian of Durham.

In 1569 the citizens joined in the Rising in the North which was intended to restore the old religion. The communion table was cast down in the cathedral, and two of the old altar stones retrieved from rubbish heaps. The English Bible and Prayer Book were removed, and for 10 or 12 days the services were sung in Latin. After the suppression of the rebellion 60 people, including the Earl of Westmorland, were executed in Durham.

In 1573 Pilkington set up the consistory court to enforce church discipline, but he was described as a man "much more angry in his speeches than in his doings", and is chiefly remembered as having left the buildings of the diocese in a ruinous condition. His successor, the unpopular Richard Barnes, observed on his arrival in 1575 that Pilkington had left the cathedral an Augean stable, "whose stink is grievous to the nose of God and man".

The advent of the learned Bishop Matthew Hutton in 1589

coincided with wanton damage to Neville's Cross during the night, and in his time at Durham we read of the decay of buildings and of the poor accommodation available for the queen's messengers. He left in 1594 on becoming Archbishop of York, and his passing was followed by an era of prosperity.

Bishop Tobias Matthew, who had been Dean of Durham for 13 years, and had acted as High Commissioner and as a member of the Council of the North, set about improving the city's trade and general well-being. He granted the first charter that really gave it independence, with a mayor, 12 aldermen, and a common council elected from the 12 chief guilds.

James I, on his way to claim the crown of England in 1603, paid a visit to the city, entering by Framwellgate Bridge. He was met in the marketplace by the mayor and corporation, and the procession then moved to the castle, where the bishop was waiting with 100 gentlemen in livery. After a sumptuous entertainment the king retired to rest in the Deanery.

When Tobias Matthew became Archbishop of York in 1606 his place at Durham was taken by William James, who also had been dean. Unlike Matthew he took it upon himself to strip the town of all the privileges he could get. In the spring of 1617 when James I again visited the city, the mayor, mounted on horseback, received him on Elvet Bridge and escorted him to the marketplace, where an apprentice recited some verses imploring the king to restore to the city its former privileges. The king spent the next few days at the castle, soundly rating the bishop for some fault, we know not what, though it has been seriously suggested that it was because the beer was too weak.

Whatever the cause, Bishop James, already worn out by his struggle with the corporation, took to his bed and in less than three weeks was dead.

Two months later Richard Neile came to Durham, his fourth bishopric. He spent much money on repairs to the buildings of Durham, and in 1627, the year of his departure for Winchester, granted various courts and fees to the city, a welcome restitution after the exactions of William James.

Neile was succeeded by George Montaigne, Bishop of London, a Yorkshireman of humble birth. Charles I sent him to Durham to make way for Laud in London, regarding him as "one that loved his own ease too much to disturb himself in the concernments of the Church". He was certainly not happy at Durham, and rejoiced when he was appointed Archbishop of York a few months later.

From 1628 to 1631 the See was in the care of John Howson, a man said to have been as vigorous in his quarrels with his clergy as in his attacks on popery. Then came Thomas Morton, who was translated from Lichfield in 1632 and was nominally bishop throughout the period of the Commonwealth.

When Charles I was on his way to be crowned at Edinburgh in 1633 he was lavishly entertained at Durham by Thomas Morton. The king attended evensong in great state, visited the graves of Cuthbert and Bede, and on leaving ordered the removal of unsightly buildings round the cathedral. He also commanded that the mayor and corporation should no longer sit in the choir.

During the Civil War Durham was seldom free from troops, and extensive damage was done by the Scots, who invaded the city in 1640 and caused Thomas Morton to flee for his life, never to return. King Charles was here again in 1647, this time on his way to Holmby House as a prisoner of the Scots; and three years later Cromwell passed through the city on his way to the Battle of Dunbar.

In 1658 a short-lived college was founded out of the cathedral revenues in accordance with the wishes of Cromwell, and it would have become a university but for opposition from Oxford and Cambridge and the Restoration of Charles II. Two centuries were to pass before the founding of Durham University.

John Cosin became Bishop of Durham after the Restoration and at once proceeded with great energy, to make good the damage done to the buildings of the diocese. He repaired the cathedral and castle, rebuilt the schools and county assize court on Palace Green, erected a library, and built almshouses for eight poor people. He erected a new conduit to carry water across the river from Elvet Moor to the cathedral and castle, rendering the Norman well unnecessary. He spent vast sums here, and also at Bishop Auckland Castle, where the chapel still bears witness to his munificence.

The next bishop, Nathaniel (Lord) Crewe, came here from Oxford in 1674, and held office for 48 years. He made Durham Castle his principal place of residence, and entertained widely. In 1677 he received the Duke of Monmouth who had been sent against the Scottish Covenanters, and himself raised the militia on the duke's behalf. He lived in great style, riding in his coach with six black horses, and being rowed on the river in his gondola. But he was noted for his charity, and the corporation got on well with him; he was a good friend to the city and presented most of the existing corporation plate.

After Nathaniel Crewe came Bishop William Talbot, in 1722, and then Edward Chandler, who was translated from Lichfield in 1730. In 1733 appeared the first local guide-book, a scholarly compilation by Dr Christopher Hunter, who was a friend of Patrick Sanderson of Saddler Street, the first Durham bookseller of whom we know. It was probably Sanderson who in 1735 started the earliest local newspaper, the *Durham Courant*.

From 1750 to 1752 Durham's bishop was Joseph Butler, author of the famous *Analogy of Religion*, which he wrote while he was parson at Stanhope. Next came the learned Richard Trevor, from St Davids, and then, from 1771 to 1787, John Egerton, who was translated here from Lichfield.

In 1780 Egerton granted the city the last charter it was ever to receive from a bishop, and he marked the occasion by entertaining the corporation and freemen inside the castle and providing wine, running from a fountain in the courtyard, for the townspeople in general.

Thomas Thurlow, brother of the Lord Chancellor, came to Durham from Lincoln in 1787, and was followed four years later by Shute Barrington, who held the See until his death in 1826 at the age of 92. It was Barrington who employed James Wyatt to pull down the Norman chapter house and carry out other disastrous restoration work on the cathedral. It was Barrington, too, who in 1809 laid the foundation stone of the new assize courts and prison which still stand in Old Elvet. John Howard had years before condemned the state of the old prison.

Still greater changes were to come. Shute Barrington was succeeded by the equally beneficent William Van Mildert, and during his episcopate (1826–36) it was decided that the time was ripe for abolishing much of the mediaeval privilege which still lingered on. Future bishops were to have a fixed income, and the palatinate powers of the bishopric were to pass to the Crown. Bishop Van Mildert was therefore the last Count Palatine.

During his term Durham University was founded with the surplus revenues of the See, and he himself contributed generously to its needs, as well as giving up the castle to its use; by 1841 the long-ruined keep had been fitted up with rooms for undergraduates.

With the death of William Van Mildert in 1836, the old order passed and the temporal powers of the bishop were transferred to the Crown. But Durham is still the capital of the County Palatine, in close and special relation to the sovereign, and one of its greatest treasures is a sword which George V granted to the city to symbolise this union.

51

So much for a brief outline of the history of Durham and its bishops from Saxon times to the Victorian era; now let us turn to the city itself and the riches with which the centuries have endowed it.

The cathedral and castle round which Durham has grown are set close together on a steep hill ringed by a long loop of the River Wear. From many viewpoints—notably the railway station, South Street, and the new Leazes Road—they are seen in all their grandeur, rising side by side from the steep wooded banks of the river.

The Wear almost encircles the old city. Flowing in from the east it takes a sharp turn to the south under Elvet Bridge and the Kingsgate footbridge, assumes a northerly direction under Prebends' Bridge, and leaves the city soon after passing Framwellgate Bridge and Millburngate Bridge. A central area of some 60 acres is thus enclosed, with the marketplace on the north side, the only side not fringed by the river.

Outside the river-girt heart of the City of Durham are suburbs as old, or older. From Elvet Bridge a dignified street called Old Elvet leads to the site of the oldest settlements we know of here—Iron Age, Roman, and Anglo-Saxon. From the same bridge New Elvet runs southward to St Oswald's, the mother church of Durham.

After the building of Elvet Bridge about 1160, New Elvet supplanted South Street as the road to London, and several inns were built by the bridge. In about 1830 the Great North Road was diverted to the west of the city by a bypass from Farewell Hall to Neville's Cross.

A good starting-point for a tour of Durham city is Framwellgate Bridge, built by Bishop Flambard in 1128 to serve his new suburb of Framwellgate. Some of his original work is still visible on the north face, though most of the bridge was rebuilt 300 years later by Cardinal Langley. It has two round arches, each with a span of 30 yards.

The remarkably narrow Silver Street winds up from the bridge to the little marketplace, also founded by Flambard. On the site of the old market house stands a spirited equestrian statue of the third Marquis of Londonderry (1779–1854). After a distinguished career of military and political service, he applied himself to county affairs, and is remembered as the founder of Seaham Harbour. The statue, set up in 1861, is of plaster coated with copper, and is the work of Raffaelle Monti, the Milanese sculptor who executed the reliefs of Music and Poetry on the proscenium arch at Covent Garden Opera House.

The church in the marketplace is St Nicholas, 19th century successor to one built by Bishop Flambard. It has a graceful stone

DURHAM CATHEDRAL

The cloister and west towers

Palace green

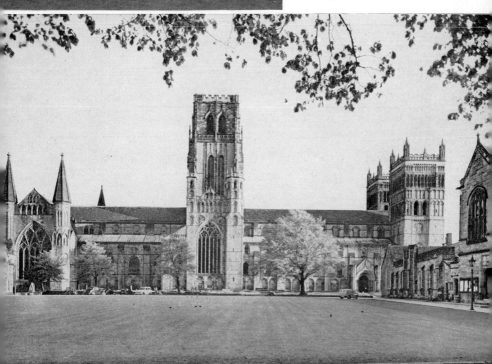

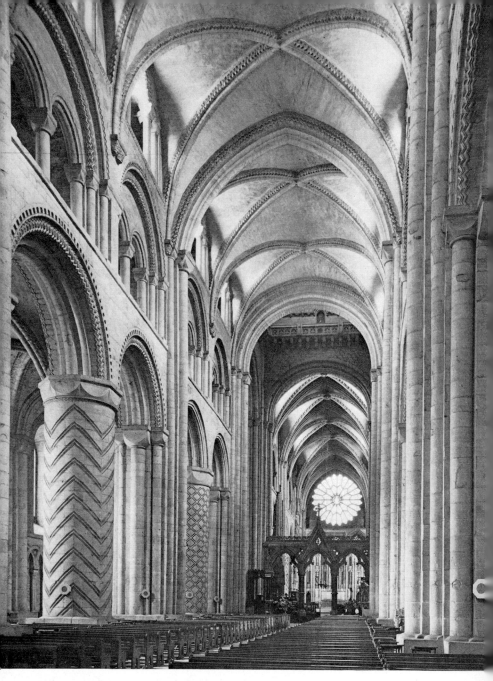

The nave of Durham Cathedral

spire and a light and spacious interior. Two striking modern windows in the south wall portray the Parable of the Sower and the Prophecy of Isaiah; they are the work of L. C. Evetts.

Below the pulpit is a stone font of 1700 which was restored to the church in 1898 after long use as a garden bird bath. In a glass case at the west end are two pewter collection plates (dated 1709 and 1714) which were found in a London shop in 1907, 50 years after the rebuilding of the church.

Next to St Nicholas' Church are various civic buildings. The Town Hall, opened in 1851, was designed by Philip Hardwick, the architect of the original Euston Station. It has an elaborate roof decorated with shield-bearing angels, and a fine west window with figures of four bishops of Durham who gave charters to the city—Hugh Pudsey, James Pilkington, Tobias Matthew, and Lord Crewe. Upper lights depict the colourful Corpus Christi procession of the guilds marching with their banners to the cathedral; below is a picture of the young Edward III, mounted on a white horse, thanking the citizens for rescuing his baggage train, which had been left unguarded while he was fighting the Scots.

The Mayor's Chamber has a fine Jacobean mantelpiece of oak which came from the Red Lion Inn, now part of Hatfield College. It is adorned with wooden statues of a crowned king and two men in armour, and also with copies of Van Dyck portraits of Charles I and Henrietta Maria.

The oldest of the civic buildings is the Guildhall; it dates from 1356, though it was largely rebuilt in the middle of the 18th century. The whole of one wall is occupied by traceried windows opening on to a balcony overlooking the marketplace. At one end of the room is some 18th century panelling capped by the royal arms of 1691.

In the lobby are a statue and a painting of Count Boruwlaski, a Polish dwarf, who died in Durham in 1837 and was buried in the cathedral. Displayed in glass cases are the little man's black suit, white stockings, shoes, embroidered slippers, hat and hat-box, cane, and violin.

In the room to the right of the entrance is a small collection of oil paintings left to the city by a Durham artist, Clement Burlison, who died in 1899. Many are copies of religious pictures made by Burlison himself in foreign galleries. Among the landscapes are several views of old Durham.

From the marketplace a road called Claypath climbs eastward towards Gilesgate, with its old church standing higher than the cathedral. Before reaching the church it joins the new Leazes Road, part of an ambitious scheme to bypass the city centre. This thorough-fare sweeps down towards the Wear, presenting an impressive view of the cathedral and castle, before passing under Claypath north of the marketplace. It is then carried across the river on the single-span Millburngate Bridge, and leaves the city by way of Framwell-gate, the ancient road to the north. Another bridge will eventually link Leazes Road to New Elvet to complete the through road scheme.

The third exit from Durham marketplace is Saddler Street. After passing Drury Lane, one of the steep narrow passages (vennels) running down to the river, the visitor will see some shops with fluted pillars supporting a classical cornice—the façade of an 18th century theatre which was destroyed by fire. Then comes Owengate, which curves steeply upwards to Palace Green and reveals the cathedral in all its glory.

Grouped round Palace Green are several old buildings occupied by Durham University. At the north-east corner is a lofty 17th century house of mellow brick, originally known as Archdeacon's Inn but now called Bishop Cosin's Hall. Next door are Bishop Cosin's Almshouses, a long low range of weather-worn stone buildings built in 1666 for eight poor men and women.

At the south-east corner of Palace Green is the plain stone Abbey House, a gracious Queen Anne building. At the south-west corner is the Grammar School building of 1661; it has a traceried east window, and also retains its original gallery and panelling. On its north side is Windy Gap, leading down to the river, and beyond this is a battle-mented building of 1820 which was originally the Diocesan Registry.

Further north is Bishop Cosin's Library, a dignified stone building of 1669, with a striking modern turret. Now part of the University Library, it still houses Cosin's books, together with 200 volumes printed before 1500. The library has also overflowed into Bishop Neville's exchequer and courtroom, a 15th century stone building with round-headed windows at the north-west corner of the green.

At this corner of Palace Green is the entrance to **Durham Castle,** the bishop's former residence, or fortress, from 1072 until the founda-tion of the university in 1831, and now the home of University College.

It was in 1069 that William the Conqueror inspected this rocky site high above the river and determined to make it the centre of the buffer state, or palatinate, he was establishing as protection from the Scots.

It was a wise choice; the Scots never took the castle, and the palatinate scheme worked well because the head of it was a bishop appointed by the king, and not a powerful and possibly disloyal hereditary noble.

Apart from the Norman chapel (which still exists) the first castle buildings were of wood, and were begun by Earl Waltheof in 1072. These were later replaced by stone buildings set up by Bishop Ralph Flambard, a favourite of King William Rufus.

As seen today the castle comprises buildings of different dates forming an irregular courtyard reached by a battlemented gateway. The core of this gateway is Norman, but the external casing and upper parts were added by James Wyatt about 1800. The heavy oak doors, with studded ironwork and massive bolts, are 400 years old.

Passing through the gateway, the visitor sees on his right the battlemented keep, which has been converted into rooms for under-graduates. The three terraces of the steep mound on which it stands were made in Restoration times for Bishop Cosin; the stone walls were renewed in 1840, when Anthony Salvin built them up from the ruins of Bishop Hatfield's 14th century keep.

On the left is the Great Hall, built by Bishop Bek about 1300. It was enlarged by Bishop Hatfield about 1350, and 150 years later was reduced to its original length by Bishop Fox. At the Restoration Bishop Cosin added the four big buttresses capped by cupolas, as well as the impressive pillared porch with his arms boldly carved on the pediment.

Bishop Bek's original pointed doorway, which still stands inside the porch, leads into one of the most magnificent dining-halls in England. Some of the stonework of the tall windows dates from the enlargement of 1350, and in the corners of the gallery are stone seats which Bishop Fox provided for musicians.

Armour and banners hang from the panelled walls, together with rows of portraits of bishops and benefactors. They make a brave display which has enhanced many a stately gathering through the centuries—from the time of Edward II (who dined here in 1322) to the time of Elizabeth II, who was here a few years before her accession. Here, too, Sir Walter Scott and the Duke of Wellington took dinner in October 1827 with the last of the prince-bishops, William Van Mildert.

Next to the hall is a kitchen with huge fireplaces and high chestnut roof. This kitchen was converted from a Norman guardroom by Bishop Fox about 470 years ago and is still in daily use. The entrance from the hall is a magnificent door with richly carved fruit and foliage which originally was either part of Bishop Cosin's Restoration choir

T021295

screen in the cathedral or, more probably, of a screen which he erected in the hall.

The central block of buildings facing the main gateway of the castle has as its nucleus the original Constable's Hall which was built by Bishop Pudsey in the 12th century. It has been divided into small rooms, but Pudsey's upper range of windows can still be seen from the courtyard, and can be studied to better advantage within the building from the wide passage called the Norman Gallery (the upper portion of Pudsey's hall). This exceptionally fine arcade, let into the thickness of the wall, has arches arranged in triplets, with coupled columns and zigzag carving.

The lower front of the Constable's Hall is hidden by Bishop Tunstall's Gallery, a battlemented Tudor range with mullioned windows which was built to provide access to his new chapel. In this gallery is the original entrance to the Constable's Hall—a beautiful and richly carved Norman doorway which was revealed again in the 19th century after long being hidden under lath and plaster.

Bishop Tunstall's Chapel was extended eastward by Lord Crewe about the year 1700, the rougher stonework of the extension being easily distinguished. The carved oak stalls with traceried bench-ends are early 16th century work, brought by Bishop Tunstall from his chapel at Bishop Auckland. One of the carved misericords shows three pigs, and another depicts a man trundling a woman in a wheel-barrow. The organ consists partly of a 17th century instrument which was once in the cathedral. Under the organ loft is a fine oak screen of Cosin's time.

Connecting Bishop Tunstall's Gallery with the Pudsey Norman Gallery above is a beautiful staircase inserted by Bishop Cosin in 1663. Mainly of black oak, it rises four storeys, and has pierced panels of willow carved with foliage. It was originally built on the cantilever principle, the supports having been added later to correct the pronounced outward slope of the treads.

One of the most splendid apartments in the castle is the Senate Room, formerly the bishop's drawing-room. It is hung with 16th century Flemish tapestry showing the life of Moses and has an oak overmantel erected in 1603, when James I stayed here on his way to London to be crowned. This woodwork, rich in heraldic devices, displays the earliest shield showing the arms of Scotland quartered with those of England.

Immediately under the Senate Room is the oldest part of Durham Castle—the beautiful little Norman chapel which was built late in the 11th century. Discoveries made in recent years suggest that the north wall may be even earlier work, a relic, indeed, of pre-Norman fortifications. Much of the original pavement remains, the flags being laid in herringbone fashion. The nave and aisles are vaulted, and the capitals are carved with geometrical designs, together with serpents, flowers, human figures, and leopards. One carved capital in the north arcade has stag-hunting scenes.

The Common Room, formerly the bishop's dining-room, has a 400-year-old oak ceiling with odd-looking gilt battlements added in the 18th century. The Judges' Apartments, used by the two judges staying here for the Durham Assizes, are notable for the 16th century tapestry on their walls.

From Durham Castle it is only a short step across Palace Green to the city's crowning glory, the cathedral which not only contains the noblest Norman architecture in England but also has the noblest site.

It is strange to reflect that all this magnificence began quite simply, a thousand years ago, with a temporary church of branches built over the coffin of St Cuthbert. The first **Durham Cathedral** was a Saxon building dedicated in 998 and served by a community of married clergy called the Congregation of St Cuthbert.

Walcher, the first Norman bishop, started to renew the domestic buildings of this community, and on August 11, 1093, his successor, William de St Carileph, laid the foundation stone of the present cathedral. Workmen were brought from Normandy; the stone came from the river bank below. Forty years later the cathedral was complete, much as we see it today except that the three eastern apses have given place to the Chapel of the Nine Altars, and that the Galilee Chapel has since been added to the west end.

Most of the new monastic buildings were finished about the same time as the cathedral, and when Bishop Galfrid Rufus arrived in 1133 he had only to complete the chapter house. Bishop Pudsey built the Galilee Chapel, at the west end of the cathedral, about the year 1175, and Richard de Marisco probably completed the west towers in the next half-century. When Richard Poore came fresh from the rapidly rising Salisbury Cathedral in 1229, the serious state of the choir vault decided him to do away with the old apses and to substitute the splendid Chapel of the Nine Altars. This work was completed by 1280.

About 1350 the Jesse window was inserted in the west wall of the nave, and fifty years later the cloister was rebuilt, together with the great dormitory on the west side. Early in the 15th century Cardinal

Langley altered the Galilee Chapel, and between 1470 and 1490, after damage by lightning, the central tower was rebuilt.

At the end of the 18th century James Wyatt carried out various "improvements"—including the demolition of most of the Norman chapter house, which fortunately was rebuilt on the original lines 100 years later.

With those essential dates in mind, let us now survey the outstanding features of the exterior of Durham Cathedral.

The impressive central tower is 40 feet wide and over 200 feet high, with a twin pair of lancet windows in each face. At the corners are crocketed buttresses with statues of saints in niches, and rising above them is the belfry with an open battlemented parapet.

The twin western towers have Norman lower stages, with wide windows and blind arches, and 13th century upper storeys famed for their tiers of wall arcading. Framed by the two towers is the great west window with fine flamboyant tracery of about 1340. Buttressing the whole west front which soars above the steep wooded bank of the river is the low Galilee Chapel.

The wide and impressive east end (the Chapel of the Nine Altars) was much altered by Wyatt and has a great rose window dating from about 1800. Above it is a gable lit by a triplet of lancets, and below it are three rows of pointed windows.

Just round the corner on the north side of the cathedral is a wide window of the Chapel of the Nine Altars, with two rows of arcading above it. Here, in a canopied niche in the north-west corner turret of the chapel, can be seen a high-relief carving of the Dun Cow, whose finding first led the monks of St Cuthbert to Durham. This work, probably designed by Wyatt or an assistant, replaced an earlier carving set up by Ralph Flambard. Beyond stretches the north transept, with six lights soaring to an arcaded gable flanked by two turrets with beautiful balustrades.

The great north doorway of the cathedral dates from the first half of the 12th century, but it was severely maltreated by Wyatt, and perhaps the only authentic Norman work remaining is on the inner side. This has Norman shafts carved with interlacing foliage framing little beasts and human figures: a man riding a lion, two centaurs, two figures embracing, a boy being whipped, a man strangling another with a rope, a man performing gymnastics, and Samson and the lion.

On the north door itself is the 12th century sanctuary knocker of bronze—a grotesque head with staring eyes, protruding ears, ray-like mane, and ring in mouth. Fugitives from the law could claim protection once they had laid hold of this knocker, and it is recorded that some 331 people did so between 1464 and 1524. Over the door in mediaeval times was a room for the two monks who received the seekers of sanctuary and after a week or two gave them a safe-conduct to the coast.

On passing through the north doorway the visitor may find himself rather overwhelmed by the sheer majesty of this vast interior, particularly by the nave, which is unspoiled Norman work from end to end. The great round arches (adorned with zigzag ornament) are supported by clustered round columns rising to the roof, alternating with immense round pillars with a circumference—23 feet—equal to their height. The stonework of these pillars is deeply cut in rugged patterns of spiral, flute, lozenge, and chevron.

Each bay of the triforium above the arcades has a pair of small round arches within a larger one enriched by four rows of zigzag ornament. Still higher is the clerestory with each of its round-headed lights, flanked by a pair of little arches on round pillars, and a processional way running through the wall, from window to window, the whole length of the nave.

The vaulting of the nave rests on shafts which rise above the lofty clustered columns, the ribs being ornamented with zigzag work and springing from grotesque human heads.

The nave aisles, also Norman work, are crossed by flying buttresses which are perhaps the oldest in England; they are hidden by the triforium roof. The walls are adorned with round-arched arcading, and one bay in the south aisle has been restored with the red and black decoration which originally coloured all the wall surface.

At the west end of the south aisle is part of Bishop Cosin's splendid 17th century choir screen of oak, which was replaced by Sir Gilbert Scott's screen of marble. Together with Cosin's massive organ case, it covers a recess which was the spot set apart for those taking sanctuary in the cathedral.

At the west end of the nave is the Galilee Chapel built by Bishop Pudsey to accommodate women worshippers denied free access to the main body of the cathedral. In the floor near the font is a cross of Frosterley marble which marks the line beyond which no woman was allowed to pass eastward lest St Cuthbert be offended—a strange ban of which no one has ever been able to explain the origin. The font is a big fluted vase of white marble placed here in 1633 to replace one destroyed by the Scots, and quite dwarfed by the lavishly carved oak canopy with which Bishop Cosin adorned it after the Restoration.

The Galilee Chapel is one of the most exquisite examples of late

Norman work in this country—Norman masonry at its most graceful. It has fine aisles composed of lofty round arches richly decorated with chevron ornament and supported on slender clustered columns. Some of these columns are of Purbeck marble, its earliest use in the north of England; others are of sandstone added about 1430 by Cardinal Langley, who also built the enormous buttresses at the west end to prevent the chapel from collapsing into the river. In the west wall is a low recess of his day lit by two small windows giving a beautiful view of the Wear; and in this recess is the Galilee Well, 34 feet deep, and lined with lead.

Beside the north altar of the Galilee Chapel are some well-preserved Norman paintings which may represent St Cuthbert and St Oswald, and on the wall of the nearby aisle are 13th century paintings of the Crucifixion of Christ and St Peter, Peter being shown head downwards. On the wall near Bede's tomb are two sculptured panels of the 12th century; they represent the Resurrection and the Transfiguration, and were originally part of the nave screen of the cathedral.

Immediately east of the nave, soaring majestically on huge clustered pillars, are the four lofty Norman arches supporting the central tower. Above them is the impressive 15th century lantern, with a gallery at its base and vaulting which rises to a height of 155 feet.

At the entrance to the choir there are two modern pulpits—a marble one designed by Anthony Salvin, and another of black oak which is a memorial to Canon Geoffrey Gordon, Bishop of Jarrow, who died in 1938.

More early Norman work is in the transepts, both begun before Bishop de St Carileph's death in 1096. Each has an eastern aisle with chapels, but the western sides are plainer, owing to lack of money following his death. The clerestories and triforiums are similar to those of the nave.

Over the door of the south transept is a gaily painted and richly carved astronomical clock, with a face above the main dial showing the phases of the moon. Originally set up about 1500 on the south side of the roodscreen, it was moved to its present position in the reign of Charles I, much new woodwork being made for it.

The very earliest Norman work in Durham Cathedral is to be seen in the choir, the two round-arched bays at its west end being the work of de St Carileph. East of these Norman bays are richly moulded pointed arches dating from the 13th century, when Carileph's apses were removed to make way for the Chapel of the Nine Altars.

A notable feature of the choir is the range of blind arcading on each of the piers between the old work and the new, each having a line of six little trefoil-headed arches below, and three lofty ones above with ornately carved capitals and canopies. Above the upper arcade a figure of an angel adorns each pier.

The altar screen, the bishop's throne, and the choir stalls also repay close study.

The lofty altar screen, fashioned of Caen stone, is one of the most elaborate in the world. Made about 1375, it has niches for 107 statues, and nine finely carved canopies rising tier upon tier into soaring spires. On either side is a doorway (formerly leading to St Cuthbert's shrine) and flanking it are canopied stone sedilia. In front of the screen, concealed by a magnificent embroidered frontal, is a marble altar dating from about 1630.

The screen was made in London, brought to Newcastle by sea, and set up by seven masons working for nearly a year. As the greater part of the cost was borne by Lord John Neville of Raby Castle (son of the victor of the Battle of Neville's Cross) it is often called the Neville Screen. Shorn of its statues and colour, it is still a thing of beauty.

The splendid bishop's throne, glorious with gilding and colour, occupies the central arch of the choir's south arcade. It is said to be the highest in Christendom. The older part was built of Dorset stone in the 14th century; the wooden portion was made about 1700. The ornate staircase, guarded by an oak door bearing the arms of Bishop Crewe, leads to a stone gallery supporting the actual throne, which is flanked by seats for chaplains. But the most astonishing part of the throne is the lower portion—a tiny chantry chapel containing a panelled tomb bearing an alabaster figure of Bishop Thomas Hatfield in mitre and vestments. Hatfield died in 1381 and his body was brought here from London.

The magnificent 17th century choir stalls, a gift of Bishop Cosin, are remarkable for the blending of Gothic features with Classic details. They have elaborate carved canopies with light openwork spires soaring upwards in diminishing stages, and panelled backs adorned with blind arcading and heads of chubby cherubs. The desk-ends have foliated poppyheads, and the seats are misericords with carvings of a huge crab, a barking dog, a man sucking his fingers, a monkey eating a nut, a dolphin, a dragon, two men with a fish, a squirrel eating nuts, and a lion chasing a man.

The choir also has a six-sided pulpit of Restoration date and two brass chandeliers made in 1751.

The vaulted aisles of the choir are impressive in their simplicity. The eastern bays, finished before 1096, have what is believed to be the earliest ribbed vaulting in Europe. Nearly 200 years after the erection of these vaults each of these bays was adorned with a single stone boss with richly carved foliage, the one in the south aisle having the extra adornment of two dragons eating fruit.

The great eastern transept of Durham Cathedral is called the Chapel of the Nine Altars. Based on the eastern transept of Fountains Abbey, it was begun in 1242 and finished in 1280, and it has been described as the greatest triumph of the architecture of its period, the last and grandest building in the Early English style. Certainly it has a delicacy and grace contrasting strongly with the massive Norman work in nave and choir.

The architect of this exquisite chapel was Master Richard of Farnham in Surrey—probably a relative of Bishop Nicholas of Farnham. Heads of two of the masons (in dust-caps) who carried out his orders are carved on the arcading below the two windows in the south wall.

This arcading, of trefoiled arches on round marble columns with foliated capitals, runs right round the lower walls of the chapel. Soaring high above this are beautiful clustered columns of grey Frosterley marble supporting a noble vault with richly-carved ribs and bosses.

In the east wall, framed by the clustered columns, are three groups of triple lancets, the centre group being crowned by a big rose window inserted by Wyatt in the 18th century. Occupying the whole width of the north wall is a magnificent six-light window.

Part of the foundations of the original Norman eastern apses can be seen under trapdoors in the floor. It is possible that these apses weakened under the thrust from the vaulted roof, but rebuilding was also demanded by the need for accommodating the increasing crowds of pilgrims to the shrine of St Cuthbert, which stood on the big stone just behind the high altar. A great gravestone let into the floor marks the resting-place of the bones, now buried beneath, and in the surrounding pavement are hollows worn by the feet of countless pilgrims. At the corners of the grave stand four silver candlesticks, and over it hangs Sir Ninian Comper's magnificent canopy, with a painting of Christ in Majesty.

Having studied the wonderful architectural features and the chief fittings of Durham Cathedral, the visitor is recommended to take two further walks round the building before passing into the cloister—first to see the stained glass, and then the monuments.

The biggest array of ancient glass in the cathedral is in the three centre windows in the west wall of the Galilee Chapel. The middle window has 18 panels of beautifully-coloured fragments with little figures in the tracery at the top, and there are other little figures in the upper lights of the side windows. The great west window of the nave, a fine example of leaf tracery of about 1350, has brightly-coloured Victorian glass showing a Jesse tree.

The west window of the north aisle has one of the cathedral's many modern compositions by Hugh Easton, designer of the Battle of Britain window in Westminster Abbey; it portrays St Cuthbert looking upward at a flock of seagulls forming a halo round his head. Close by is the county's war memorial window (also by Hugh Easton) showing an airman, guarded by an archangel, being borne by a black eagle over the city of Durham—"As birds flying so shall the Lord of Hosts protect Jerusalem".

The window to the east of the north door has bright Victorian glass showing scenes in the life of Bernard Gilpin, the Apostle of the North; he is depicted giving his horse to a farmer, quelling the tumult in Rothbury Church, and inspecting the school which he founded at Houghton-le-Spring.

The most striking glass in the north transept is in the lower west window, commemorating Basil Phillott Blackett, Knight Commander of the Star of India, who died in 1935. It portrays St Gregory Nazianzen, one of the Fathers of the Eastern Church, standing on the Earth, with Sun, Moon, Stars, and Saturn beh nd him.

The central rose window at the east end of the cathedral contains a few fragments of glass from the 15th century window which it replaced, but its dominant feature is the ruby centre radiating innumerable spokes of colour.

More old glass—a wonderful patchwork of blue, yellow, and white —is to be seen in a window in the south choir aisle.

The great south window of the south transept has harmonious Victorian glass illustrating the Te Deum, and in two upper lights are angel figures from the 15th century Te Deum window.

Incidents in the early history of the Church in Northumbria are illustrated by the Victorian glass in the south aisle of the nave: Bede instructing his disciples and translating the Gospels on his deathbed; Benedict Biscop visiting a scholar and superintending the building of the church at Monkwearmouth; St Cuthbert preaching in a mountain village and praying before his cell in the Farne Island; St Aidan being received at Bamburgh by King Oswald and embarking on his mission from Iona; and Paulinus baptising converts in the River Swale.

The west window of the south aisle, portraying St Oswald, is another splendid work by Hugh Easton; it commemorates Patrick Alington (son of Dean Alington) who died on active service in Italy in 1943.

Returning to the Galilee Chapel, the visitor can now begin a final tour of the cathedral to study the monuments. Outstanding here is the tomb of the Venerable Bede, who died at Jarrow in 735. In the 11th century the bones of this devout historian were stolen from Jarrow by a Durham sacrist named Elfrid; they were placed in the shrine of St Cuthbert and later encased by Bishop Pudsey in a shrine of gold and silver. In 1370 they were transferred to the Galilee Chapel, but the tomb in which they lay was destroyed at the Reformation. The present tomb dates from 1831, when the remains were transferred to an inner chest of oak.

Close by is the great plain altar tomb of Cardinal Langley, Bishop of Durham from 1406 to 1437, and the restorer of this fine Norman chapel. It is of blue marble, probably from Egglestone on the Tees, and stands in front of what used to be the west door of the cathedral.

In the middle of the chapel is the grave of John Brimleis, an organist who died in 1576. He played the organ for Roman Catholic services temporarily re-introduced at the Rising in the North of 1569; but he afterwards recanted and was duly forgiven. The inscription on the gravestone runs:

> *John Brimleis body here doth ly*
> *Who praysed God with hand and voice*
> *By musickes heavenlie harmonie*
> *Dull myndes he maid in God rejoice*
> *His soul into the heavenes is lyft*
> *To prayse him still that gave the gyft.*

Let into the floor at the west end of the north aisle is a little square bearing the initials J.B. and a tiny cross. It covers the grave of Count Joseph Boruwlaski, the Polish dwarf who wrote of himself:

> *Poland was my cradle,*
> *England is my nest,*
> *Durham is my quiet place*
> *Where my bones shall rest.*

(In the church of St Mary the Less, South Bailey, is a commemorative brass to the little man, inscribed with an epitaph which was thought unworthy of a place in the cathedral.)

Under an arch at the other end of the north aisle is a tomb with a reclining marble figure of kindly-looking James Britton, in long flowing gown and buckled shoes, an open book in his left hand. He died in 1836, after serving as headmaster of Durham School for 30 years.

Along the north wall of the north choir aisle runs a bedesmen's bench originally built for the pensioners of Bishop Skirlaw, who was buried close by in 1405; on the front are twelve traceried panels bearing the arms of this bishop, builder of bridges and churches.

A striking sight in the Chapel of the Nine Altars is the white marble statue (carved by John Gibson at Rome) covering the grave of Bishop Van Mildert who died in 1836. It portrays the bishop seated pensively in an armchair, book in hand.

Let into the floor at the foot of Van Mildert's statue is a blue stone marking the grave of Anthony Bek, Bishop of Durham from 1283 to 1311, Patriarch of Jerusalem, and King of the Isle of Man. On a brass plate is a little rhyming inscription in Latin, copied in 1834 from the original. Near this inscription is the gravestone of Herbert Hensley Henson, Dean of Durham from 1913 to 1918 and Bishop from 1920 to 1939. "He fed them with a faithful and true heart, and ruled them prudently with all his power."

On the south side of the chapel is the grave of Bishop Richard de Bury, marked by a marble slab with an engraved figure of the bishop in full robes, his right hand raised in blessing, his left arm hugging a copy of his work, the *Philobiblon*, a little book about books. The inscription states that

Richard d'Aungerville, commonly styled de Bury from Bury St Edmunds, was Bishop of Durham 1333–45. This monument is the gift of members of the Grolier Club of the City of New York to commemorate the author of the 'Philobiblon' and the munificent friend and patron of books in England.

Edward II appointed Richard de Bury tutor to his son, later Edward III, and on the accession of his pupil he was made Bishop of Durham despite the fact that the chapter had elected another. In 1334 he became Lord High Chancellor, and as ambassador carried to Paris Edward III's declaration of war in 1338. He was several times employed in negotiations with the King of Scotland.

Another relic of mediaeval times in the Chapel of the Nine Altars is the 13th century cross of red stone from the site of Neasham Priory, beside the Tees at Hurworth; on one side is a carving of the Crucifixion, and on the other are the symbols of the Evangelists surrounding the Lord in Glory.

Apart from the figure of Thomas Hatfield in the lower part of the bishop's throne, already noted, the outstanding monument in the choir is the white marble effigy of Bishop Joseph Barber Lightfoot, who was buried at Bishop Auckland in 1889. Begun by Edgar Boehm and finished by Alfred Gilbert, it shows him in long gown and skull-cap, with three books at his feet. On the wall beside the bishop's throne is William Gladstone's eulogy of Joseph Butler (1692–1752) *"Surpassed by none in the long line of bishops of the see or among the Christian philosophers of England"*.

Three of the finest monuments in the cathedral now come under review. The first, in the south transept, is Chantrey's lifesize kneeling figure of Bishop Barrington, who died in 1826 at the age of 92. The others, framed in two arches on the south side of the nave, are the Neville tombs which were shamelessly defaced by Scottish prisoners shut up in the cathedral after the Battle of Dunbar. The older bears the battered figure of Ralph, second Baron Neville, the victor of Neville's Cross, who died in 1367; beside him is the headless figure of his wife. On the other tomb are fragmentary figures of their son John, third Baron Neville (donor of the Neville Screen), and of his wife Matilda.

In the south aisle is a massive wall memorial of black Spanish oak which was set up in response to a suggestion made by an unknown miner. An inscription in golden letters asks us to

Remember before God the Durham miners who have given their lives in the pits of the county, and who work in darkness and danger in those pits today.

On the wall of the south-west tower is a white marble bust of the much-travelled Sir George Wheler, who was buried in the Galilee Chapel in 1724. During 1675 and 1676 he made a collection of antiquities in Greece and Levant, and also brought home many new plants. He became a canon of Durham in 1684, and in 1709 received the rectory of Houghton-le-Spring, where he founded a school for girls.

On the south side of the cathedral is the cloister, which was begun late in the 14th century by Bishop Walter de Skirlaw and completed by his successor, Cardinal Langley, who held the See from 1406 to 1438. Almost the only original feature is the panelled oak roof, adorned with floral bosses and gaily painted heraldic shields. The pavement of Yorkshire stone was laid in the 18th century, when the mediaeval stonework lights were replaced by traceried windows of three lights each, all open to the garth. In the middle of the garth is an eight-sided basin of Eggleston marble—all that is left of the monk's laver of 1432, which had 24 bronze spouts and a dovecot in the roof.

Two magnificent Norman doorways lead from the south aisle into the cloister. Every Sunday the procession of monks left the cathedral by what is called the Prior's Doorway, passed right round the cloister, and re-entered by the Monks' Doorway.

The Prior's Doorway, looking down the east walk of the cloister, has richly-moulded round arches and cushion capitals carved with foliage and bead ornament. The Monks' Doorway, looking down the west walk of the cloister, is as plain as the other is elaborate, but it frames a magnificent door (dating from about 1160) with ironwork forming a broad flowing pattern over the entire surface.

For a tour of the cloister and the monastic buildings surrounding it the visitor should start in the east walk, passing the stone bench where on Maundy Thursday 13 poor men used to sit while their feet were washed by the prior. A few yards along on the left is the barrel-vaulted parlour where the monks were able to meet their relations and buy wares from visiting pedlars. In earlier times it was merely a slype, or passage, leading to the monks' cemetery. Beyond it is the round-arched Norman doorway of the rebuilt chapter house.

The original chapter house, built in the time of Bishop Rufus (1133–40), was almost completely destroyed by James Wyatt. The present building, with its finely vaulted roof and arcaded walls, is a late 19th century restoration in Norman style—a work carried out in memory of Bishop Lightfoot.

Round the walls is a stone bench on which the monks sat when they assembled here twice daily. In the apse is a plain throne of stone representing the one in which the bishops used to be installed; the arms, found under the floor in 1874, are the only remaining part of the original throne. Let into the floor are stones commemorating 10 early bishops who were laid to rest beneath the chapter house: Aldhun, Walcher, Flambard, Rufus, de St Barbara, de Farnham, de Kirkham, de Stitchill, de Insula, and Kellaw.

Seven of the windows have splendid glass by Hugh Easton. The first shows Adam and Eve at the Tree of Life, and below them, Walcher, the first Norman bishop, who was murdered by a mob at Gateshead in 1080. Next comes an Annunciation scene and a green-clad figure of Bishop Pudsey (also buried here) holding a model of his Galilee Chapel; it is a memorial of Arthur Harrison, who built the cathedral organ. The third window is a beautiful Madonna and Child with a kneeling figure of Bishop Rufus, holding a model of his Norman chapter house.

The central window shows St Benedict gazing up at the Cross, and to the right of this are the Ascension and a kneeling figure of Bishop Flambard, builder of the Norman nave. Next comes a window to Bishop Westcott (1890–1901), his firm features being portrayed in the kneeling figure of Bishop William de St Barbara who points to St John. The seventh represents the Heavenly Jerusalem, with the north front of the cathedral and its builder, William de St Carileph, shown below.

In the chapter-house windows on the cloister side, originally unglazed, are three panels of the old heraldic glass and a fourth with a small group of standing figures.

To the south of the chapter house are three dark little rooms which were once used as cells for monks found guilty of small offences.

Along the south wall of the cloister runs the refectory undercroft, dating from about 1300. It has a vaulted roof resting on short square piers, and contains an outstanding collection of Roman altars and inscriptions brought together by Canon Greenwell.

The west walk of the cloister is flanked by the fine early 13th century undercroft of the monks' dormitory. Its eight southern bays (originally containing the monks' common room and the great buttery) now form a single apartment, with an impressive vaulted roof resting on a row of short columns. Many carved stones from the cathedral and various churches in County Durham are to be seen here; and also a great curiosity—the skeleton of a whale, which was probably stranded on the coast and sent to the prince palatine as a "royal fish".

The next two or three bays of the undercroft have been converted into vestries, and then comes a chamber once used as treasury and muniment room; it still has its sturdy 15th century door.

At the north-west corner of the cloister a plain Norman round-headed doorway leads to stairs which give access to the New Library, formerly the monks' dormitory. This magnificent chamber, 65 yards long, was built about 1400 and still has its original roof. A noble roof it is, fashioned of sturdy oak brought from Bear Park, two miles north-west of the city.

At the north end is the doorway through which the monks would descend to the cathedral in the small hours, probably passing along a wooden gallery which led to the tower staircase. By this doorway the sub-prior would take his rest, for it was his duty to keep watch on the monks and "see that none of them shall be lacking or stolen forth to go about any kind of vice or naughtiness".

After the Restoration the southern portion of the dormitory was converted into a house for one of the prebends. The northern part

The Chapter House

DURHAM CATHEDRAL

The Galilee Chapel

DURHAM CATHEDRAL   The monks' dormitory

                        The monastic kitchen

Durham city, from the north-west

DURHAM CATHEDRAL

The sanctuary knocker on the north door   The carving of the dun cow

The remains of St Cuthbert's coffin

became a covered playground for the children of the prebends. Dr Valerian Wellesley, brother of the Duke of Wellington, was the last prebend to occupy the house, but on his death in 1848 the whole of the great dormitory was converted to its present use as a library. The walls were restored, a new floor was laid down and the long lines of oak bookcases were set up round the room.

Today the library displays a fascinating collection of Durham's priceless treasures, including perhaps the most precious relic of all —the reconstructed oak coffin of St Cuthbert.

When Cuthbert died in 687, worn out from self-imposed hardships, he was buried in a stone coffin under the floor of the church at Holy Island (Lindisfarne), but eleven years later his remains were transferred to this wooden coffin, which was kept on the floor of the church for "better observation and greater reverence".

In the year 875 fear of a new onslaught by Viking invaders caused the monks to leave Holy Island, bearing the coffin of St Cuthbert and its many relics. For seven years their wanderings continued, and then they settled at Chester-le-Street.

From 882 until 995 St Cuthbert's coffin was enshrined at Chester-le-Street, and then, after a brief stay at Ripon, it was removed to Durham. In 1069 when Durham was threatened with the wrath of William the Conqueror, the coffin was taken back to Holy Island; but it was returned to Durham in the spring of 1070, there to remain.

It was opened in 1104 for an inspection of the body and was then transferred to a special shrine in the cathedral. In 1537 it was reopened by the King's Commissioners, and five years later was enclosed in two other coffins and buried under the spot which for centuries had been visited by pilgrims. In 1827 the coffin was once more unearthed, the relics this time being removed and the bones reburied. More fragments of the coffin were found in the grave in 1899, and in 1939 all the pieces were reassembled and mounted on new oak boards.

It is five feet six inches long, and completely covered with simple and vigorous carving representing a pictorial Litany for the protection of St Cuthbert. This is the earliest example of Christian carving in England to which a specific date can be given. The style of decoration is derived from the Mediterranean, though the Northumbrian artist produced some entirely new features. The standing figure of Christ on the lid is surrounded by full-length symbols of the four Evangelists. One side depicts the Apostles, with their names written in runes, and on the other side are angels. At one end of the coffin stands the

Madonna and Child, and at the other are the Archangels Michael and Gabriel.

The pectoral cross found in the coffin is a delicate and beautiful piece of workmanship in gold cloisonné set with garnets. It was probably made by a British craftsman in the province of Strathclyde, perhaps in the 5th or 6th century, and by the time of St Cuthbert had been considerably patched and mended. With it are exhibited the remains of St Cuthbert's little portable altar of oak, the earliest existing example of its kind, together with fragments of the silver plate applied to it by an Anglian silversmith after the saint's death.

Another case contains long narrow strips of embroidery, woven with gold thread, which were found in the coffin. Made within 10 or 15 years of the death of Alfred the Great, it is the earliest English embroidery in existence. The biggest object is the stole, with woven figures of the prophets and of St John the Evangelist and St Thomas. On the back in Latin are inscriptions which reveal it was made by command of Queen Aelflaed of Wessex for Bishop Frithestan of Winchester, who was enthroned in 909. A similar inscription is on the accompanying maniple, which was given by King Athelstan in 934, when he visited Cuthbert's shrine at Chester-le-Street during the course of an expedition against the Scots.

Other exhibits from the coffin consist of a woven girdle, two gold bracelets, a double-sided comb, and fragments of Byzantine textiles made about the year 600.

Another of the glories of this library is the collection of Anglo-Saxon sculpture assembled by Canon William Greenwell (whose story we tell at Lanchester). Here are wonderful carved crosses found during the restoration of Gainford Church in 1864. From Benedict Biscop's church at Jarrow is part of a cross-shaft which bears signs of burning, perhaps a relic of devastation caused by William the Conqueror. From the sister house of Monkwearmouth are two limestone shafts which probably formed part of a decorative feature in the church there. From the monastery of St Hilda at Hartlepool is a little gravestone 1300 years old.

Broken crosses and grave-covers discovered in the foundations and walls of the chapter house also form part of the striking collection in this library. They appear to have been memorials to the Congregation of St Cuthbert (the body of married clergy which preceded the Benedictine monks) which were broken up and used as building material soon after 1100, when they were little more than a century old. One elaborately carved cross-head shows the Lamb of God standing on the Gospels, with monsters beside him and a four-winged angel above; another has the Crucifixion scene, and on the other side a lion with an extra head at the end of its long twisted tail.

Two ancient log coffins are preserved in the library, and also two chests hollowed out from trunks of trees 700 years ago. One has four compartments for the money of the monastic bursar, almoner, sacrist and hosteller. The other, some six feet long and plated with iron, held the title deeds of the monastery and of neighbouring landowners.

Displayed in glass-covered cases are several volumes of manuscripts, relics of the monastic library. The oldest is an incomplete Gospels of the late 7th century, comparable with the famous Lindisfarne Gospels, now in the British Museum. Adorned with lovely illuminated initials, it was written in Irish, probably in Northumbria. Another early volume is the 8th century "Bede" Gospels, written in short regular lines of neatly formed capitals.

The 10th century Rituals written in Latin with a red interlinear version in Anglo-Saxon is specially notable, for it is a transcription of a work by King Alfred. Augustine on the Psalms, with elaborately illuminated initials, is one of 39 books given by Bishop de St Carileph about the year 1090; no fewer than 19 of them are still preserved in this library.

Among a host of other bibliographical treasures are Bishop Pudsey's great Bible (in four volumes), a little book of the lives of Cuthbert, Oswald, and Aidan which was written at Durham in the 12th century, and several 15th century printed books in their original bindings. The cathedral library is also fortunate in possessing some early catalogues of its books; the oldest dates from about 1170, and there are two others made at the end of the 14th century. No less precious are the manuscripts of cathedral music, some of them centuries old.

A splendid series of seals down to the time of Van Mildert, last of the Prince Bishops, displays some astonishing craftsmanship. The earliest genuine episcopal seal is that of Ralph Flambard (1099–1128) and shows him standing in his robes, crozier in hand. The beautiful seal of Richard de Bury, remarkable for its richness of detail, portrays him in dignified pose beneath niches filled with figures of saints. The seal of Anthony Bek, in whose time the power of the Bishops of Durham reached its zenith, shows him seated on his throne.

No less interesting is the collection of richly-embroidered copes, four of them dating from pre-Reformation times and a fifth bought for the visit of Charles I to the cathedral in 1633.

One unique exhibit in the library is the Conyers Falchion which was presented to each Bishop of Durham on the occasion of his first crossing the Tees to enter his palatinate. The last bishop to receive it was Van Mildert—on Croft Bridge in April 1826. A falchion is a broadsword with one cutting edge, of a type thought to have been introduced into England at the time of the First Crusade. Engraved on the wooden handle of this specimen, probably made about 1250, are the arms of Henry III and his younger brother, Richard, Earl of Cornwall.

Of the smaller objects on view in the cathedral library we will mention only five of exceptional interest: a little gold plate which was found in a heap of rubbish outside the Roman fort of Lanchester; an iron-gilt ring from the tomb of Bede, probably placed there in 1538 by the King's Commissioners as a substitute for a more valuable ring; and three massive gold rings found in 1874 in the graves of the Norman bishops Rufus, de St Barbara, and Flambard when the ruined chapter house was excavated.

South of the cloister is the College, a secluded, well-shaped enclosure with old stone buildings surrounding a trim plot of grass, and, in the centre of it all, a homely pump.

Protruding into the north-west corner of the College is the monastic kitchen built towards the end of the 14th century. A striking octagonal building with battlemented walls, heavily buttressed, it is now a muniment room used by one of the university departments.

On the site of the passage which linked the kitchen to the Prior's Lodging on the east is the Durham Light Infantry Memorial Garden, with an inscription on the south wall of the old refectory and under-croft in the background. The Prior's Lodging, now the Deanery, is a plain-looking house with an 18th century torch-extinguisher by the front entrance. Its old apartments have been converted to new uses.

The chapel crypt dates from the 13th century; in the 18th century the chapel itself was divided into separate rooms, and the prior's great chamber transformed into a drawing-room and lobby. A small chamber with a late 15th century ceiling of oak is now the library, and the great hall has become a dining-room with bedrooms above. The prior's old bedroom, with a panelled oak ceiling of 1515, is called King James's Room, for it was here that James VI of Scotland stayed in April 1603 when on his way to London to receive the English crown.

The imposing gatehouse at the north-east corner of the College was the main entrance to the monastery. Built by Prior Castell about the year 1500, it has a vaulted archway with painted and gilded bosses displaying heraldic angels, a flaming sun, a Tudor rose, and fighting dragons. Over the archway was the Chapel of St Helen and the bedroom of its priest.

Beyond the gateway, bounding the cathedral precincts on the east, is the Bailey, one of the loveliest streets in England, graced by many delightful Georgian houses.

At its northern end stands the Halmote Court Office, a grey Gothic building of 1850 with corbel heads of a king and a judge beside the door. In this building are also the offices of the Durham Court of Chancery.

Number 7 North Bailey is a new university building which in 1966 replaced an old house with a dignified Georgian entrance; this was for some years the home of John Gully, a 19th century prize-fighter who became a colliery owner and represented Pontefract in Parliament. Behind stands Hatfield College, named after Thomas Hatfield, the great patron of learning who was Bishop of Durham from 1345 to 1381. The older central block of red brick was once a popular coaching inn called the Red Lion.

On the same side of the road, further south, is the Church of St Mary-le-Bow, thought to stand on the site of the wattle church in which St Cuthbert's body rested when it was first brought to Durham. The present building, dating from 1683, has a dignified interior, with some fine early 18th century woodwork—panelling, altar rails, font cover, and seating. The oak chancel screen of 1707 is a particularly fine piece of craftsmanship.

Beside the church Bow Lane, an ancient cobbled way, leads to Kingsgate footbridge, a light and graceful piece of modern architecture which spans the Wear at a height of 60 feet to link the old buildings of the university with the new.

In the South Bailey, tucked away in a quiet corner beyond St Chad's College and St John's College (both 20th century founda-tions), is the little church of St Mary the Less. Originally Norman, it was largely rebuilt in the middle of the 19th century, the old materials being used. The rector who watched over this rebuilding was Dr James Raine, a well-known antiquary and topographer who died in 1858. A few years later the church had an even more distinguished rector, the archaeologist Dr William Greenwell.

The church is the chapel of St John's College, and its beautiful modern east window of Mary and John at the Cross commemorates its various benefactors.

Over the vestry door is a stone panel with carvings of Christ in

73

Glory and symbols of the Evangelists. Thought to be early Norman work, the panel was brought here by Dr Raine from St Giles's Church, Durham, in 1829. Let into the wall of the chancel is a mediaeval tombstone carved with a sword and a very beautiful floral cross.

Commemorated here, though buried in the cathedral, is the Polish dwarf, Count Boruwlaski, who died in 1837 at the age of 98. An inscribed brass, which was prepared for his tomb but rejected by the dean as being unsuitably worded, states that he "measured no more than three feet three inches in height, but his form was well-proportioned and he possessed a more than common share of understanding and knowledge".

The Bailey ends at the Water Gate, an archway in the city wall which incorporates some mediaeval masonry and was built to take carriages when the new Prebends' Bridge was opened in 1778. The first bridge was thrown across the Wear in 1574 to replace a ferry; the west abutment is still visible slightly higher upstream. That bridge was destroyed in the great flood of 1771, and in the following year the present beautiful bridge was designed for the prebends of the cathedral by George Nicholson. The weir below the bridge was constructed in ancient times.

One of the grandest of all views of Durham Cathedral is the one from this bridge. It is a noble sight, and it inspired Sir Walter Scott to write the verse (from *Harold the Dauntless*) which is inscribed on a stone let into the approach to the bridge from the west:

> *Grey towers of Durham*
> *Yet well I love thy mixed and massive piles*
> *Half church of God, half castle 'gainst the Scot,*
> *And long to roam these venerable aisles*
> *With records stored of deeds long since forgot.*

At the Water Gate the wall which once completely surrounded the city stands to its original height and width. A good section extends from here to Kingsgate Bridge, high above the river, and to the north the upper path follows the line of the wall for some 50 yards towards the cathedral.

At the west end of the cathedral is another imposing stretch of the wall—the original Norman work of Bishop Pudsey, strengthened by huge buttresses added in the 15th century by Cardinal Langley. High up we can see the round-headed window of the monastic prison for major offenders, and a little to the north of it is the mouth of the main drain of the monastery, covered by a wooden grating.

Beyond is the doorway of a passage built in the thickness of the wall to enable soldiers to enter the castle without passing through the monastery; nearby is an observation slit.

A grating in the stonework below the Galilee Chapel covers the nearly dried up Galilee Well, once reached by a flight of steps; water could be drawn up through a trapdoor in the floor of the Galilee Chapel.

A little way down the bank below the north-west corner of the cathedral are some steps leading to a round-arched recess fed with water from a little pipe; above it is a stone inscribed *Fons Cuthberti, 1690.*

The path continues to Framwellgate Bridge, passing a spot known as Broken Walls, where quarrying long ago led to the destruction of the city's defences. Below the bridge little is left of the later wall built round the marketplace area after the invasion of Robert Bruce in 1312, but a few remains of it can be seen close to the lower weir.

From here the wall ran across the peninsula to Elvet Bridge, originally built about 1160 by Bishop Pudsey; his work is still visible between the modern ribs and the southern half of the bridge. Bishop Fox repaired the bridge in 1495, and in 1805 it was widened, the four bit cutwater buttresses then being added. At the south-east corner of the bridge is a modern brick building standing on the stone foundations of the vanished chapel of St Andrew; and under the approach leading to the centre of the city is a gloomy basement which was part of an old House of Correction.

Southward from Elvet Bridge runs New Elvet, leading to Church Street and the mother Church of St Oswald, which stands in a beautiful churchyard looking across the river to the south-east side of the cathedral. Much of the church, including the stately tower, was built early in the 15th century, but the aisles and most of the chancel had to be rebuilt in 1834 owing to subsidence caused by coal workings. The nave has a clerestory and a fine oak roof with carved wooden corbels displaying crowned heads of bearded men and shield-bearing angels.

In the rebuilt chancel are some handsome 15th century stalls of oak with foliated poppyheads, and fine old chairs with richly carved backs. But the most remarkable feature of the church is the tower staircase with 20 steps made from mediaeval grave-covers; a dozen of them have carvings in relief—crosses, swords, a horn, a battleaxe, a book, and a spade.

Across the road, in a garden which was formerly a churchyard, is

75

the grave of Dr John Bacchus Dykes, vicar here from 1864 until his death in January 1876. A founder of the Cambridge University Musical Society, he was also one of the editors and compilers of Hymns Ancient and Modern. He wrote many popular hymn tunes, including *Jesu, Lover of my Soul* and *Nearer my God to Thee*.

Two other ancient Durham churches which no visitor should miss are St Giles's and St Margaret's.

St Giles's, which serves the high eastern arm of the city, stands in a churchyard sloping steeply towards the Wear and affording a splendid view of the city when the trees are bare. The north wall of the nave, with two narrow round-headed windows, is part of the original church built by Bishop Ralph Flambard in 1112. During the usurpation of "Bishop" Cumin between 1141 and 1144, it was fortified by the lawful bishop, William de St Barbara, and sustained a siege. The chancel dates from about 1180; the tower is 13th century work, with an upper storey which was built by Cardinal Langley early in the 15th century and contains two pre-Reformation bells. The massive cup-shaped font is 700 years old.

In the sanctuary is a remarkable wooden figure of a thin man in armour, gazing calmly upwards. It is a memorial of John Heath (d. 1591), founder, with his friend Bernard Gilpin of the Kepier School at Houghton-le-Spring.

A quarter of a mile to the north of the church are the scanty ruins of the tiny chapel of St Mary Magdalene, which served a small hospital founded here in the 13th century; only the west wall and a tall pointed doorway remain.

Still farther north, standing by a pretty bend of the Wear where the water ripples noisily over a rocky bed, is Kepier Hospital. Founded in 1112 by Bishop Flambard as a religious house for 13 brethren, the hospital was burned down a few years later by Roger Cumin, but was restored later in the century by Bishop Pudsey. A picturesque fragment of mediaeval times is a weatherworn 14th century gatehouse with pointed arches and two bays of vaulting.

Below St Giles's Church, overlooking the river and the recreation grounds on the old Racecourse, is the College of the Venerable Bede, one of the colleges of the university and primarily for the training of schoolmasters. The college chapel, dedicated in 1939, is an outstanding work of modern architecture, with an interior of austere beauty.

St Margaret's Church is in the western part of the city, between Crossgate and South Street. It dates from the middle of the 12th century, and the nave arcades, the chancel arch, and the north wall of the chancel are all Norman survivals from the original building. So is the font, of Frosterley marble; but the most remarkable Norman feature is the westernmost window on the south side of the clerestory; it is the oldest clerestory window in County Durham.

The tower is 15th century and remarkable for its period in having no buttresses. Two of the bells, inscribed to St Augustine and St Margaret, were probably made in London about 1450.

A large grey stone in the middle of the nave marks the grave of Sir John Duck, a Durham Dick Whittington. He came to Durham to be a butcher's apprentice, and on being refused admission to the guild wandered down to the banks of the Wear. There a raven dropped a golden sovereign at his feet. It was an omen: he became a rich butcher and coal-owner, and in 1680 was made Mayor of Durham.

From the upper end of the churchyard is the finest view of the cathedral from the north-west.

Other delightful glimpses of the cathedral are to be had from South Street, which leads to the famous Durham School, removed here from Palace Green in 1842.

Overlooking the cricket field is the headmaster's house, a big, creeper-covered building which is older than the rest of the school buildings. Originally called Bellasis House, it was the home of William Cooke, who in 1833 became Reader in Medicine to Durham University. His son, Sir William Fothergill Cooke, is said to have made some early experiments here in connection with the electric telegraph which he developed with Sir Charles Wheatstone.

A pointed archway leads from the road into the school quadrangle, which also affords a magnificent view of the cathedral. Here, perched on a grassy mound and reached by 90 steps, stands the chapel built in 1925. It has an imposing east end with big buttresses and slender windows.

Durham School is probably as old as the cathedral, and the list of headmasters is complete from 1414, when the school was reorganised by Cardinal Langley. In 1541 Langley's School was incorporated in a new royal foundation which was endowed from the forfeited revenues of the monastery.

In Restoration days the old school buildings on Palace Green were renewed, and from a local grammar school it grew into a public school of great repute to which the leading families of Northumberland and County Durham sent their sons.

One of the great distinctions of the school is the number of local historians and antiquaries it has produced. Foremost among them was James Mickleton, who came here about 1650 and later laid the foundations for historians of 17th century and mediaeval Durham. Thirty years later came Thomas Baker, a Lanchester boy who went on to St John's College, Cambridge, and there stayed for the rest of his life. He was a famous student on British antiquities, but his best-known work is *Reflection on Learning*.

Headmaster Elias Smith preserved the cathedral library during the Commonwealth. His successor, Thomas Rudd, made an admirable index of the cathedral manuscripts, and in 1732, in conjunction with John Smith, the editor of Bede, brought out a splendid edition of Simeon of Durham's history of the cathedral. Thomas Randall, headmaster 1761–68, was a big collector of manuscripts for local history; and James Raine and Canon Greenwell carried on the great tradition. Among other famous Dunelmians were Mandell Creighton, Bishop of London; Sir Hugh Walpole, the novelist; and Robert Smith Surtees, creator of Jorrocks.

Perched on a green hill south of Durham School is Salvin's little University Observatory of 1840, a building of grey stone with four gables and a central dome. It was here, about the year 1900, that Professor Ralph Sampson made the standard observations on the satellites of Jupiter. Nowadays the work of the observatory is confined to recording earthquakes and the state of the weather. The meteorological records go back to 1841, Greenwich and Oxford being the only older weather-recording stations in the country.

Further south, also on rising ground, are five new colleges of the University—St Mary's, St Aidan's, Van Mildert, Trevelyan, and Grey. In their contrasting styles they afford an interesting study in contemporary architecture.

Also here, between Potters Bank and South Road, is the Gulbenkian Museum, containing an astonishing display of oriental art which no visitor should miss. The only museum of its kind in the country, it houses important collections of Egyptian antiquities, Chinese jade, and Tibetan, Indian, and Chinese paintings.

A mile to the north of the observatory, rising above the road to Newcastle, is a graceful stone obelisk erected in 1850 by William Lloyd Wharton to provide a north reference point. It bears a Latin inscription stating that it is dedicated to astronomy.

Durham's most imposing public building is County Hall, finely situated on the northern edge of the city; it was opened in 1963 by His Royal Highness the Duke of Edinburgh. From this vast modern office block the county of Durham is administered.

Many chapters in the Durham story are portrayed in two mural paintings, a mosaic, and a series of sculptures which adorn County Hall. Inside, the two murals depict the Building of the Cathedral and the Miners' Gala. The mosaic panel, on an outside wall facing south, represents several episodes, including the Viking raids, the monks carrying St Cuthbert's coffin, Sir John Duck and the Raven, and the legends of the Dun Cow and the Lambton Worm. On the north wall of the six-sided Council Chamber thirteen small stone carvings symbolise Durham's close links with the Church, and the many industries to be found in the county; also shown are Bede's History, and the North Country Maid.

One sculpture is of the bugle badge of the Durham Light Infantry, and many relics of this famous regiment are to be seen in the DLI Museum and Arts Centre, a modern building to the south of County Hall.

Lower down the hill, near the railway station, is the park which William Lloyd Wharton gave to the city about 1860. It commands a view which Ruskin called one of the Seven Wonders of the World. In the foreground is the fine railway viaduct of 11 round arches, and in the middle of the scene looms Durham City, with cathedral and castle on the skyline and the Wear winding round the outskirts.

In Wharton Park is a metal statue of Neptune which was removed in 1920 from the marketplace. The god stands in spirited pose upon a dolphin thrusting his trident into the waves beneath him. The figure was first set up in 1729 and is said to symbolise the proposed union of the city with the sea by making the Wear navigable for ships of 20 tons.

At Red Hill, not far from the station, is the Durham Miners' Hall of 1915, with a central copper dome rising from a balustraded roof. Beside the drive stands a line of four stone statues—frock-coated figures of John Forman, W. H. Patterson, Alexander Macdonald, and William Crawford. It was Crawford who founded the Durham Miners' Association in 1870 and later started the annual miners' gala, first held in Wharton Park.

Easington. A big village on high ground overlooking a huge colliery by the sea, it has a sloping green, and on its upper edge a spacious church which has served the villagers for many centuries.

Though heavily restored last century, the church has retained its ancient character. The heavily buttressed tower, a landmark for miles around, is Norman work, with a fine round-headed arch. The chancel and clerestoried nave date from the 13th century, the arcades and aisles from the 14th. The chancel has an east window of five tall

79

lancets which date from the restoration of 1852, and a little low side window with Victorian glass portraying St Cuthbert, St Hilda, the Venerable Bede, and Bernard Gilpin, who became rector here in 1556, and ministered for some months before leaving for Houghton-le-Spring.

In the middle of the nave is a fine series of early 17th century oak pews; the ends have poppyheads, and are carved with foliage and fruit hanging from ribbons. In the south aisle is a 13th century stone figure of a knight in chain mail, with sword and shield; probably representing Geoffrey FitzMarmaduke of the neighbouring Horden Hall, it shows him with mailed head resting on a carved cushion, his hands joined in prayer, his legs crossed, and his feet resting on a lion. Beside this effigy is a huge stone coffin found under the floor, and on a windowsill above is a 16th century tilting helmet.

On the floor at the east end of the north aisle is a 13th century figure of a woman, carved in Frosterley marble. With her right hand she gathers up her long mantle, and beneath this is an inner robe bearing her coat-of-arms; at her shoulders and feet are the remains of three small figures. It is believed to represent Isabel, wife of John FitzMarmaduke of Horden Hall, and sister of the famous Robert Bruce.

Horden Hall, now a farmhouse, stands beside the road about a mile south-east. Built about 1600, it has a projecting porch with a pair of round columns on each side and an upper room. Carved on the porch are the arms of Conyers.

Eastgate. This neat and delightful village is scarcely more than a cluster of houses at the spot where a bridge carries the main road to Alston across the Rookhope Burn. The burn rises at Rookhope Head on the Northumberland border, and runs into the Wear at Eastgate.

The village church is a dignified Victorian building with a central stone spire, massive font of Frosterley marble, and an impressive east window portraying the Ascension.

Close by are the lovely Low Linn Falls, where the Rookhope Burn rushes over rocks worn to the shape of a horseshoe; and just above the falls is another white cascade framed in the bridge of pipes carrying water from the Burnhope Reservoir to the Sunderland area.

It was hereabouts, on November 15, 1869, that Thomas Moore, Eastgate's schoolmaster and innkeeper, found a Roman altar dedicated to the god Silvanus by the Prefect Aurelius Quirinus, who was in charge of the first cohort of Ligones at Lanchester. The altar is now in the possession of Durham University.

The name Eastgate refers to the eastern entrance of Old Park, a former hunting ground of the Bishops of Durham. It is now rough and hilly moorland cut into by quarries and mines, but up to the 16th century some 200 deer were kept in the upper part of the park.

In the 15th century there was a semi-permanent hunting lodge on a steep bank above the Wear at Cambokeels, between the main road and the river. Grassy banks of masonry in a field still remain to outline some of the buildings.

It is recorded in documents that the main occupation of the site was between 1430 and 1460, and the spot is known as a type-site because excavations have revealed bits of pottery and various objects which hitherto had not been dated. The finds include horseshoes, spurs, harness buckles, a fish-hook, an iron tripod, knives, hones of local stone, shears, a sickle, keys, silver coins, and perhaps the only mediaeval thimble ever found.

It was along the Wear between Cambokeels and the village of Eastgate that in 1327 the army of Edward III encamped for 24 days opposite the Scots. Froissart tells how the English heralds were unable to bring the enemy to an engagement, while Edward's men had to lie uncomfortably on the hard ground with their armour on. The Scots busied themselves with stealing and eating English cattle, making such good use of the skins that when they finally decamped they left behind them 10,000 pairs of worn-out shoes.

Ebchester. It is pleasantly situated on the edge of a hill above the River Derwent, here separating Durham from Northumberland. The river scenery is lovely, and it is good to know that 10 acres of the wooded banks are in the safe keeping of the National Trust.

Just above the present narrow bridge Dere Street, the Roman road from York to Hadrian's Wall, crossed the Derwent. The crossing was guarded by a square fort of four acres which the Romans called Vindomara, and the northern part of the old village stands on its site. Roman stones carved with lettering are built into some of the garden walls and houses, and part of the mound of the south-east side of the fort can be traced in the churchyard.

Ebchester's church, a Norman building, is in the southern corner of Vindomara, and the greater part of it is of square stones from the fort. There are some huge stones in the lower parts of the east and north walls of the chancel, and built into an inner wall of the tower is a worn Roman stone with a carving of a fish; this was once in the walls of a grey cottage opposite the church, now called Fish Cottage. Also in the tower is yet another relic of the fort—a Roman altar with an eagle carved on it.

The church is narrow and dark, the deeply-splayed windows being no more than slits. It still has its little Norman font, and on the floor beneath the altar is the original altar stone.

The west window portrays a company of kneeling saints adoring the Risen Lord. It is of special interest because one of the saints has the calm face of the widow of Robert Smith Surtees, the sporting novelist, and another has the youthful features of his eldest son, Anthony, who died at Rome when only 23. Robert Surtees died at Brighton in 1864, but his body was brought here for burial, and a white marble cross marks his grave in the churchyard, not far from his old home.

The Surtees' home was Hamsterley Hall, which stands in well-wooded grounds away from the village to the east, looking across the Derwent to the Chopwell Woods of the Forestry Commission. Part of the mansion dates from mediaeval times, but the front is in 18th century Gothic style; some of the leadwork bears the date 1769, the year when the house was reconstructed by young Henry Swinburne, son of Sir John Swinburne of Capheaton Hall in Northumberland.

Henry Swinburne spent most of his life abroad, and when he died in Trinidad, in 1803, Hamsterley Hall was bought by Anthony Surtees, who lived across the Derwent. He brought with him his four-year-old son, Robert Smith Surtees, who was to live here for half-a-century, writing his rollicking tales of the sporting grocer John Jorrocks. The house is said to be the original of the Hillingdon Hall in his famous books.

An even more famous man who spent many happy boyhood days here was Field-Marshal Viscount Gort, VC, eldest son of the fifth Viscount Gort, and of Eleanor, youngest daughter of Robert Smith Surtees.

Edmundbyers. This is an airy moorland village in a beautiful setting in a north-western corner of the county, its cottages spread out on a hillside above the Burnhope Burn.

North of the village is the dam of the Derwent Reservoir, which stretches three and a half miles to the west along the border between Durham and Northumberland. This remarkable man-made lake, completed in 1967, has a capacity of 11,000 million gallons. Visible for miles around, it is a striking feature of a fine landscape.

The neat little village church was founded about 1150, but little is left of the original Norman work save the rugged north wall, two big stone heads of chubby-cheeked men on either side of the porch, and the stone altar which was found under the chancel during restoration work in 1859 and is now back in place again; the original consecration crosses can be seen at the corners. Near it is a carved 17th century armchair of black oak.

One curious feature of the church is the round chancel arch with a smaller arch on either side. Another is the wooden enclosure in the north-west corner, fashioned of wood from the chapels of Auckland Castle and Durham Castle, organ cases in Durham Cathedral and St Mary Redcliffe, Bristol, and a door from Riding Mill Hall. Set in its open panels are five richly-carved poppyheads, one of them with a little dog shown crouching on top. The panelled door has carved cherub-heads, and the door-frame has a pair of fluted classical pillars supporting a cornice adorned with foliage and the snarling heads of three lions.

Built into the west wall of the porch is the gravestone of a mediaeval priest; a cross with arms of foliage is carved upon it, and beside this is a chalice.

The view from the churchyard is memorable—a glorious panorama of heather-clad hills stretching far away to the south.

Egglescliffe. A village with pleasant old houses round a sloping green, it looks across to the Yorkshire town of Yarm from its perch on the steep and lofty left bank of the Tees.

The river is tidal up to this point, and is here crossed by a mediaeval stone bridge and a 19th century railway viaduct with 43 arches. The bridge was built by Bishop Skirlaw of Durham about the year 1400, and although much widened and repaired, still retains some of the original work in the ribbed arch on the Yorkshire side. The arch on the Durham side, rebuilt in 1799, was turned into a drawbridge during the Civil War.

On the green are the base and shaft of an old cross, and close by, the battlements of its 15th century tower emerging from the trees on top of the slope above the river, stands the dignified church. The south porch, bearing a modern replica of the original wooden sundial, shelters a doorway with a hollow-moulded pointed arch beneath a plain round one of Norman date. Parts of the north wall of the nave, with rugged stonework of red, yellow, and grey, are also Norman.

The chancel dates from the 15th century, and is notable for its arch (of alternate red and white stones) and for its fine 17th century barrel roof of oak with carved bosses displaying human heads, a hunting horn, shields, a Tudor rose, and foliage.

The outstanding feature of this church is its array of fine wooden fittings. The carved chancel screen, the choir stalls, and the panelling on the sanctuary walls all date from the Restoration period, and close to the 18th century altar rails (a single heavy beam supported by an arcade of pointed arches) are three finely carved old armchairs.

The nave is filled with a wonderful collection of 17th century oak pews with open backs, and the plain mediaeval font has an elaborate oak canopy of the same date. The pulpit, with reading desk attached, is 18th century work; and so also is the panelling in the Perpendicular Aislaby Chapel on the south side of the nave.

This chapel contains two chained books (Bishop Jewell's *Apology*, and the *Eikon Basilike*) and in a recess below them lies a worn stone figure of about 1300 showing a knight in chain armour with a winged dragon biting the bottom of his shield. The figure possibly represents Thomas Aislaby, who fought at the Battle of Lewes. A similar effigy, even more worn, lies on a stone bench in the porch, where a mediaeval grave-cover bearing a floriated cross is also preserved, together with part of a Saxon cross covered with scrollwork.

One of the bells in the tower dates from about 1400.

Elton. It is a tiny village, quietly situated away from the Stockton–Darlington road, with a small wayside church which was restored in 1841 but still has its original round-arched Norman doorway and a Norman chancel arch with beakhead decoration.

Filling the chancel arch and the two smaller arches on either side is a gaily painted roodscreen designed by J. N. Comper in 1907; in traceried panels in the lower part of the doors are pictures of six saints.

On the north side of the sanctuary, within the altar rails, is a cross-legged figure of a knight in chain armour, with a lion at his feet and two reclining angels with open books supporting the pillow beneath his head. The figure is thought to represent Robert Gower, who lived close by at Coatham Stob; he died in 1315.

The register records the burial of Mary Benton in 1853 at the age of 116.

Elwick Hall. This charming place, some three miles west of Hartlepool, has a small 13th century church of considerable interest. The tower was rebuilt in 1813, but still has its original doorway, and to the left is the carved head of a bishop, thought to represent Bishop

The Norman doorway

DURHAM CASTLE

The gateway

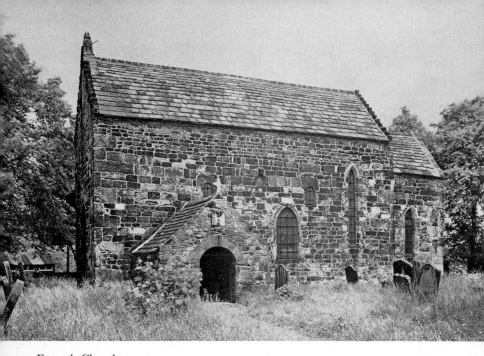

Escomb Church

Finchale Priory

Pudsey. High up on either side of the chancel arch (also rebuilt) are two little reliefs from a Saxon cross (one showing Adam and Eve driven from Paradise). On the altar is the original altar stone of Frosterley marble, and at the east end of the south aisle is a worn stone crucifix which once stood on the west wall of the tower. Another ancient relic is the graceful font with an eight-sided bowl, and there are also eight 17th century bench-ends with carved foliage.

In the north wall of the church is a fine window by the A. K. Nicholson Studios "in memory of the faithful ministries" of George Worthington Reynolds, rector 1891–1916, and his sister, Lucy Frances Reynolds. The rector is shown as St George standing with a spear; his sister, in a red robe, holds a lighted lantern.

John Cosin was rector here from 1624 to 1660, when he became Bishop of Durham.

Escomb. It is only a small village by the Wear, nestling at the bottom of a steep bank a mile to the west of Bishop Auckland; but amid its modern houses it has one of the most ancient churches in the land.

This venerable building, recently restored to regular use, is thought to date from the second half of the 7th century, and although England has several other churches which are as old—St Martin's at Canterbury, indeed, is considerably older—this is the only one which has survived in almost its original form. We see this house of prayer almost exactly as our Saxon forbears saw it.

Small, simple, and of austere dignity, Escomb Church consists of a long and narrow high-walled nave, and a tiny square chancel with 17th century porch and later bellcot.

Nave and chancel are constructed of worked Roman stone which almost certainly came from the fort of Binchester, across the Wear, one and a half miles to the north-east. Some of the blocks are five feet long, and many bear marks of the Roman tooling called brooch pattern or cross-hatching.

The high walls, leaning slightly inwards, are about 30 inches thick and retain five of the original round-headed windows, two on each side of the nave and one at the top of the west gable—all placed high for defensive purposes and to avoid weakening the walls.

On the north side of the nave is the original doorway, formed of simple stones arranged in the style known as long-and-short work. In the chancel is another doorway, now filled in, and set upside down in the wall near it is a stone bearing the inscription LEG VI, a reference to the Sixth Legion, the Victorious, which started to garrison York about the year 122, and on the evidence of this inscription was also associated with Binchester. On the south wall is a worn Saxon sundial, surrounded by a carving of a strange serpent; it is the oldest sundial in England still in its original position.

The most striking feature of the interior is the strong, solid-looking chancel arch. Tall and narrow, it may originally have stood in one of the Roman buildings at Binchester. On the underside of the arch are traces of 12th century painting.

Above the altar is a grey stone with a cross carved on it, and lying along the north wall of the nave are fragments of other Saxon crosses which once stood in the churchyard; one has a bold carving of a bird perching on some foliage.

At the west end of the church, which still has part of its original floor of small cobble-stones, a Norman font rests on stone steps marked with Roman diamond tooling.

The rude stone seats on either side of the porch are formed of massive blocks of stone bearing Roman tool marks; also in the porch are two mediaeval grave-covers removed from the floor of the nave.

Esh. This is a windswept village on a ridge between the valleys of the Browney and the Deerness, and it affords a magnificent view across the Browney to the north. On the green is a 17th century cross said to mark one of the resting-places of St Cuthbert's body. Near the cross, at the end of a sycamore avenue, is a pair of dignified 17th century gateposts of stone; they bear the arms of the Smythe family, whose home, long since vanished, was at the other end of the avenue.

Surrounded by trees on the opposite side of the green is the small church, modernised but still keeping one or two witnesses to its antiquity. It has a single bell bearing the date 1695, and lying beneath a window in the south transept is a fine stone figure dating from about AD 1300. It portrays a woman in embroidered mantle, resting with her head on two cushions and her feet on a little dog. On a nearby windowsill is the headless figure of an infant in swaddling clothes.

At Waterhouse, about a mile away, a Roman Catholic priest named John Boste was arrested after saying his last Mass. He was tortured in the Tower of London and executed at Durham in July 1594.

Ferryhill. Like Ferndown in Dorset, this industrial and market town takes its name from an Old English word, "fiergen", a wooded hill. Beside it runs the Great North Road—in a strikingly deep cutting which was commenced in the coaching era, abandoned with the advent of the railway, and resumed with the coming of cars.

At the top of the hill is the old marketplace, and lower down (near the railway) is a farm with a fragment of historic stone built into the coping of its roadside wall. An inscription states that *The large stone just above, part of Cleves Cross, marks the site where by tradition the Brawn of Brancepeth was killed by Roger de Fery about the year 1200.* Roger is sometimes known as Hodge of Ferry; the Brawn was the fabulous boar said—dubiously—to account for the name of the village of Brancepeth (Brawn's Path) six miles to the north-west.

At Rushyford, two miles or so up the Great North Road, is the Eden Arms, a long white building with a red roof. It was once a posting house called the Wheatsheaf, and it was here that the great lawyer Lord Eldon spent many vacations in his last years. He kept a private cellar here, and it is said that he and Holt the landlord between them used to account for seven bottles of port a day. Here, too, one snowy January day in 1815, Byron and his wife stopped for a glass of port when on their way from their wedding at Seaham to spend their honeymoon at Halnaby Hall.

At Rushyford, nearly 500 years earlier, Louis de Beaumont, Bishop of Durham, was captured by Sir Gilbert Middleton; he was carried off to Mitford Castle in Northumberland, and there held to ransom.

Finchale Priory. The loveliest ruin in the county, it is situated in a glorious bend of the Wear, three miles north of Durham City. The waters rush noisily over the rocks, and on the other side of the river is a steep and rocky wooded bank reached by a footbridge.

Finchale's story starts with St Godric, who was born in the year 1065 and on coming of age turned from the precarious life of a pedlar to the equally precarious life of a sea captain. In 1102 he made a pilgrimage to Compostella in Spain, and two years later resolved to leave all worldly affairs behind him and to start life anew as a hermit.

Godric's first hermitage was near Carlisle, and from there he went to Wolsingham to share a cave with a former monk of Durham. At Wolsingham he had a vision in which he learned that he was later to found a hermitage at Finchale.

On the death of his companion he left for Durham Priory, and there for the first time learned where his destiny lay. About 1110 Bishop Flambard granted him permission to live at Finchale, and here, a mile

87

or so upstream from the present priory, Godric built himself a turf-covered hut and a little rude chapel of timber which he dedicated to St Mary.

A stone chapel (dedicated to St John the Baptist) was later built on the present site, with humble living quarters attached, and here Godric lived for the rest of his days.

He was buried here in 1170 at the patriarchal age of 105, and the buildings were eventually taken over by Durham Priory. About 1237 they were extended on the plan we see today in order to accommodate up to 15 monks. From the 14th century until the Dissolution, the establishment consisted of a prior and four monks living here permanently, with four other monks from Durham in turn taking a three-week country holiday in this delightful spot.

The ruined chancel of the priory church contains traces of St Godric's stone chapel; the walls are outlined in the turf, and by the north wall is a cross marking a stone-lined grave enclosing the hermit's empty coffin.

The chancel measures 33½ feet by 15½, and most of the walls still stand almost to their original height. At the east end is an opening for a cupboard, with a groove in the stone for a shelf. In the south wall are remains of a double piscina. (Piscinas with two drains were in use for only a short period in the 13th century, when the earlier custom of using a piscina for the drainings of the chalice overlapped its later use for the ceremonial washing of the priest's hands. It was not thought fit that the same drain should be used for both purposes, so another was provided when hand-washing was introduced. After a short time the priest was ordered to drink the contents of the chalice after Mass instead of emptying it down the drain on consecrated ground; hence the need for two drains disappeared.)

Of the central tower of Finchale Priory Church four massive round piers still stand, the north-west one having a staircase which led to the upper storey. The east and west walls of the north transept rise to their full height, the west wall having unusually long and narrow lancet windows. All the walls of the south transept are still standing, and there are foundations of the staircase which led through the doorway halfway up the south wall into the monks' dormitory.

The aisles of both nave and chancel were demolished in 1364, and we can see that the arcades were blocked and fitted with traceried windows. The north wall of the nave (which was 15 feet shorter than the chancel) rises to its original height, but the upper half of the south wall has gone. From the west end, where the original 13th century doorway still stands, with remains of three lancet windows above it, there is a particularly beautiful view of the whole church.

East of the church is a rare survival—the ruins of the temporary buildings used when the establishment was undergoing its great extension early in the 13th century. At its south-west corner stands part of the 14th century vaulting of what may have been a guest-house.

The cloister is to the south of the nave. Its north walk, still partly standing, was the original south aisle, adapted for the cloister in 1364.

On the east of the cloister, reached through a pointed doorway flanked by two windows, is the chapter house; a stone bench runs round the wall, and at the east end is a seat for the prior. On the south side of the cloister is the roofless refectory, with pointed windows on both sides and a fireplace at the west end; in the vaulted lower storey are many carved fragments of stone found in various parts of the priory.

East of the cloisters are extensive remains of the great house of the prior, where the visiting monks lived and had their meals. The round pillars of the cellar are still here, and there are traces of the hall fireplace. An upper room, the prior's study, still retains the base of the bay window which gave a delightful view of the River Wear. The walls of the prior's chapel are also standing, with traces of its gallery.

Frosterley. This Weardale village is noted for its marble, a black limestone, speckled with fossils, which has been quarried here for hundreds of years and is to be seen in many churches in this county, fashioned into fonts and effigies, altar stones and grave-covers. A small marble plaque on the north wall of Frosterley Church records the use of this stone throughout the world.

Over the river is a dignified stone bridge with three round arches; built in 1813, it affords a good view across the broad bed of the Wear to the spire of the church rising from among the trees. Below the village the river is joined by the Bollihope Burn, lovely with juniper and yew springing from the limestone crags above the stream.

Gainford. A neatly-built village on the Tees, eight miles west of Darlington, it is a place of considerable antiquity.

It is gathered round a big village green and boasts some dignified rows of Georgian houses, an Elizabethan mansion, and a church with its roots in Saxon England. On the north side of the green is a 12-foot cross set up on the base of the ancient village cross to mark Queen Victoria's jubilee. At the south-west corner is the old church, so close to the river's edge that even within the building the water can be heard rushing over the stones; and beyond the green is the many-gabled Gainford Hall, built in 1600 by John Cradock, vicar of Gainford from 1593 to 1627, and restored about 1850.

Gainford's church, successor to one built early in the 9th century by Edred, Bishop of Lindisfarne, dates from about 1200, and has several lancet windows of that period. But the walls consist largely of Roman stones from the fort at Piercebridge three miles away to the east.

During restoration work in 1864 a Roman altar of AD 217 was found serving as capital of a pillar in the tower; it bore a carving of an eagle with a wreath in its beak and was dedicated to Jupiter. This altar and two more carved Roman stones, together with a tall Saxon cross and several other Saxon carvings found at the same time, were later sent to Durham Cathedral and there adorn a magnificent collection.

Fragments of the shafts of two Saxon crosses, however, are still preserved here, and in the walls of the rebuilt north porch are relics of mediaeval gravestones with carved crosses, swords, and shears. There is also one with a chalice, a priest's memorial which was mutilated in 1768 when used again for an inscription to Lawrence Brockett, a Cambridge professor of history who lived at Headlam Hall, a fine Jacobean house about one and a half miles north of Gainford.

A striking feature of the spacious interior are the 13th century nave arcades, each consisting of three very wide and lofty pointed arches on round pillars. At the west end of the nave are three more arches, supporting a tower which has a big projecting stair turret. At the other end, a tall chancel arch frames a lovely east window of three lancets, filled with modern glass depicting the Annunciation, the Nativity, and the Crucifixion. The graceful 13th century font has a Jacobean oak cover carved with foliage.

Gateshead. To the first Saxon settler it was a headland frequented by wild goats; to Dr Johnson it was "a dirty lane leading to Newcastle". Now it is a sprawling Tyneside town with a host of engineering and allied industries. Within its boundaries is the fine 700-acre Team Valley Trading Estate, with well over 100 factories in a garden city environment.

Of the five bridges which Gateshead shares with Newcastle the one with the longest history is the Swing Bridge. There was a bridge at this point in Roman times, and this was replaced in 1250 by a stone bridge which was guarded by a fortified tower. The mediaeval bridge was swept away in 1771 by a disastrous flood and replaced by a nine-arched stone bridge, which in turn was demolished a century later to make way for the present Swing Bridge. It has a great span which can be swung round in 90 seconds to enable deep-sea vessels to travel further up the river.

To the west of the Swing Bridge is Robert Stephenson's six-arched High Level Bridge, which was opened by Queen Victoria in 1849; trains run on the upper deck and road traffic below. Further upstream are the King Edward VII Railway Bridge, opened in 1906 for main-line traffic, and the Redheugh Bridge, built in 1871 and reconstructed in 1901.

To the east of the Swing Bridge is the imposing Tyne Bridge, opened by King George V in 1928. The roadway is suspended 84 feet above the river from a gigantic and graceful arch containing 4000 tons of steel; with its span of 531 feet and rise of 170 feet, it was, when built, the longest single-span bridge in the world. The foundations are nearly 70 feet below water level.

Gateshead's mother church (St Mary's) is perched on the bank of the river near the Tyne Bridge; the churchyard gives a fine view of Newcastle quay and the shipping on the river. The first church on the site was the scene, in 1080, of the murder of Bishop Walcher who had aroused anger by refusing to bring to justice the murderers of a Saxon nobleman named Liulph. He was holding a council when a mob assembled outside the church, and when he emerged to plead with them he was slain and the church set on fire. His remains, terribly maltreated by the mob, were subsequently buried in the chapter house at Durham.

The present building, of Norman origin, displays notable 14th century work in its lofty arcades, and also has a dignified 18th century tower; but the chancel was rebuilt, and the rest of the church drastically restored, after heavy damage caused by a dreadful fire and explosion in a worsted factory fronting the river in Hillgate, in October 1854. The east window, portraying Christ and the Four Evangelists, commemorates those who lost their lives in the disaster; and in the churchyard is a little heap of stones which together with burning timber and red-hot iron bars were blown on to the roof and into the church.

Attached to the north wall of the chancel, which retains its Norman masonry and one Norman window, is a modern room called the Anchorage, a name handed down through the years, and recalling

91

the fact that in 1340 Bishop de Bury of Durham granted a licence for an anchoress's house in the churchyard. This hermit's cell later became a school, probably the first school ever attended by Gateshead children.

Fragments of Gateshead's early history are illustrated in a big window on the south side of the chancel. It was set up by the Master and Brethren of King James Hospital in 1899 *to the glory of God and in thankfulness for the benefits received from this ancient charity*, which was in existence as early as the 13th century. The three senior brethren are portrayed in a little panel below the main subjects.

The central light shows a man in a brown robe laying the foundation stone of a monastery on this site early in the 7th century. The founder, Bede tells us, was Utta, "renowned priest and abbot". In this window he is portrayed with the kindly features of Archdeacon Prest, rector of Gateshead when the window was erected, and to the left of him is the wooden bridge built across the Tyne by the Romans.

Another light shows the mitred figure of St Aidan presenting a crozier to the kneeling Utta. The firm features of Aidan are those of Bishop Lightfoot, and the other three figures standing near him bear the features of Lord Northbourne, a benefactor of the church, James Turner, who was parish clerk for over 40 years, and Canon Moore Ede, rector of Gateshead and later Dean of Worcester.

The third light shows the baptism at Wallbottle of Peada, son of Penda, King of Mercia, in AD 653, an event which marked the virtual triumph of Christianity in the north. The red-robed Bishop Finan, who is baptising Peada, bears the features of Bishop Westcott.

St Mary's Church has a particularly fine array of woodwork. The nave has a fine 15th century roof of dark oak, with foliated bosses, and is filled with a magnificent set of oak pews dating from 1634. At the back of the church are two big oak chests, one bearing the date 1647.

Above the modern oak chancel screen are the royal arms of Charles II, placed there in 1660; and under the chancel arch is an oak armchair of 1666 with the arms of the borough boldly carved on the back. On the backs of the choir-stalls is a little carved head of the young Queen Victoria, and another of Archbishop Howley who announced to her the news that she was Queen.

Built into the wall of the church are several old carved stones. One, with a carved cross and a dagger, is in the north side of the chancel arch; let into the south wall is another, with carved sword and sheath; and in the west wall of the porch is a remarkable mediaeval tombstone with a boldly carved foliated cross rising from a trefoil base. Another, with a foliated cross and a pair of shears, stands on the other side of the porch, and near it is a rudely carved cross thought to be Saxon.

Of modern memorials perhaps the most notable is a tablet in the baptistry wall which was set up by St George's Society of Halifax, Nova Scotia, in honour of a Gateshead man, James Renforth, champion oarsman of England, who died at the age of 29 while rowing on the Kennebecasis River in 1871 for the championship of the world. He was buried in Gateshead's East Cemetery, and a monument there portrays his tragic end.

Gateshead's only other historic building is Holy Trinity Church, in the busy High Street, though this also has largely been rebuilt, the south aisle being the only remaining fragment of a monastic chapel founded by Bishop Nicholas de Farnham in the middle of the 13th century. This building was nearly destroyed in 1746 when an infuriated mob set fire to the neighbouring Gateshead House. It is said that the people had climbed the walls round the mansion to catch a glimpse of the Duke of Cumberland (then on his way to deal with the Jacobite rebels at Culloden), and that the gardener unwisely set some dogs on them. The stone gateway outside the church belonged to Gateshead House.

The roads going south from this crowded part of Gateshead climb to the highest parts of the town, culminating in Sheriff Hill which reaches a height of 538 feet. There are many fine viewpoints in this neighbourhood, and here also is the finest of Gateshead's open spaces—the 58-acre Saltwell Park, with its sweep of lawn sloping down to a big lake.

The 19th century mansion in this park is now a Local and Industrial Museum, containing many fascinating exhibits. One is a bow window from an 18th century shop front in the High Street; another is a glass case devoted to three of the inventions of Sir Joseph Wilson Swan—the incandescent lamp, the carbon print photograph, and cellulose filament.

For 14 years Swan lived in Gateshead, and his house—Underhill, Low Fell—was the first in England to be lit by electric lamps. The key to the problem of the incandescent lamp was solved in 1878 at this house when Swan found that carbon sealed in a vacuum did not waste away. On December 18 he exhibited his invention to the Newcastle Chemical Society, and three months later he gave a public lecture at the Gateshead Town Hall. For the first two experimental years the delicate work of forming the filament for carbonisation was performed by the ladies of Swan's household, while the only glassblower in England sufficiently expert to make the bulbs was young Fred Topham of Birkenhead. With the introduction of German glassblowers in 1881 the commercial manufacture of the lamp was started at Benwell near Newcastle, but Gateshead was the cradle of what is now a vast industry.

Among the other attractions of Gateshead Museum are models of Tyne ships, exhibits illustrating the local manufacture of paper, pottery, soap and glass, a delightful Victorian room, a splendid collection of British birds, and a remarkable assembly of dolls illustrating 1000 years of British costume.

Near the north-east corner of Saltwell Park stands the Shipley Art Gallery, named after the donor, Joseph Shipley, a Newcastle and Gateshead solicitor who died in 1909. Its colonnaded entrance is surmounted by two colossal groups of statuary representing the instruction of youth in the Arts and Sciences.

The gallery now contains about 1000 works of art, including some fine religious pictures by artists of the Dutch, Flemish, and German schools. British painters of the last 300 years are well represented, and there is an interesting display of the work of notable local artists —Myles Birkett Foster and George Bulmer of North Shields, and James Peel, J. W. Carmichael, John Atkinson, and the Richardsons of Newcastle.

Near the Shipley Gallery is the Central Public Library. It houses a particularly fine collection of books, manorial documents, letters, deeds, maps, and plans which are of inestimable value to all who are interested in delving into the history of Gateshead and County Durham in general.

Greatham. Much of the salt we use in our homes comes from the great salt works here, which draws brine from beds over 1000 feet below the surface. Greatham saltmarsh is a wide area of flat ground beside the Tees estuary, cut up by a network of winding waterways and old salt pans.

The most remarkable building in the village is Greatham Hospital, which was built in 1272 by Robert de Stitchill, Bishop of Durham, and rebuilt in Gothic style by Jeffry Wyatt in 1803. It stands among tall trees beside a green on the north side of the churchyard. Over the porch in the centre is a clock-tower, capped by an eight-sided bell-turret; behind the porch lies the hall, and on either side are alms-houses for 13 men and six women.

On the western edge of the churchyard is the hospital chapel, rebuilt in 1788; and to the south-west is the master's house (Greatham

Hall), a plain stone building of 1725. It was once the home of Ralph Ward Jackson, to whose enterprise the modern port of Hartlepool owes its origin.

Greatham Church was largely rebuilt in 1792, enlarged in 1855, and given a tall tower in 1909. But it dates from the 12th century, and still has its round Norman nave arcades and a round Norman font of local marble. The altar of Frosterley marble, a relic of the mediaeval church, is supported by two turned balusters which must have come from the window of a Saxon tower.

In the south aisle are other Saxon and Norman relics found during the building of the tower. They include a pre-Conquest cross-head with interlacing ornament, and part of an early Norman grave-cover carved with a cross-shaft.

The church also has two fine pieces of 17th century woodwork: a carved chest and massive armchair with a curious canopy formed by a male and female figure with linked arms.

Great Stainton. This is a tiny hilltop village on the Roman road from Newcastle to York; its red roofs can be seen peeping out above the trees from a considerable distance.

The church stands in a secluded graveyard, reached by a grassy road lined with fine old beeches. It was completely rebuilt in 1876, but still has its original Norman font with shallow octagonal bowl. Built into the base of the tower are some 17th century tombstones and fragments of mediaeval grave-covers with carved crosses.

Hamsterley. It stands on a long narrow ridge overlooking the Bedburn Beck—its dwellings gathered round a sloping green and its church solitary in a field half a mile to the east. From the churchyard there is a fine view towards the Yorkshire border.

The church is chiefly 13th century work, much restored, but within the porch is a reconstructed Norman doorway with a narrow round arch and an ancient door studded with iron.

The walls of the church are remarkable for the mediaeval monuments built into them. Two of the most astonishing project at ground level from the west wall of the south transept; the inside portions have been removed, but those in the churchyard have carvings of a praying woman and an elaborate floral cross. Also built into this wall is a grave-cover with a cross and a plough-share, and facing it in the east wall is a sculptured cross with sword, hammer, and pincers.

Inside the north transept are two fine crosses with swords. On the south side of the chancel a fine floral cross commemorating a priest rises from steps carved over a wheel, and beside it are shown a chalice, a book, a spear, and a dice-box.

Among other antiquities preserved here are the graceful 13th century font, a paten of 1520, and a 17th century panelled oak chest with carved foliage.

The east window is a splendid composition in modern glass: the middle lancet depicts Christ in Majesty, and on either side are medallions representing symbols of the Crucifixion.

About a mile north of Hamsterley the Bedburn is joined by the Harthope Beck, which once fed a moat surrounding the strong earthwork called the Castles. Here are the overgrown remains of a big, stone-walled, post-Roman camp about 70 yards square.

Hart. This pleasant little place has one long sloping street with a distant view of the sea, and a grey stone church which is the mother church of Hartlepool and dates from Saxon times.

The nave represents the body of the original pre-Conquest church, which had no aisle; the typical quoin stones at the four angles of the Saxon nave can just be distinguished on the exterior. The remains of Saxon windows can also be seen over the north arcade and above the chancel arch.

The low tower and its stately arch, the wide chancel arch, and the north arcade are all Norman work, a notable feature of the arcade being a series of 10 corbel heads of men and monsters facing the aisle.

The chancel, rebuilt in the 19th century, has an attractive little window with a finely coloured figure of an angel holding a book—a memorial of the Second World War.

Built into the west wall of the south aisle is an early stone sundial with raised lines, and near it are two fragments of mediaeval grave-covers, part of a Saxon cross, and a massive Norman font, long disused. Another ancient relic is a curious little relief of St George and the Dragon, built into the external south wall of the chancel.

But the greatest treasure of Hart Church is its 15th century font, the most elaborate in the county. Made of local limestone, it has an eight-sided bowl on an eight-sided shaft, both enriched with carved figures. The bowl bears emblems of the four Evangelists and figures of St Philip, St James, St Simon (with a spear), St Thomas, St Jude, and St Barnabas. The west side of the bowl portrays the Resurrection scene, flanked by symbols of the Passion.

Round the shaft of the font are figures of St Euphemia (with sword through her breast), Pope Gregory the Great (wearing the triple crown), St Lucy (with book and pincers), an abbot, St Elizabeth standing on a dragon, St Leonard, St Barbara, and St Petronilla. Below the bowl are eight half-figures of shield-bearing angels, and at the angles of the base are eight heads of men (four tonsured) separated by four-petalled flowers.

Hartlepool. Within the boundaries of this coastal town, south-east of the Durham coalfield, are the ancient borough of Hartlepool and the modern port of West Hartlepool. Old Hartlepool has a history dating from the 7th century; West Hartlepool is entirely a product of the Industrial Revolution.

From the writings of the Venerable Bede it is known that in AD 640 St Aidan, first Bishop of Lindisfarne, gave permission for a religious house for men and women to be established here. It was set up on the Heugh, the headland north of the old harbour, and placed in charge of Heiu, "the first woman that in the province of the Northumbrians took upon her the life and habit of a nun".

Heiu, who like many other shadowy saints of early times is believed to have been an Irish princess, presided over the monastery until 649, when she was succeeded as abbess by St Hilda, who 22 years earlier had been baptised by St Paulinus himself.

St Hilda controlled the monastery at Hartlepool for eight years before moving south and founding Whitby Abbey, where Caedmon, first of English poets, wrote his *Song of Creation*.

By 686 Hartlepool Monastery had become a religious house for women only, but it continued to hold the prestige St Hilda had won for it until about the year 800, when it was destroyed by Danish invaders—so completely that for 1000 years even its site was unknown.

The history of the settlement which grew up round the monastery is obscure, but it is known that soon after the Conquest the Manor came into the possession of a Norman knight named Robert de Bruce, ancestor of the Bruces of Annandale—the line to which King Robert I of Scotland belonged. Under the wing of this powerful family the place prospered; by 1189 the harbour was sufficiently important to be an assembly point for the fleet of Crusaders, and in 1200 the town was given a charter by King John.

Hartlepool continued to flourish through the years, and about 1330 was given the protection of a town wall with 10 defensive towers. As late as 1614 Hartlepool was described as the only port in the county of Durham, but the defences were largely destroyed during the Civil War after the town had been captured by the Scots, and by the 18th century the once-flourishing port had become a fishing village.

With the advent of the railway the decline was reversed, and although overshadowed by the rapid development of its new neighbour West Hartlepool, old Hartlepool regained some of its former importance. Today it has extensive docks and timber ponds, flourishing engineering industries, and a well-equipped Fish Quay.

The centre of old Hartlepool is the Heugh, bounded on its north side by the Headland Promenade and Marine Drive with waves breaking over the Parton rocks in front of them. Beyond are the North Sands, stretching away to the grassy cliffs at Crimdon.

From the south side of the Heugh there are fine views of Hartlepool Bay edged by docks and the ships moored at the quay; and here, running alongside the harbour, are some 600 yards of the town wall. This relic of mediaeval times, about 18 feet high and six to nine feet thick, is pierced by a pointed arch known as the Sandwell Gate because it leads on to the sands near a chalybeate spring called the Sand Well.

Another reminder of Hartlepool's antiquity is to be seen on the wall of the swimming-pool near the 440-yard-long breakwater projecting from the south-eastern tip of the Heugh. Here, inscribed on a bronze plate, are these words:

'The place whereon thou standest is holy ground.' Around lie buried the monks and nuns of the ancient Saxon monastery of Hartlepool (Heruteu) founded (circa) 640 AD. Destroyed by the Danes (circa) 800 AD. This cemetery was discovered in 1833.

At the beginning of the inscription is a copy of one of the little crosses carved on the memorial stones found on the site, known as Cross Close, during building operations between 1833 and 1834. The skulls of the nuns and monks were found resting on small flat pillow-stones, together with stones bearing crosses and inscriptions in Runic and Hiberno-Saxon lettering. One stone, now in the British Museum, is thought to have commemorated Bregusuid, the mother of St Hilda.

Hartlepool's ancient church, dedicated to St Hilda, stands a little to the north-west of the monastery site. One of the most remarkable in the county, it is believed to have been begun about the year 1185 by Robert Bruce IV, and completed about 30 years later.

Restored at various times, it still retains noble architectural features of the Transitional and Early English periods, as well as a south doorway enriched with zigzag moulding which is pure

Norman work and probably belonged to an earlier church on the site.

Externally, the dominant features are the long line of clerestory windows (seen to better advantage inside) and the massive west tower, with exceptionally big flying buttresses; the tower evidently started to sink soon after it was built, and the buttresses in turn sank owing to defective foundations. West of the tower is a modern choir vestry still containing a little masonry of the Galilee Chapel, or porch, which stood on the site in early times; it was used as a court for settling disputes, and also as an assembly point for processions through the church.

The spacious interior is even more impressive, with arcades and clerestory windows extending the whole length of the church. The varying clustered columns are like a magnificent avenue of stone running through the centre of the building, and make a noble spectacle, almost cathedral-like in proportions.

From these clustered columns a series of transverse arches cross the aisles of the outer wall, making other effective vistas on each side of the church. In the south aisle these arches are curiously contorted, indicating a change of plan while the work was in progress rather than settlement due to faulty foundations.

The chancel, lofty and spacious like the nave, is chiefly modern work by William Douglas Caröe; but original work is to be seen in the west bay and the fine pointed chancel arch with its clustered round shafts and richly carved capitals. An unusual feature of the chancel arch is that the east side has more mouldings and supporting shafts than the west.

Above the reredos three slender, pointed arches soar to the chancel roof, revealing between their graceful pillars the gay ruby-coloured glass of the east window.

Behind the reredos is the Bruce Chapel, containing an altar tomb, traditionally associated with the founder of the church, Robert Bruce IV. This huge tomb is of Frosterley marble, much weather-worn from having stood in the churchyard for two centuries; on it lies a worn figure of an unknown lady with a dog at her feet biting her gown. Also in the Bruce Chapel is part of a gravestone, badly worn and damaged, found during restoration work. On it is a carving of a single-masted ship of about 1350, probably intended for a merchant ship trading from the port of Hartlepool; it is a rare instance of a contemporary English drawing of a mediaeval vessel.

Another reminder of the Bruce family's associations with Hartle-pool is an oak stool in the sanctuary. It was used at the coronation of

George VI, and bears an inscription stating that he was *descended from the Bruce family who built this church, and that H.M. Queen Elizabeth is descended from George Bowes, mayor of Hartlepool in 1732, whose daughter married John Lyon, 9th Earl of Strathmore.*

It was George Bowes who gave the church its dignified Yorkshire marble font with round scalloped bowl and baluster shaft.

In a glass case on a shelf on the south wall of the sanctuary is a relic of Saxon Hartlepool—a gravestone from the monastic cemetery; it bears a carved cross showing the alpha and omega in the angle of the upper arms, and the name Hildithryth below.

On the wall of the north aisle, beside the organ, is a brass with an engraved figure of Jane Bell, wife of a merchant who was Mayor of Hartlepool in Elizabethan times. She wears a tall hat and a ruff, and a richly embroidered petticoat peeps through her gown.

Beneath this brass is a collection of stones of various periods, including a broken arch of Saxon origin, probably from an earlier church on this site.

West Hartlepool lies in fact to the south-west of the old town. It is a busy port, exporting millions of tons of coal from the Durham coalfield, and importing timber—much of it for use as pit-props—and iron ore, to feed the local iron and steel industries. Ships are repaired, but no longer built, here, and many light industries are established on the trading estate.

The founder of the town was Ralph Ward Jackson, the enterprising and far-seeing champion of the original West Hartlepool Harbour and Railway Company, and his memory is duly remembered. One of the many docks bears his name; on the western edge of the town is the delightful Ward Jackson Park; and in Church Square, looking towards the docks, is a bronze statue of him.

Near Jackson's statue is another of the shipbuilder Sir William Gray, a broad, bearded figure in the robes he wore as first Mayor of West Hartlepool; and close by, in Clarence Road, is the fine Art Gallery and Museum which he presented to the town. Several of the exhibits illustrate local industries; there are also attractive natural history and porcelain collections, and remarkable displays of Eastern idols and Japanese netsuke.

The pictures include works by David Cox, Stanhope Forbes, and Birket Foster, as well as examples by local artists such as James Clark, J. W. Howey, Seymour Walker, and Frederic Shields. A striking oil painting by J. W. Carmichael shows West Hartlepool in the mid-19th century.

On an island site between the statues of the town's two great men stands Christ Church, built in 1854, with a lofty tower originally intended to carry a beacon. It contains one unique feature—altar rails composed of bog-oak excavated when the first dock was being dug.

Less than half a mile south, perched on a bank above the main road, is West Hartlepool's only ancient church—All Saints. This is the old church of the village of Stranton around which West Hartlepool has grown. Much restored, it has a weather-worn tower dating from about 1280, and a chancel with Norman masonry. The north aisle of the church was once used as a school. Built into the wall of the south aisle are bits of mediaeval gravestones carved with crosses.

One of the windows, commemorating a choir master who died in 1903, has attractive figures of two angel children, with medallions of the church and a gabled house below.

In an unknown grave in the churchyard lies William Humphrey, the Barnard Castle clockmaker immortalised by Dickens.

In addition to the Ward Jackson Park, the town has the narrow Burn Valley Gardens, which stretch for a considerable distance beside a stream in the heart of the town; and at Seaton Carew, the seaside suburb south of the town, are splendid sands and a fine promenade.

Haughton-le-Skerne. A village suburb of Darlington, standing where the main road to Stockton crosses the little River Skerne, it has a street graced by pleasant old-fashioned houses and a fine Norman church.

The chief Norman features are the south doorway, the chancel arch, and the tower, which has a turret at its south-east corner and a tall, round-headed doorway in its west wall. There are also some narrow Norman windows in the chancel, one of them being particularly notable because of its attractive modern glass showing St John holding the infant Christ.

Another great feature of the church is its wealth of 17th century woodwork: the elaborate canopy of the 700-year-old font, a fine panelled pulpit with richly-carved sounding-board, a lectern to match, massive altar rails, and two finely-carved armchairs (note the dragons on the back of one of them).

In addition, the nave has a complete and splendid series of 17th century panelled pews and the chancel walls are lined with 17th century oak panelling.

Built into the south porch are some mediaeval gravestones with carvings of crosses, swords, and shears; and beside the chancel arch is a brass dated 1592 and showing Dorothy Parkington with her twin babes in her arms—a quaint figure in a long gown which reveals an embroidered petticoat beneath.

Another ancient relic is a bell dating from pre-Reformation times. But the most ancient possessions of the church are some fragments of cross-shafts built into two recesses in the north wall of the nave; they date from Saxon times and bear characteristic carvings of little animals entwined with interlacing patterns.

In the churchyard lies William Bewick, a distinguished artist who was born at Darlington in 1795. At the age of 20 he left his father's upholstery business, and in London he became a pupil of Benjamin Robert Haydon, in whose company he met Wordsworth, Hazlitt, and Keats. Bewick was a skilful copyist; Haydon employed him to make drawings of the Elgin Marbles for Goethe, and Sir Thomas Lawrence sent him to Rome to copy Michelangelo's paintings in the Sistine Chapel. He spent the last 20 years of his life at Haughton House which he himself built. He died there on June 8, 1866.

Heighington. This picturesque village is clustered round a large green on a hill, and from its outskirts there are fine views in the direction of Darlington and the broad valley of the Tees.

Much of the village church is Norman work, including the chancel and its arch, the tower with its narrow windows and dignified arch, and the south doorway, which was originally on the north side of the building. The Norman doorway, remarkably tall and narrow, has a round arch on a pair of round pillars, and is surmounted by a little stone panel with a worn relief of King Oswald and St Cuthbert. The tower has a 15th century parapet with gargoyles at the corners, and in the belfry are three 15th century bells; one is inscribed: *Do thou Peter when rung calm the angry waves.*

Standing in the tower is the old eight-sided font, and near it are three ancient gravestones and two 14th century stone figures of women in long gowns and pointed shoes.

Yet another mediaeval memorial (with a foliated cross) is in the chancel, and near it is a white marble monument with various war trophies commemorating Captain William Pryce Cumby, who fought at Trafalgar and died at Pembroke 32 years later.

The rarest possession of the church is the pre-Reformation pulpit of oak. It has six traceried linenfold panels and a cornice with a Latin inscription asking prayers for Alexander Flettchar and Agnes his wife.

In the neighbourhood are two 16th century houses in beautiful parks—Redworth Hall and Walworth Castle. The castle, a lofty building with two prominent round towers, was built by Thomas Jennison, auditor-general in Ireland. James I stayed here on April 14, 1603, while journeying south to mount the English throne.

Heworth. A busy industrial place on the outskirts of Gateshead, it has a wide view of the valley of the lower Tyne.

In 1813, when it was little more than a village, an important discovery was made here. A little red earthenware jar was dug up in the churchyard, and in it were several stycas of Ecgfrith, King of Northumbria from 670 to 685. The earliest known coins of Northumbria, they are the only examples of their kind ever found. One of them is now in the Museum of Antiquities at Newcastle upon Tyne.

At the time they were found John Hodgson, the historian of Northumberland, was living at High Heworth Farm (since rebuilt), which looks northward across the Tyne. Hodgson was perpetual curate of Jarrow and Heworth (which until 1834 were linked), and this farmhouse was his home from 1808 until he left for Kirkwhelpington in Northumberland, 15 years later. Here at Heworth he began his important historical work.

When Hodgson came to Heworth the church was in a state of decay, and he diligently set to work to design and build a new one, acting as his own clerk of works. On May 5, 1822, he preached the first sermon in the finished church, a sombre building at a busy bend of the main road by the Tyne. Over the south entrance is the boldly-carved Latin inscription placed here by Hodgson, stating that the church was founded in the reign of King Ecgfrith and rebuilt in the reign of George IV.

On the chancel wall is a marble inscription in Latin to Richard Dawes, a headmaster of Newcastle Grammar School and a fine Greek scholar, who died in 1766 having spent his last 17 years in retirement at Heworth. Above the inscription rests a carved copy of his book, *Miscellanea Critica*, which threw entirely new light on the Greek language. On the boulder over his grave by the lych-gate is a brass inscription: "The burial-place of Richard Dawes, MA. Let no man move his bones."

Between this grave and the church stands an early 18th century canopied table-tomb carved to represent a four-poster bed. Under an embroidered counterpane lie stone figures of three sleeping children, apparently of the Haddon family.

The most poignant memorial here is a stone obelisk rising above the wall at the west end of the churchyard. It commemorates 91 people, including several children, who were killed in Felling Colliery on May 25, 1812.

The High Main Colliery at Felling was exhausted in 1811, and the Low Main was then started. These deeper workings were unfortunately subject to firedamp, and as safety lamps were not yet in use, an accumulation of gas caused the explosion which led to this awful tragedy. John Hodgson preached the funeral sermon.

High Coniscliffe. Perched above the River Tees, about four miles west of Darlington, it stands, a village of considerable antiquity.

It is recorded in the Anglo-Saxon Chronicle that in 778 a high sheriff called Eldulf was slain at Ciningesclif, "the King's Cliff". That cliff is the rocky river-side spur where the church stands, and the king was Edwin of Northumbria, to whom the church is dedicated; it is, in fact, the only one in England dedicated to Edwin.

The building has fragments of carved Saxon stonework in its walls and a Norman north doorway surmounted by a curious little relief showing the Holy Lamb in a circle held by two angels. Otherwise it dates almost entirely from the 13th century. It has a long and narrow nave with north arcade of three pointed arches on remarkably low round pillars, a lofty chancel arch, and an octagonal stone spire—one of the county's five ancient spires.

Over the vestry is a priest's room; and in the chancel are old stalls and desks with carved poppyheads displaying foliage, little heads of men and women, a fierce-looking animal, and angels holding shields. There is also a fine 17th century armchair with carved foliage.

Houghton-le-Spring. This busy little town is sheltered from the north-east by the long steep hill which terminates in Warden Law. At nearly 650 feet this is the highest point in east Durham, and it has a fine all-round view of land and sea; to the south-west, nearly eight miles away, Durham Cathedral is clearly seen.

Towards the higher and older part of the town, in Church Street, stands Houghton Hall, a three-storied Elizabethan mansion now used as a club. It was built by a rector named Robert Hutton, whose son, a Roundhead captain, was buried in the garden near his favourite horse in 1681. His gravestone is now in the churchyard, near the almshouses.

Another notable old house is the former Rectory, a low battlemented building of stone across the road from the church, in a pleasant walled garden which is now a public park. Rector George Davenport rebuilt the house soon after the Restoration.

Preserved at its north-west corner is a big thorn tree, split into two and with gnarled limbs propped up with timber supports, which is said to have been planted by Bernard Gilpin, the Apostle of the North. Rector here from 1556 until his death in 1584, he is still remembered for his piety and benevolence.

Bernard Gilpin was born near Kendal in 1517, and after a grammar school education was sent to Oxford. There he won esteem for his scholarly mind and his cheerful disposition, and for the moderation of his views at a time when there was much fanaticism.

In 1552 he accepted a modest living at Norton-on-Tees, a gift of his great-uncle, Bishop Tunstall; but before taking up office he was called upon to give a sermon to the Court of Edward VI, and during the course of it rebuked the "mighty men, gentlemen, and rich men' who "rob and spoil the poor". Brave words indeed!

After this, instead of going to Norton, he decided to continue his studies on the Continent, but after a year or two abroad he returned home and in 1556 was appointed vicar of Easington and Archdeacon of Durham. A year later, he became rector of Houghton-le-Spring, and here he remained for the rest of his days.

It was one of the richest livings in the county, and his generosity was prodigious. His guests ranged from the highest in the kingdom to the 24 poor men he fed every week. Every Sunday from Michaelmas to Easter he kept open house, providing dinner for all who came.

But Bernard Gilpin saw much further than his own parish; he set himself the task of evangelising the remote districts of Northumbria, and travelled through the wilds of Tynedale and Teesdale "where the word of God was never heard to be preached". Hence his title— Apostle of the North.

Many thought that Gilpin should have been a bishop, and he was indeed offered the See of Carlisle; but he refused, feeling that he could do more good in the humbler office of parish priest.

At 66 Gilpin, already a sick man through constant and unsparing labour, was knocked down by an ox in Durham market. He never wholly recovered, and a few months later he was laid to rest in his church, mourned by a vast flock.

Rector George Davenport, the rebuilder of the Rectory, seems to have been a worthy follower of the saintly Gilpin.

> *If the soul's transmigration were believed*
> *You'd say good Gilpin's soul had he received.*

So runs the inscription on his tomb in the north transept of the church.

Tangible witnesses to the generosity of both men are still to be seen near the church. At the north-east corner of the churchyard stands the rebuilt Kepier Grammar School founded by Gilpin and John Heath in 1574. A building with a projecting gabled wing, it has a Latin inscription over the entrance, and the date 1724. At the south-east corner of the churchyard are the almshouses founded by Davenport—a picturesque 17th century building of stone with mullioned windows and red-tiled roof.

The large and imposing church where these two men ministered watches over a busy crossing in the middle of the town. Largely 13th century work, it has a central tower with a modern upper stage, a nave with two arcades of pointed arches on dignified clustered columns, a chancel with a fine row of lancet windows in its south wall, and a Norman window and doorway facing them. The doorway, exceedingly narrow, has a tympanum with a relief carving of two entwined monsters fighting among waving foliage.

A remarkable feature of the church is the battlemented building set in the angle between chancel and south transept, and linked to the rest of the church by a passage. Now used as a vestry, it was originally built in the 15th century for the Guild of the Holy Trinity; the guild met on the ground floor and the attached chantry priest lived in the upper room.

Other tokens of the church's antiquity are the eight-sided mediaeval font and an Elizabethan altar table of oak in the north aisle. It also has some interesting old monuments.

In the south transept is a white marble inscription extolling Sir Francis Blake, a distinguished mathematician who died in 1780. On the wall facing this is a brass to Margery Bellasis who *becoming widow so continued the rest of her life the space of 58 years, bestowing her whole time only in hospitality and relief of the poor, and being of the age of 90 deceased the 20th day of August 1587.* Above the inscription is an engraved portrait of her kneeling on a squared floor, her long headdress falling over her shoulders, and her children, all in ruffs and long gowns, kneeling dutifully in the rear.

There are also two effigies in the south transept. One, in a recess, is a much-worn figure of an armoured knight with his legs crossed and his feet on a lion; it may represent the Sir Rowland Bellasis who was knighted at the Battle of Lewes in 1264. The other figure, on the floor, portrays another 13th century knight in surcoat and chain armour, returning his sword to its sheath.

The last monument to be noted here—last but not least—is the huge altar tomb of Bernard Gilpin; its panelled sides, much worn, are ornamented with chainwork carving forming circles and squares, and at one end is carved Gilpin's coat-of-arms—a boar under a tree.

It is a remarkable fact that Houghton had only two rectors over a period of 106 years. Edward South Thurlow, who was appointed in 1789, ministered here until 1847, and was succeeded by John Grey, fourth son of Prime Minister Earl Grey, of Reform Bill fame. John Grey was rector here until his death in 1895, and during his ministry saw seven new parishes with churches carved out of the old parish of Houghton.

Hurworth-on-Tees. This big village stretches for more than half a mile along the north bank of the Tees, about three miles south of Darlington. It is an attractive place, with some fine Georgian houses round its spacious green, and a church in a dominating position on a steep cliff above the river.

To the west of the village is a dignified railway bridge with four lofty arches, each 20 yards long, carrying the London-Edinburgh line across the Tees. It took seven years to build, the keystone of the last arch being placed in position on April 9, 1840.

Half a mile upstream is Croft Bridge, with seven boldly ribbed pointed arches, linking Yorkshire and Durham. Its origins are not known, but it is thought to have been rebuilt by Bishop de Skirlaw about 1400, much restored in 1673, and since enlarged to twice its original width. The upstream arches are of a cold grey stone; downstream they are of warm red sandstone.

At one time newly-appointed Bishops of Durham arriving at Croft Bridge used to be presented with the Conyers Falchion by the lord of Sockburn, a tiny village three miles to the south-east. The presentation was made with these words:

My Lord Bishop, I here present you with the falchion wherewith the champion Conyers slew the worm, dragon, or fiery flying serpent which destroyed man, woman, and child; in memory of which the king then reigning gave him the manor of Sockburn, to hold by this tenure, that upon the first entrance of every bishop into the county the falchion should be presented.

Taking the falchion (broadsword) into his hand, the bishop immediately returned it, wishing health, long life, and prosperity to the owner of Sockburn. The last bishop to receive the falchion (now in the library of Durham Cathedral) was Van Mildert in 1826.

In earlier days the falchion was presented at Neasham Ford, lower downstream, where a grassy track leads down to the wide and swiftly flowing river. In the field by the ford stood Neasham Priory, founded as a house for nuns in the middle of the 12th century. A modern house stands on the site, but in the west wall of Hurworth Church are two stone figures of armoured knights which are thought to have come from the priory.

Hurworth Church was almost entirely rebuilt in the 19th century, the nave pillars being practically the only relics of the mediaeval building. The effigies from Neasham Priory are in arched recesses. One, showing a warrior, cross-legged and bearing a shield decorated with three chaplets of flowers, represents Ralph Fitz-William, first Lord Greystoke, who died in 1316, grandson of the founder of Neasham. The other figure, of grey Frosterley marble, wears a curious closed helmet with a remarkable narrow slit for the eyes. In the right hand is an upright sword which passes under the shield and then reappears to rest on the helmet.

The choir-stalls are notable, for they are of ancient oak taken from the rectory tithe barn when it was pulled down about 1880. Beside the organ is a fine portable screen made of 17th century oak panels with carved foliage.

In the churchyard, at the west end of the tower, is the tomb of William Emerson, the eccentric mathematician, who was born at Hurworth in 1701 and died here in 1782.

Emerson learned much from his father, the Hurworth schoolmaster, and from the village curate who lodged with them he learned still more, including Greek and Latin; but his bent was entirely towards mathematics.

Finishing his studies at Newcastle and York, William Emerson failed wholly in his attempt to assume his father's mantle as schoolmaster. His school having come to an end, he tramped to London and arranged for the publication of a series of manuals for beginners in mathematics. But the books were useless: Emerson just could not teach—his lessons were beyond the comprehension of any mind less able and mature than his own.

Emerson's strangeness of manner, the emphatic brusquerie of his address, his uncouth costume and general bearing stamped him as a complete eccentric. But his mathematical skill gained the esteem of the foremost members of the Royal Society, and he was offered membership. He answered rudely that it was a hard thing that a man should burn so many farthing candles as he had, and then have to pay so much a year for the honour of FRS at the end of his name.

Fishing was this strange man's abiding delight; he would stand waist-high all day in the water working out his problems, landing as few fish as solutions.

William Emerson died at the age of 81, leaving as his chief memorial several outstanding mathematical works, such as *Mechanics*, *Method of Increments*, and *Doctrine of Fluxions*.

Jarrow. The history of this sprawling town near the mouth of the Tyne is an eventful one; indeed, 13 centuries ago, Jarrow was a cradle of English literature and learning, the most illustrious name in its long story being that of the Venerable Bede. This devout historian passed nearly all his life in the monastery founded here in AD 681 by his beloved teacher, Benedict Biscop.

Jarrow's only visible links with those far-off days are the Church of St Paul and a few other fragments of the monastery, standing close to the spot where the waters of the little river Don flow into the Tyne. The shallow estuary, known as Jarrow Slake, covers 470 acres, and is largely used for storing and seasoning timber.

For the rest, Jarrow is a modern industrial town and as unprepossessing as most of its kind, although post-war rebuilding has done much to improve its appearance. The new shopping precinct is watched over by two Viking warriors (sculpture by Colin M. Davidson) recalling the Danish raids on the north-east coast in the dark days after the death of Bede.

There was a colliery here from 1803 to 1845 but the town's real rise to commercial importance began in 1852, when Charles Palmer opened his shipbuilding yard. That shipyard won a world-wide reputation for fine vessels and speedily developed into a vast enterprise, employing nearly 10,000 people. No fewer than 900 ships were launched from Palmer's Yard before it was finally closed. That was in 1933, during the Great Depression which brought distress to many parts of Tyneside. Jarrow itself suffered bitterly, with its people struggling on year after year without work. A plaque on the Town Hall recalls the Jarrow Crusade of October 5, 1936, when 200 unemployed marched to London to draw attention to the region's plight.

Gradually, with the help of good friends—public-spirited men like Sir John Jarvis, who as High Sheriff of Surrey organised a relief fund in that county—Jarrow emerged from the shadows. Now she has new and varied industries, new parks and playing-fields, new housing estates, and new tunnels running below the bed of the Tyne and linking the town with its neighbours in Northumberland.

Of its great shipbuilding days Jarrow has vivid reminders in its active ship-repairing industry, and in the ships continually passing by on the Tyne waterway. It also has a memorial of its leading citizen in those days, a bronze statue (near the railway station) of kindly-looking Sir Charles Mark Palmer in his mayoral robes. The inscription says that he was

Born at South Shields November 3rd 1822. Founder of the Palmer works and of the town of Jarrow of which he was first mayor in 1875. Originator of the first steam screw collier built at Jarrow in 1851. Member of Parliament for North Durham from 1874, and subsequently for the Jarrow division. This statue, erected in 1903 by the workmen of Palmer's company and a few friends, commemorates a life devoted to the social advancement of the working classes, the prosperity of Jarrow, and the industrial progress of Tyneside.

Below the statue are bronze reliefs depicting a miner and two of the ships of which Jarrow folk were so proud: the collier *John Bowes*, which was launched here in 1852 and gave good service until 1934, when she ran ashore on the north coast of Spain and was broken up; and HMS *Resolution* (forerunner of HMS *Queen Mary*), the Jarrow-built 27,000-ton battle cruiser which was sunk in 1916 at the Battle of Jutland.

As a reminder of its remote but illustrious past, Jarrow has the Church of St Paul, principal relic of the famous monastery founded here in 681 by Benedict Biscop and his friend Ceolfrid. Bede, who was born about 673, entered this monastery as a boy and here, with occasional visits to the sister house at Monkwearmouth, he remained until his death in 735.

Dark days followed the death of Bede; in 794 and again in 866 Jarrow Monastery was sacked by the Danes, and in 1069 the rebuilt parts were razed by the Conqueror. Five years later it was again rebuilt, this time by three monks, Aldwin of Winchcomb and Elfwins and Reinfridus of Evesham.

In 1083 the 23 monks of Jarrow were moved to Durham, and Jarrow became a cell of that great house, the priors of Durham occasionally coming here for a holiday. In 1144 the usurper William Cumin attacked Bishop de St Barbara here, but the buildings successfully withstood a siege. Later its importance gradually waned, and at the Dissolution it suffered the fate of all the old English monasteries and vanished into history.

Apart from the church the few traces of the monastery that remain probably date from the restoration by Aldwin and his fellow monks. They consist of a high wall running north and south, and terminating near the south-west corner of the church. This wall was the east side of a two-storey building; it has a big round-headed doorway with round shafts and, at the south end, a narrow triangular-headed doorway. There is another wall at right angles to it running eastward and forming the south side of what was the cloister; this wall still retains a little blocked doorway and three windows.

St Paul's Church is of great length, with a west porch and wide nave of the Victorian era, a slender central tower dating from early Norman times and a Saxon chancel. The tower, rebuilt by Aldwin, may originally have been a western porch of the Saxon church. It has round arches on the east and west, and much narrower ones on the north and south.

Above the western arch of the tower, lit by a little electric lamp, is a unique treasure—the original dedication stone of the church. Found in the north wall of the nave during a rebuilding in 1783, and in splendid preservation, it has a Latin inscription recording "The dedication of the basilica of St Paul on the 9th of the kalends of May in the 15th year of King Ecgfrid and the 4th of Abbot Ceolfrid, founder under God of the said church".

The Saxon chancel, which still has its original rugged stone walls, is the only remaining part of the church known to Bede. It is quite spacious—41 feet 6 inches long, and 15 feet 9 inches wide.

The blocked round-headed doorway in the north wall of the chancel is Saxon, and so are the three round-headed windows in the south wall. Two of the windows are still partly blocked with stone slabs pierced to let in the light.

Built into the outer part of the east wall (in the angles made by two later buttresses) are two upright slabs rising about three feet above the ground; they are thought to be marks to which Bede refers, placed here at the command of King Ecgfrid to show where the altar was to be placed. The east window (magnificent modern work by Leonard C. Evetts of Newcastle) depicts the crucified Lord, flanked on one side by St Peter, sword in hand, and on the other by solemn-faced Bede in a blue robe, holding a book.

Against the north wall of the sanctuary stands the relic known as Bede's Chair; it has been much mutilated, chips having been removed for luck by expectant and superstitious mothers. Also in the chancel is a graceful armchair of about 1700 with a tall richly carved back, and close by are four fine 15th century bench-ends of black oak with elaborate carved tracery. One end has a poppyhead carved with a pair of little human heads with wrinkled foreheads and protruding tongues; below, on the east, a pair of dragons bite their tails, while on the west is the badge of Prior Castell of Durham—a heart pierced by a sword.

Above the pulpit hangs a big painting of the Crucifixion which was brought from Hylton Castle in 1846, and in the north porch are many turned baluster shafts which were taken from the walls of the nave in 1866 and are thought to have adorned the church in Saxon times. There are also three pieces of carved stonework from Saxon crosses; two of them are 10th century work, and depict a hunter walking in a wood, with birds and beasts climbing branches. Also preserved here are a massive stone coffin and a mediaeval grave-cover with a graceful cross.

By the churchyard gate are the old village stocks, now enclosed in an iron cage.

Bede, whom we call the Venerable, is pre-eminent in our island story as the first example of the way in which the coming of Christianity transformed the nation's life.

He was born about AD 673, somewhere between Wear and Tyne, and he grew up in an atmosphere alive with religion. At Jarrow he saw the rising of the monastery in which, together with the house at Monkwearmouth, he was to spend most of his life. Travellers from the Continent brought holy pictures, craftsmen from Italy came with rare and beautiful glass; artists were making pictures for those who could not read; and Bede, who entered Jarrow Monastery as a boy, must have been stirred by it all.

Though Bede wrote more than any other man of his time, he tells us little of himself. He was too busy making knowledge known. He loved learning and music and beauty, and he was tireless. "I am my own secretary; I make my own notes; I am my own librarian," he said. He had 600 monks in his school at Jarrow and the textbooks he wrote for them were the wonder of his time. They contained all that was known in England about astronomy, meteorology, physics, music, grammar, arithmetic, medicine, and philosophy.

His greatest book, the *Ecclesiastical History of the English People*, must have taken him at least 2000 hours merely to write, apart from all the thinking and research that went into it. He wrote essays—one on time fills 200 pages—on such subjects as why the sea is salt, rainbows and volcanoes, lightning and thunder and the winds, and the working of the calendar.

He left behind 79 books, every one written laboriously with his own hand or dictated when he could write no more; and when death came to him, on Ascension Day in the year 735, it found him still writing out the Bible in the language of the English people.

For weeks the old man had been short of breath, but every day he gave thanks to God and was wonderfully cheerful, reading and singing psalms. Knowing that he was dying, he hastened on with his translation. In the afternoon of his last day he called his friends and gave them his little gifts—small personal possessions from his store-chest. Then he told them they would see his face no more.

That evening, he reached the translation of the last chapter of St John. Bede urged his boy to write quickly, and after a while the boy exclaimed, "One sentence, dear master, is left unfinished". The old man summoned up his strength and gave him the translation. "It is finished", said the boy, and Bede said, "True, it is finished", and closed his eyes, and died.

So passed our first great scholar, our first historian, and the father of English learning.

Kelloe. It is a scattered parish, scarred by quarrying and coal-mining, but here and there, in hill and valley, it still retains some pleasant rural scenery. It also has a church of more than passing interest.

Kelloe Church is chiefly 13th and 14th century work; but the low tower and the south doorway are both relics of the original Norman building, and in the sanctuary is a remarkable Norman cross which came to light, in six pieces, during 19th century restoration.

In this cross, which is of sandstone, are a number of holes which it is thought were intended to hold holy relics. The top portion is a wheel cross, and stretching down the stem are little scenes carved in relief: an angel revealing the position of the True Cross to the sleeping St Helen, figures of St Helen and the Emperor Constantine, and St Helen commanding Judas to dig for the Cross with a spade. At the base is the Cross itself. Nearby are two mediaeval grave-covers which were unearthed at the same time as the Norman cross.

On the south side of the church, next to a magnificent window depicting the parable of the Good Samaritan, is a marble monument inscribed with these words:

To commemorate the birth in this parish of Elizabeth Barrett Browning, who was born at Coxhoe Hall, March 6, 1806, and died at Florence, July 29, 1861. A great poetess, a noble woman, a devoted wife. Erected by public subscription, 1897.

The church still has the dignified little 18th century font at which Elizabeth Barrett was baptised, together with her brother, on February 10, 1808. Coxhoe Hall has been demolished in recent years.

In the shaded extension of Kelloe churchyard is a monument recalling a terrible mining tragedy; it marks the burial-place of 26 of the 74 men and boys who lost their lives in the Trimdon Grange colliery explosion on February 16, 1882.

A curious discovery was made at Kelloe Law Farm in 1948 when a tractor crushed the large covering-slab of a Bronze Age cist. This stone-lined grave contained the partially-burnt skeletons of a family of five; the bones have now been set up, and are in the Bowes Museum at Barnard Castle. With the bones were fragments of a Bronze Age beaker.

Kirk Merrington. Set on a lofty ridge six miles south of Durham, this village commands a magnificent view which embraces Durham Cathedral, Brancepeth Castle, the valley of the Wear, and the Yorkshire hills. Its own church tower is visible up to 20 miles away.

The church, rebuilt in 1851 in Norman style, stands on the site of the building which the usurping bishop William Cumin started to convert into a fortress in 1143. Cumin had got as far as digging a ditch and erecting outworks when he was attacked by loyal supporters of the rightful bishop, William de St Barbara. Heedless of darts and arrows, the attackers forced their way to the church windows and then drove out the defenders by throwing in burning brands.

The great treasure of the church is a magnificent 17th century chancel screen of black oak; the lower part has plain panels capped with graceful tracery, the cornice has carved flowers and foliage, and there is a cresting of scrolls and garlands. The altar rails, an armchair in the sanctuary, the graceful font, and two old box pews with panelled sides and massive ends carved with fruit and foliage, also date from the 17th century. The altar table of oak is Elizabethan work.

Outside the south door are two mediaeval gravestones with coped tops; one is carved like a tiled roof, and the other has a crown. On the south side of the churchyard is a massive stone table tomb inscribed with the names of John, Jane, and Elizabeth Brass, who were murdered by their father's servant, Andrew Mills, in January 1683, at a farmhouse still standing on a ridge north-east of the church. Poor Mills, a madman, was hanged on a gallows in sight of the house, and the story goes that he swung alive in his chains for several days, sustained with food brought to him by a devoted sweetheart.

On lower land to the south of Kirk Merrington lies Windlestone Hall, a brown stone mansion built by Ignatius Bonomi about 1835 for Sir Robert Johnson Eden, 5th Baronet of West Auckland.

The Edens, who are among the oldest and most respected of all the great families in the north, have an outstanding record of public service, and this tradition has been upheld in recent years by Lord Avon, formerly Sir Anthony Eden, who was born here in 1897.

Lamesley. A faintly old-world, country air still lingers about this village, though it is now skirted by a huge railway marshalling yard, and linked to Gateshead by the Team Valley Trading Estate stretching for nearly two miles towards the Tyne.

On higher ground overlooking the valley once stood one of the stately homes of England—Ravensworth Castle, 19th century successor of a feudal castle which belonged in turn to the noble families of FitzMarmaduke and Lumley, Gascoigne and Liddell. It was a Liddell—Sir Thomas, later Lord Ravensworth—who with the help of John Nash rebuilt the castle. In recent years, however, Ravensworth was demolished, and now only two 13th century towers of the old castle remain.

Some of the owners of Ravensworth were laid to rest in Lamesley Church, which stands in the old part of the village. It has been rebuilt, and the only relics of mediaeval times are two grave-covers with finely carved crosses, and a plain round stone font, long disused.

Colourful modern glass portraying St Peter and St Andrew fills a window in the north aisle of the nave; it is a particularly fine example of the work of L. C. Evetts of Newcastle.

On the south wall of the chancel is a memorial to Thomas Henry Liddell, second Baron Ravensworth, who died in 1855 at the age of 80. The inscription states that:

The barony of Ravensworth, which had become extinct on the death of the first lord, in 1784, was restored by favour of His Majesty King George IV for the day of his coronation, July 17th 1821. During the long period of his possession Lord Ravensworth augmented and improved his estates, rebuilt Ravensworth Castle, and to the honour of God rebuilt and embellished this chapel within whose walls his ashes lie.

Lord Ravensworth was a wealthy coal-owner, and he spent with a lavish hand. He took a great pride in his castle, and was never more delighted than when he was entertaining distinguished people there. In October 1827 he had as guest for a few days no less a personage than the Duke of Wellington.

Generous host and shrewd man of business, the second Baron Ravensworth deserves remembrance above all for his faith in the genius of George Stephenson. The great engineer freely acknowledged this help in later life when success was his. "The first locomotive that I made was at Killingworth Colliery" he would say, adding, "and with Lord Ravensworth's money."

In the churchyard is the grave of John Croft, vicar of Lamesley from 1898 until his death in 1951. In 1949 he fell from a ladder while pruning fruit trees, and on his recovery began to read the New Testament through again in Greek. He was then 98. In 1950 he and his wife celebrated their 75th wedding anniversary. In 1951 he died, a valiant centenarian, mourned by everyone in the Durham village he had served for so many years.

Lanchester. This pleasant old village, eight miles north-west of Durham, takes its name from the long fort built by the Romans high on the hill to the west. It measured 180 yards by 140, with an enclosed area of some eight acres.

The Roman encampment has never been thoroughly excavated, although several inscribed stones and altars have been found on the site from time to time; most of them are preserved at Durham in the Dean and Chapter library. Another fine Roman altar found in 1893 in a field on Margery Flatt's Farm is preserved in Lanchester Church.

Most of the ruins have been incorporated in farm buildings and field walls, as well as in the old parish church, and the site is now pasture land; but there are still some stone ramparts eight to 12 feet high, and on the west side are traces of a deep ditch. The turf-covered foundations of a small building can be seen inside the rounded south-west angle, and in the middle of the fort is some masonry of an underground chamber which was reached by stone steps.

In the field next to the fort is a wet hollow where stood a reservoir fed by two aqueducts, each starting four miles away, and uniting half a mile before reaching the fort. The southern aqueduct can be seen as a narrow bank along the south side of the Wolsingham road near Hollinside Hall. Few traces are left of the Roman road which on one side ran from the fort to York and on the other to Hadrian's Wall.

Other evidence of habitation in this vicinity in ancient times was revealed in 1891 on Hurbuck Farm, about two miles north-west of the Roman fort. The most important series of Anglo-Saxon weapons ever found in Durham were brought to light there by a farmer fishing in the Smallhope Burn. Among the finds were a sword, four scythes, and eight axe-heads.

As might be inferred from Lanchester's history, its magnificent church at the corner of the green is of exceptional interest. In the spacious south porch is the Roman altar found here on the farm.

Gateshead Church, with the Tyne Bridge

High Force, near Langdon Beck

Monkwearmouth Church, Sunderland: tombstone and Saxon pillars

Bede's chair in Jarrow Church

About five feet high, it is adorned with patterns of circles and has an inscription indicating that it was set up in AD 244 to the British goddess Garmangabis. Three carved mediaeval grave-covers are also kept in the porch, and the door it shelters is notable for some 700-year-old ironwork.

The tall 15th century tower contains some Roman stones from the fort, and the monolithic pillars of the graceful Norman north arcade are also Roman. The lofty chancel arch with three lines of zigzag moulding is Norman; the chancel itself is largely 13th century work, but its panelled roof, adorned with richly carved floral bosses, is modern.

In the side walls of the chancel are two arched recesses; they were designed to accommodate the vicars choral appointed when Bishop Bek made the church collegiate in 1283. One of the six old oak stalls preserved in the south recess has a human head with projecting ears carved on its misericord seat.

Set into a south window in the chancel are some panels of 13th century glass; originally in the east window, they colourfully portray the Adoration of the Shepherds and the Flight into Egypt. Beside the altar are six ancient candle-brackets, much mutilated, but still showing carving of crowned and mitred heads; and there is more old carving—a headless figure of Christ in Judgment with a flying angel on either side—on the tympanum of the vestry door.

At the west end of the south aisle is a window containing an old glass shield with the arms of Tempest and Umfraville, the six birds shown on the shield being storm-finches, birds of *tempest*. At the other end of this aisle (in a recess with a round arch which was probably removed from a Norman doorway in the church) lies a worn figure of a 14th century priest in long robes, holding a chalice.

John Hodgson, historian of Northumberland, lived at Lanchester from 1804 to 1806. He came here as a young man of 25 to take charge of the village school, which consisted of two rooms, the lower one for the girls, and the upper, reached by a ladder, for the boys. Within a few months he obtained Holy Orders and became curate of Esh and Satley, two chapelries in the parish of Lanchester, but in between his duties of teaching the village children and ministering to the needs of his parishioners he found time to study the history and archaeology of the district and also to write poetry. His *Poems Written at Lanchester*, published in 1807, include one called "Longovicum", a fanciful narrative (with long historical footnotes) of Lanchester under the Druids, Romans, and Saxons.

Another learned delver into the past was buried in Lanchester churchyard in 1919 at the age of 97. This was Dr William Greenwell, the distinguished archivist and archaeologist, who was born in this parish at the old house called Greenwell Ford, half-hidden among the trees above the River Browney.

Educated at Durham School and University, Greenwell became a canon of Durham Cathedral in 1854, and eight years later became librarian to the dean and chapter, an office which he held for 46 years. He did invaluable work in arranging the cathedral records and edited some of the more important for publication.

In 1865 he was given the four-acre parish of St Mary in the South Bailey, with its population of 100, and in the same year was elected president of the Architectural and Archaeological Society of Durham and Northumberland.

His many activities included angling, and several salmon- and trout-flies, notably Greenwell's Glory, are named after him.

William Greenwell's sister Dora, the religious writer, was born here on December 6, 1821. Friend of Christina Rossetti and Elizabeth Barrett Browning, she is perhaps best known for her book of poems *Carmina Crucis*, but it is in her prose work *The Patience of Hope* that her wonderful spiritual insight is most patently revealed.

She died at Clifton near Bristol in 1882.

Langdon Beck. Hereabouts is Durham at its wildest and grandest, a landscape of green pasture, grey stone walls, and whitewashed farms, backed by the broad sweep of the Pennine fells. The main road to Alston crosses the Langdon Beck as it rushes madly downhill towards the Tees. Overlooking the glorious stretch of bare hills at the head of Teesdale is a fine Youth Hostel. On every side there is magnificent scenery.

A few miles to the west, at the wild meeting-place of Cumberland, Westmorland, and Durham, the River Tees flows through a broad basin, rushes past rocks originally smoothed by the Teesdale Glacier, and then enters on a straight stretch of water broken by the irregular rocks of the Whin Sill. Soon it reaches the Cow Green reservoir, three miles long, and covering some 650 acres. Below the dam the river tumbles through a rocky gorge of the Whin Sill in a series of cataracts, the final step in the descent, where the white foam cascades over the rocks into the pool below, being the famous Caldron Snout, one of the most impressive waterfalls in England.

The Tees then flows for two miles below Falcon Clints, high rugged cliffs of basalt rising like grey pillars from a green base of heather and bilberry, with here and there the yellow saxifrage growing in damp places on the rocks. At the end of the Clints the river curves under Widdybank Fell, famous for its rare alpine plants, the best known being the little blue Spring Gentian, one of the most beautiful of all English wild flowers and also one of the rarest. The elusive Bog Sandwort, a small five-petalled white flower on a long stalk, is also to be found growing in the limestone, but much more abundant are the Stone Violet and the Bird's-eye Primrose.

Two miles below Widdybank Fell is High Force, the highest waterfall in the North of England. A mighty black-marble rock divides the stream into two, and the water falls violently into a deep pool shut in by grim walls of dark rock overhung by shrubs. When the central rock is covered by flood-water the fall of the river is 70 feet, and the roar can be heard for a considerable distance.

In the Bowes Museum at Barnard Castle are 13 Roman coins of Constantine which, with the upper stone of a Roman quern, were ploughed up near High Force in 1944. Other important finds were made about 1885 in the Teesdale Cave on Langdon Common. James Backhouse here found some of the first lynx bones ever discovered in England, and also the skull of a woman who may have lived here in the Stone Age. The entrance (called the Fairy Hole) has been blocked by a limekiln, and shepherds have filled in the dangerous pot-holes descending from above, so the beauties of the cave are now all too little known.

Long Newton. This pleasant and well-shaded village, situated near the main road halfway between Stockton and Darlington, is divided into two by a big field surrounded by a wall of mellow red brick. In this field once stood the manor house of the Vanes, a branch of the famous family which has owned Raby Castle for over 300 years.

Their memory is kept in the village church, which stands in a churchyard graced by many fine sycamores. It was rebuilt in 1857 by the Marchioness of Londonderry, and its only feature of note is the stone-vaulted chapel of the Vanes, guarded by massive iron railings capped with gilded fleurs-de-lis. In the floor of the chapel is a brass plate inscribed to the first of the Vanes of Long Newton: Sir George Vane, who died in 1679, father of thirteen "hopeful children":

> *His honour wonne ith feild lies here ith dust.*
> *His honour got by grace shall never rust.*
> *The former fades, the latter shall faile never;*
> *For why? he was Sr George once but St George ever.*

Sir George Vane, who was Sheriff of Durham County, raised about 300 men to support the cause of Parliament and led them with distinction; but his fame is eclipsed by that of his father and his elder brother, lords of Raby Castle.

His father, as the inscription here states, was none other than Sir Henry Vane, sometime principal Secretary of State to Charles I. He later transferred his allegiance to the Parliamentary cause. His brother, Sir Henry Vane the Younger, became Governor of Massachusetts when only 24 and later was an able Treasurer of the Navy. A lifelong Puritan and Republican, the close friend of Cromwell, Pym, and Hampden, he was much to the fore during the Civil War; but, growing hostile to the increase of Cromwell's power, became a thorn in the Protector's side. He drew from Cromwell the famous exclamation: "Sir Harry Vane, Sir Harry Vane, the Lord deliver me from Sir Harry Vane."

Although, like his father, Sir Henry Vane had strenuously opposed the king's execution, he himself was executed after the Restoration; Charles II thought him a dangerous man, better out of the way.

A later Sir Henry Vane served as rector of this church and is commemorated by a mural tablet in the chancel; and yet another bearer of the proud name (Sir Henry Vane, d. 1813) has a white marble monument by Richard Westmacott; it portrays a kneeling woman and three cherubs looking down from the sky.

Low Dinsdale. It is a quiet village in a bend of the Tees, with a corner of Yorkshire lying to the north of it; but it was not always so quiet, for it once had quite a reputation as a spa.

In a wooded ravine running down to the Tees at Fishlock Cottage bubbles a little sulphurous spring which broke out with much smoke and smell in 1798, when a boring for coal had reached a depth of 72 feet into the whinstone. The healing waters became quite famous, and were much visited in the summer. Not far off there used to be another strong-smelling spring called the Leper's Bath, which is said to have turned the bathers green.

The oldest building here is the manor house; it has 13th century walls, and in the green field at the side can be seen the banks of the double moat which once protected it. From this riverside domain the Surtees ("sur Tees") family almost certainly took their name. They settled here soon after the Conquest.

A mile upstream is the site of Fish Lock Weir, where the water rushes over the stones below red sandstone cliffs. Wordsworth and his sister came here in 1799, when they were at Sockburn, and watched the salmon leaping.

By the bridge stands the church, originally built about 1200 on the site of a Saxon church. It was drastically repaired in 1875 with red sandstone, but still retains many ancient relics.

In the east wall of the modern porch are four pre-Conquest stone fragments with interlacing work, together with part of a mediaeval grave-cover, and the traceried head of a two-light window. In the west wall of the porch are more carved mediaeval stones, including one with cross and sword and an inscription to Goselynus Surtees, who died in 1367.

Beside the lofty chancel arch is a 1000-year-old gravestone—a hogback stone carved with interlacing work and the head of a bear. In the south chapel is a Norman font, no longer used; and in the churchyard lies a Norman stone coffin with a coped lid and a raised cross.

Medomsley. This breezy hilltop village looking over the Derwent Valley into Northumberland has a 13th century church which was considerably modernised in Victorian times. In the porch are some pictures of the church before its restoration, and some carved stonework which formed part of it; another notable survival from the early church is the east window of the chancel, with three lancets separated by round stone shafts. The oddest relics are four carved stone heads built into the wall of the sanctuary to serve as candlesticks.

One son of this village who won a measure of fame was the antiquary, Dr Christopher Hunter. Born here in 1675, he was educated at Houghton-le-Spring and St John's College, Cambridge, and then set up as a physician at Stockton-on-Tees.

But Hunter was an antiquarian at heart, and when, a few years after his marriage, he went to live at Durham, he regularly pursued his studies in the library of the Dean and Chapter. His topographical researches and first-hand knowledge of Roman remains proved invaluable to later historians, being used by Horsley in his *Britannia Romana* and by Bourne in his *History of Newcastle*.

In 1757 Christopher Hunter retired to his wife's house at Shotleyfield in Northumberland, and in the same year was buried in Shotleyfield Church.

A great day in the history of Medomsley was February 28, 1644, when an army of no fewer than 20,000 Scots under the Earl of Leven here crossed the Derwent by means of a bridge of tree-trunks on their way to join the Roundheads in England in accordance with the Solemn League and Covenant.

Middleton-in-Teesdale. Once the centre of a flourishing lead-mining industry, this little town is a gateway to some of the loveliest scenery of Upper Teesdale and in recent years has developed as a quiet holiday resort.

Symptomatic of this change is a solid-looking stone building with a clock tower, set among tall trees overlooking the town. It was built about 1820 as the head office of the London Lead Company; now it is a hotel. The Quakers who ran the company looked after their workpeople well, providing a school, chapels, a library, and substantial cottages which are still as sound today as when they were built.

The town has a dignified, one-arched bridge with two round openings at each end to relieve the pressure of floods. The former bridge collapsed in 1811. Lower downstream is Eggleston Bridge, spanning a lovely reach of the river where the water rushes noisily over a rocky bed. It has two arches, and the massive cutwater between them forms a triangular refuge on each side. In the 15th century there was a chapel on the Yorkshire end of the bridge, which dates from about 1450 and has been less altered than any other bridge across the Tees.

Middleton's old church was rebuilt about 1876 but still retains a few relics of its predecessor. Let into the north wall of the nave are some remarkable mediaeval gravestones—one with a beautifully carved floral cross rising from a shield, another with arrow, hammer, and sword, and a third with cross, sword, dagger, and a long-handled mining tool. There is also an old font with no fewer than 16 sides.

The east window of the 13th century church has been re-erected near the churchyard gate; also by the gate are the steps of the old cross, now supporting a sundial on a round stone shaft. An iron band on the lower step is a relic of the stocks.

On the slope a few yards above the church stands the only detached belfry in County Durham. It was built in Elizabethan times to hold three bells, the bequest of a parson named William Bell. One of the original bells is still here, with two modern ones; they are rung by a man using both hands and one foot.

Middleton-in-Teesdale could boast its own poet last century—Richard Watson, born here in 1833. Son of a lead-miner, and himself a lead-miner from the age of 10, he is remembered for his *Poems and*

Songs of Teesdale, expressing in local dialect the joys and hopes and fears of himself and his fellow dalesmen.

Middleton St George. This is a pleasant village, beautifully situated on a height above the Tees; it has a lovely line of old-fashioned houses (Middleton One Row) on a terrace sloping steeply down to the water.

To the east of the village is Teesside Airport; less than half-a-mile to the west is a ford where the Roman road from Durham to Northallerton crossed the Tees, probably by a bridge. This was later known as Pons Tesie or Pounteys Bridge, and before the building of Croft Bridge was the chief entry into County Durham from the south. It was fortified on both sides; a big conical earthwork (now covered with fir trees) which was once part of a Norman castle is to be seen in the grounds of Tower Hill above the ford.

In the village, its little stone spire rising above the trees, is the church of St Lawrence, a 19th century building which possesses two features of interest. One is an attractive modern window depicting the Nativity and the Flight into Egypt; the other is a roughly-carved Saxon sundial, which came from the old parish church of St George.

This simple little building stands in the fields about a mile to the south-east. It has a 13th century chancel arch of pink stone with corbel heads portraying a man smiling at a woman who is putting out her tongue. The plain round font is probably Norman.

South of this old church is Low Middleton Hall, an old house with a red brick garden front of 1721; near it is an eight-sided pigeon-house with mellow brick walls, pantiled roof, and no fewer than 1500 nesting holes.

Muggleswick. Consisting of a farmhouse and a few cottages near some deep wooded bends of the Derwent, which here forms the boundary between Durham and Northumberland, it is reached by a gated road from a wild area of high moorland where horned sheep graze among the heather and bracken.

This moor is the Muggleswick Park (three miles long and two wide) which Hugh de Darlington, Prior of Durham, enclosed in the 13th century; and in a farmyard are the impressive ruins of the hunting lodge which he built—a massive gabled end wall of stone, still with a fine fireplace and part of a traceried window.

Approached by a green track leading from this farmyard is the simple little church, rebuilt in the 19th century. In the churchyard is the grave of John Ward, who died in 1717 after having been pastor for 52 years at Rowley Baptist chapel, about three miles away to the south-west. Established in 1652, this was one of the earliest Baptist churches in the North of England.

Neville's Cross. There is history in the name of this breezy residential suburb of Durham, but it is hard to realise now that it was once a battlefield, the scene of a Scottish defeat as decisive as that at Flodden.

The Great North Road here skirts the western side of the city, and perched above it, opposite the church, is a heap of stones supporting the eight-sided base and three feet of the shaft of what now passes for Neville's Cross.

This was originally one of several crosses set up around the city and it was here that in 1346 Ralph, Lord Neville, decided to set up his command post during the battle. After his victory he erected another cross at this place, but in 1589 this was maliciously broken up; now only these few wayside fragments remain.

The Battle of Neville's Cross was the most important ever fought in County Durham. On August 26, 1346, the French were defeated at Crecy, and the King of France appealed to young David II of Scotland to create a diversion while Edward III was besieging Calais.

Queen Philippa rallied the northern nobles, and some 15,000 men were soon assembled at Bishop Auckland. Leading them were the Archbishop of York, the Bishops of Durham and Lincoln, and, perhaps more directly, the Lords Neville, Mowbray, and Percy.

King David and 20,000 Scots came into England through Cumberland, destroying Lanercost Abbey and looting the countryside. Then, on October 16, flushed with victory, they sat down to enjoy a respite at Bearpark, to the north-west of Durham.

The next day a Scottish raiding party was routed near Kirk Merrington, and by following the retreating survivors the English discovered the Scottish camp. The English army was then drawn up at the spot where today the Great North Road crosses the railway.

Just before the battle was joined, strong moral support arrived from an unexpected quarter; a procession of monks came from Durham Cathedral to the Maiden's Bower, a little hill near the Scottish line, and there planted a spear with the sacred cloth of St Cuthbert held aloft on the point. There they prayed, unmolested by the Scots, while their brethren watched from the cathedral tower.

The English army was in a better position than the opposing force, and it was soon found that Scottish pikes could not withstand the English longbows. After three hours of fighting King David slipped away wounded and unarmed, but he was found hiding under the narrow bridge which still crosses the Browney to the east of Bearpark, and taken to London. He was imprisoned in the Tower, and many years passed before he was allowed to return to his kingdom.

Newbiggin. This is a small main road village in Teesdale. It has a chapel, a school, a post-office, and a few grey stone or white-washed cottages, amidst beautiful scenery; to the north rise the high moors stretching across to Weardale, and to the south of the road runs the River Tees forming the boundary between Durham and Yorkshire.

Crossing the river into the North Riding is Wynch Bridge, normally 20 feet above the water, but washed by the stream in time of severe flood. An earlier bridge, built here for lead-miners and said to have been the first suspension bridge in Europe, collapsed in 1820 while nine people were crossing, one man falling to his death in the narrow, rocky gorge below.

Above the bridge are the falls of Low Force, where two or three torrents of rusty foam roar over the rocks. The falls are divided by a delightful wooded island called Staple Crag, where gorse and heather grow. The field path to Wynch Bridge leaves the main road at the Three Brothers, three enormous sycamore stumps growing from one stem.

Less than half-a-mile below the bridge the Bow Lee Beck joins the Tees, and we can follow the Beck up to Gibson's Cave, a damp recess reached by passing behind a waterfall.

Another climb upwards is by Brocker (Badger) Gill, a lovely little wooded ravine behind a whitewashed farmhouse. High on the hill is Red Grooves, a great gash caused by "hushing" for lead. It was formerly the practice of prospectors to dam up water on the hillside, and then to release it suddenly to wash away the surface and expose the underlying lead-bearing rocks.

North Biddick. In this hamlet by the Wear is a hill associated with a piece of folklore known all over County Durham as the Legend of the Lambton Worm. It is by the bridge—an artificial mound crowned by a little war memorial and known as Worm Hill.

One Sunday, so the tale runs, the heir of the Lambtons was fishing in the Wear and hooked a small worm, which he threw into a nearby well. When this worm grew too large for the well it returned to the river, and for part of each day lay coiled round a crag in the middle of the stream. It would also coil itself nine times round the Worm

Hill, and unless the milk of nine cows was brought there daily it would devour man and beast.

In the meantime young Lambton had joined the Crusaders, but on his return he at once tried to kill the monster, which now terrorised the whole countryside. As his valiant efforts were unsuccessful, owing to the worm's power of joining up its severed limbs, he was then advised by a witch to put on armour studded with razor-blades, and to await the worm on its crag in the river.

When the creature wound itself round Lambton's armour it was cut to pieces, and as these were carried away by the stream they could not be joined again.

In return for the advice the witch had given, Lambton had promised her that he would slay the first living thing he saw after his victory. He had arranged that his father on hearing his triumph announced by three blasts on a bugle should send a greyhound to meet him. But the overjoyed old man himself ran to congratulate his son, and as a penalty for young Lambton not slaying him the witch decreed that seven generations of Lambtons should be destined not to die in their beds.

Penshaw. This straggling village is on high ground sloping towards the Wear Valley a few miles above the mouth of the river. Above it, crowning the steep green slopes of Penshaw Hill, is the magnificent Doric temple of blackened stone which was erected by public subscription to the memory of the first Earl of Durham, John George Lambton, who died in 1840. It has 18 hollow columns, 35 feet high, and in one of them is a staircase to the roof. Now the property of the National Trust, this monument is a landmark for miles around, and affords a wide view over most of north Durham.

Another striking spectacle here is the Victoria Viaduct, which was finished on the very day of Queen Victoria's coronation—June 28, 1838. Carrying the original main line across the Wear to Newcastle, it is 270 yards long, with four graceful arches carrying the line nearly 150 feet above the river. The design was based on the pattern of Trajan's bridge at Alcantara in Spain, and its grey stone came from the neighbouring Penshaw quarry, which also supplied the stone for London Bridge and the High Level Bridge at Newcastle.

Penshaw's 19th century church contains one extremely ancient relic—a fragment, indeed, of one of the Seven Wonders of the World. This is a stone which once formed part of the Great Pyramid of Ghizeh near Cairo, the tomb of Cheops who died about 4500 years ago. Now bearing an inscription to the father, mother, four brothers, and son of Sir George Elliot, MP, it was part of a block of granite brought home by him in the late Victorian Era by permission of Ismail Pasha, Khedive of Egypt. A similar stone is in the church at West Rainton.

Peterlee. It is a new town, 10 miles east of Durham City, with modern houses of varied design disposed around a natural amphi-theatre of hills, and, at the centre, the traffic-free town square. The foundation stone of its first house, bearing a facsimile of the signature of Peter Lee, whose memory the town honours, was laid at Eden Hill in the autumn of 1950.

Between the town and the North Sea lies the site of the Saxon village of Yoden. Pottery, whetstones, and a bronze buckle were among the relics unearthed when the site was excavated in 1884.

On the southern edge of the town are three fine new churches. St Cuthbert's Anglican church, a dignified brick building crowned by a flèche, dates from 1957. It is in the form of an early Christian basilica —at the west end is a portico, the nave has a clerestory with small windows, and at the east end is a semi-circular apse in which the bishop's throne stands. The altar table is in front of the throne, beneath an ornately decorated canopy; the stone font, with its cover of polished brass, stands in the middle of the nave.

Near the west door is the foundation stone, surrounded by cobbles, which came from the Holy Island of Lindisfarne, off the Northumber-land coast.

The Roman Catholic church was opened in 1966. It is a spacious cruciform building in grey brick and white stone, and from its low tower soars a slender copper spire.

The Peter Lee Memorial Methodist church, built in 1958, commemorates an outstanding figure in the history of County Durham.

Peter Lee of Trimdon Grange was set to work as a pony-driver in the coal-mines at the age of 10. As a youth of 19, standing over six feet, he attended night school and learned arithmetic alongside little boys.

A traveller throughout his life, he worked in America and South Africa, gaining knowledge about mankind, before returning, at 33, to the pits of Durham.

In 1909 he was elected chairman of the first Labour County Council; in 1930 he became secretary of the Durham Miners' Association, and three years later was elected President of the Miners' Federation. He was also a first-rate Methodist preacher.

Peter Lee died in 1935, and was buried at Wheatley Hill, respected throughout Durham by the miners he had served faithfully and well.

Piercebridge. Consisting mainly of low white houses grouped round a green this little village has the distinction of standing on the site of a Roman fort. Most of it, indeed, is within the rampart walls, the village green occupying the central area of the fort, which covered about 10 acres.

Nearly a quarter of a mile below the present bridge, the Roman road from York to Corbridge—later called Dere Street—crossed the Tees; the remains of oak piles which supported the Roman bridge have been seen at low water. From the Durham bank the road ran through what is now Tofts Field, and it was here that the first fort was built, probably about AD 125, in the reign of the Emperor Hadrian. The many Roman coins found on the site have been given the name of Toft Pennies.

About AD 300 stronger defences became necessary, and a new fort was built to the west of the Roman road, where the present village now stands. The green mounds of its north-west ramparts can still be seen, and at the north-east corner some masonry of the outer wall is exposed, with the little stone arch of a culvert.

Remains of a bath-house have been found, and there are traces of an aqueduct which led from the direction of Hopewell Farm, a mile to the north. A mile to the west of the village is the spot called White Cross, where a Roman altar stood.

The Bowes Museum at Barnard Castle has a collection of Roman objects from Piercebridge, among the best being a bone pin with a head carved in the form of an altar, a tiny portable altar, and part of a stone coffin-cover with remains of a leaden casket and a little broken cosmetic bottle of green glass. From bones found in the casket it is known that this was the burial of a woman between 25 and 30 years of age.

But the finest of all objects from Piercebridge is in the British Museum. (A replica can be seen in the Museum of Antiquities at Newcastle.) It is a small bronze statuette of a cloaked and hooded British ploughman with a team of oxen; he is using the plough called the aratrum, the light wheel-less type used all over the Roman Empire.

The three-arched bridge which links the village with the Yorkshire side of the Tees is of great antiquity, but was rebuilt in the 16th century. In September 1642 it was the scene of a skirmish which resulted in some Roundhead horse of Fairfax being heavily defeated by Royalists. Skeletons of men and horses were found here last century when the railway was being constructed.

By the bridge is a red-roofed house with a bow window and the date 1704. This was the home of Michael Aislabie Denham, the famous collector of Durham folklore, who died in 1859 and was buried in Gainford churchyard.

Since 1873 Piercebridge has had a small church of its own; it boasts a pre-Reformation bell from Gainford, inscribed in ancient lettering *St Cuthbert save us unhurt.*

Pittington. This straggling village shelters under a broad green hill from which Durham Cathedral can be seen, four miles to the south-west. The last prior of Durham had a summer residence here, beside the ancient church, which stands secluded in a quiet corner known as Hallgarth.

Pittington's church is one of the most interesting in the county, displaying fine Norman work and incorporating one or two relics of the original Saxon building. The rugged tower is Norman, with an embattled upper storey containing three pre-Reformation bells; but the most famous feature is the north arcade, which has six round arches enriched with bold zigzag ornament. The south arcade, which like the tower arch dates from about 1230, has six pointed arches on plain round pillars; the spandrels are decorated with little carved heads of men and women.

Above the arcades are some narrow Norman windows, and over one of the arches in the south aisle can be seen a little blocked Saxon window, with a round head formed from a single stone. In the splay of the westernmost window which looks into the north aisle are traces of red murals painted about 1100; they show the consecration of St Cuthbert by Archbishop Theodore in 685, and the vision of St Cuthbert at the table in Whitby Abbey.

The font, with crude round bowl, is a Norman one with a curious history. It was sold in 1809 for half-a-crown and used as a cattle-trough at Belmont Farm. In 1885 it was brought back, but remained unused for many years because a 17th century marble font from Durham Cathedral had been installed. Now the cathedral font has been returned, and Pittington's simple Norman font again does service. It has a handsome 17th century oak cover which according to the records cost 10 shillings.

The church's two most notable monuments are in the aisles. In the north aisle lies a worn stone figure of a knight who died about 1250, and, from three popinjays once visible on the shield, is thought to have been a FitzMarmaduke of Horden Hall near Easington.

On the floor of the south aisle lies a massive tombstone of grey Frosterley marble boldly carved with a Latin inscription meaning: "One having the name of Christ is buried in this grave. Let the beholder pray for him". It is the monument of Christian, one of the master masons of Bishop Pudsey. He was the builder of Sherburn Hospital, the famous almshouse between Pittington and Durham, and is also thought to have been responsible for the original Norman decoration on the round pillars of the north arcade.

On the floor under the tower stands a stone curiously carved in the form of two little coffins about a foot long, each with a dagger incised in the top. It is thought to be a 12th century grave-cover of twin boys who died in infancy. On the north wall of the nave is a marble inscription commemorating 18-year-old Mary Westrop, who was murdered by a fellow servant on an August Sunday evening in 1830.

Outside the church, let into the south wall, is a Saxon sundial with six carved lines. Beside a window in the north wall are two grotesque heads of Norman date, one having a protruding tongue.

Redmarshall. Though within a mile or two of Stockton, it still keeps its village aspect, with houses sheltered among fine old trees on a little hill. In mediaeval times it was Rodmerehil—"hill by a reedy lake".

The church is an attractive little building with some fine Norman work. The tower, which contains a 14th century bell, has a round Norman arch of great height. The beautiful round-headed outer entrance to the porch, with zigzag carving on its tympanum, is the original Norman doorway moved forward. The nave, the round chancel arch, and the font with its beautiful bowl of Frosterley marble also date from Norman times.

A notable feature of the church is the 15th century transept, called Claxton's Porch, which was originally a chantry chapel. It has a wide pointed arch with corbel heads of a curly-haired man and a woman in buttoned dress supporting the arch with her hands. On an altar tomb in this transept lie much-damaged figures of Thomas Langton of Wynyard, who died in 1440, and his wife Sybil. Thomas, portrayed with his head resting on a helm and his feet on a lion, wears an SS collar over his plate mail; his wife wears a short jacket and mantle.

In the 700-year-old chancel are three 15th century sedilia adorned with worn stone heads of a king and a bishop. Let in the floor beneath the communion table is the mediaeval altar stone, and in a recess in the north wall is a 14th century priest's gravestone with cross and chalice carved in relief.

The fine seating of the church dates from about 1700. The backs of the pews are open, with short, turned balusters, and the upper parts of the doors are treated in the same way. The ends of the pews in the nave are crowned with fleur-de-lis.

Rookhope. Its name means the Valley of Rooks, the valley through which the Rookhope Burn runs down to the Wear.

The village straggles along both sides of the quiet moorland road from Stanhope to Allenheads, and is marked by conspicuous spar-mines whose dark grey banks of spoil run along the hillside. The lead-smelting mill has long been closed, but we can trace the track of its long underground chimney for a mile and a half across Redburn Common.

On a grassy hillside overlooking the village stands the plain stone church. It was completely rebuilt in 1905, and the only relic of former days is the 17th century font-cover of oak, with six curved panels rising to a carved finial.

The ballad of Rookhope Ryde, composed in 1572, deals with a famous raid of the men of Tynedale, who crossed into Weardale on December 8, 1569, taking advantage of the confusion caused by the Rising in the North. The second canto of Sir Walter Scott's poem, *Harold the Dauntless*, also has Rookhope for its setting.

Ryton. Despite its industrial surroundings, this village on a hill above the Tyne preserves much of its rural charm, and is a favourite holiday haunt of Newcastle folk and other Tynesiders. On summer Sundays the 54-acre stretch of riverside common called Ryton Willows is gay with picnickers, and the river is lively with little boats.

Prominent on the thickly-wooded hill is the lead-covered church spire, soaring 120 feet. Chiefly 13th century work, and one of the finest in the county, the village church has two arcades with pointed arches on tall columns alternately round and eight-sided.

Its chief treasures are the chancel screen and stalls of oak, the work of painstaking and skilful 17th century craftsmen. The screen, panelled below, has six beautiful bays divided by slender round shafts, with circles of tracery suspended from the carved cornice. Two old desk-ends have carved medallions with scaly sea monsters, and over one of the stalls is an elaborate carving of the Nativity.

Set in the south wall of the chancel is an inscribed slab brought here from the tomb of Bernard Gilpin in Houghton-le-Spring church.

On the north wall of the sanctuary are brass inscriptions with coloured coats-of-arms of the Bunny family. One was Francis Bunny, rector here from 1578 to 1617, who, as the inscription states, *having buried here his four sons, and his daughter at York, hasteneth to Heaven after them.*

A later rector was Thomas Secker, who left in 1735 to become Bishop of Bristol, and was afterwards Archbishop of Canterbury.

A memorial of a much earlier churchman lies on the floor of the sanctuary. This is a striking Frosterley marble figure of a 13th century deacon in a wide-sleeved gown. His tonsured head is on a cushion supported by two headless angels: his pointed shoes rest on a lion, and in his hands is a big book with a carved dove.

In the northern part of the churchyard is a striking round tumulus, 20 feet high. At the west end of the village green, where John Wesley once preached, is an 18-foot cross which was set up in 1795 on the base of a much earlier cross.

Sadberge. A village on a hill, with a fine view of the country between Stockton and Darlington, this was a place of considerable importance in mediaeval times, the headquarters of a large district with its own sheriffs and assize courts.

The earldom of Sadberge is still one of the titles attached to the Crown, and one of its rare uses can be seen on a grey boulder on the village green; it bears a brass inscription stating that:

This stone was placed here to commemorate the jubilee of Victoria, Queen of the United Kingdom, Empress of India, and Countess of Sadberge, June 20, 1887. It was found 12 feet below the surface in making the reservoir. It had been detached from the rock in the West and deposited by a glacier.

The reservoir mentioned is the one to the west of the village, holding 12 million gallons for the use of Teesside.

Sadberge's church was built in 1831, but it has one or two relics of the ancient church which stood close by. These include two inscribed pre-Reformation bells (one in the turret and the other in the vestry), and two little carved stones built into the walls of the porch after being found in the Glittering Star, an inn at Darlington. One of the stones has little carved figures of Adam and Eve in the Garden; the other bears traces of a carving which may have represented Christ trampling on Satan.

Monkwearmouth Church,
Sunderland

The Penshaw Monument

St Cuthbert's College, Ushaw

Washington Old Hall

The materials of the ancient church were given away, much of the stonework being used for an embankment along the River Skerne at Darlington, and also for building the kitchen of the Glittering Star.

St Helen Auckland. A neighbour of Bishop Auckland, and practically inseparable from West Auckland, this scattered industrial place by the little River Gaunless still retains something of its old rural aspect.

The church itself wears the look of a veteran, as becomes a building which has stood 800 years or more. The most imposing external features are the big nave clerestory and the 500-year-old porch, which has a battlemented upper chamber and shelters a massive iron-studded door believed to be Norman. Within the church the dominant features are the round Norman arches of the nave—six on each side—and the massive roofs of black oak, dating from about 1500.

Among the old possessions of the church are a plain round font, the carved 16th century choir-stalls, and an oak almsbox with three slots; in the vestry (the room over the porch) are an altar table dating from late Tudor times and an eight-sided table made from the sounding-board of the old pulpit. The richly-carved pulpit now in use, together with the brass eagle lectern, was the gift of Sybil, Lady Eden, mother of Lord Avon. Many generations of the Eden family have lived at West Auckland, and their old Hall still stands to the north of the broad village green.

On the north wall of the nave is a brass plate from the tomb of Ralph Dalton who was buried in this church in 1558. He possessed the manor of West Auckland before it passed to the Edens in the late 16th century. The Latin inscription records that he "held three offices under that most learned man of blessed memory, Tunstall, Bishop of Durham, namely as Excheator, Receiver of Howden and Clerk of Works; he was also Receiver General of the Cathedral Church".

Half-hidden by the altar steps is one of the county's few monumental brasses. Engraved about 1450, it portrays a man in a long cloak, holding a rosary, with a fragmentary figure of his wife and a little group of three daughters below her. Figures of his six sons are hidden by the steps.

The east window portrays the Crucifixion, with flanking figures of St Cuthbert and St Helen; it commemorates Matthew Chester, vicar here from 1820 until his death in 1871.

K

Near the church is the 17th century Hall, with three little gables protruding from its stone roof; it is now a farmhouse.

About three miles south-east of St Helen Auckland, in a field beside the Roman road from York to Corbridge, stands an ancient monument called Legs Cross. It consists of a rough shaft (with Saxon knotwork still discernible on one side) supported by a massive base resting on a flat stone which bears Roman tool marks and may be part of a Roman milestone. One of the more plausible explanations of the name Legs Cross is the theory that LEG (Legion) was once carved on this stone.

From the cross there is a magnificent panorama of the Tees Valley, backed by the Yorkshire hills.

St John's Chapel. A small town in upper Weardale, it takes its name from a chapel founded here in 1465.

Towards the end of the 18th century the chapel was replaced by the present church overlooking the little green—a plain Georgian building with a square nave which has four tall round pillars supporting the roof. The long churchyard has a remarkable number of trees, planted about 1880 when the church was restored.

To the south of the town rises Chapel Fell, 2294 feet high.

Satley. A little village on the Steeley Burn, about 11 miles north-west of Durham, it has a 19th century church with a fine tower. By the door is the font (no longer used) of the 15th century chapel which formerly stood on the site; and set in the west wall near it are two fragments of mediaeval grave-covers—one with carved cross and sword. In the sanctuary is a 17th century armchair of oak.

Seaham. In this tiny coastal village the poet Byron was married; but coal-mining has transformed it since his day, and the only two buildings which remain much as he knew them are the ancient church and the hall which was his bride's home.

Least changed is the high and narrow 11th century church on the edge of the wooded dene leading to the sea. In the walls of the nave are stones with Roman markings—probably from the fort at South Shields—and high up, near the roof are three little round-headed windows, which may be pre-Conquest work. The tower and the porch date from the 13th century, features of the porch being a stone roof supported by two massive pointed arches, and a sundial of 1773 with this inscription:

The natural clock-work by the Mighty One,
Wound up at first, and ever since has gone,
No pin drops out, its wheels and springs hold good.
It speaks its Master's praise, though once it stood.
But that was by the order of the Workman's power,
And when it stands again it goes no more.

The chancel arch is modern, but fixed to it are two old corbels with carvings of sad-looking human faces. At the back of a recess in the south wall of the sanctuary is a stone with a carving of a priest's hand raised in blessing.

The church is nearly filled with old box pews, and it also boasts a Jacobean pulpit and a 17th century font-cover. The font, with a band of foliage carved in its round bowl, is 700 years old.

Lying outside the south wall is a stone coffin found early last century in the neighbouring dene.

In the marriage registers are the signatures of Lord Byron, his bride, Ann Isabella Milbanke, and his best man, John Cam Hobhouse. The wedding took place not in the church but in the bow-windowed drawing-room on the first floor of the neighbouring Seaham Hall, a long plain building now used as a hospital.

Byron wrote afterwards: "I shall never forget the 2nd of January 1815! Lady Byron was the only unconcerned person present; Lady Noel, her mother, cried; I trembled like a leaf, made the wrong responses, and after the ceremony called her Miss Milbanke."

From Seaham Hall the ill-matched couple started off on their honeymoon. Such happiness as was theirs on that January day was to be short-lived; in a little over twelve months they were separated—for ever.

Seaham Harbour. Still a thriving little port, it is a product of the Industrial Revolution, owing its existence entirely to the neighbouring coalfield. Before 1828 there was scarcely a cottage on this desolate coast; but in that year Charles, third Marquess of Londonderry, laid the first stone of the harbour, and a new town was born.

Apart from its harbour, with its docks and lofty wooden staiths for loading vessels with coal, it has little to show a visitor. The North Pier, which has a lighthouse at the end, is 450 yards long; the South Pier measures 300 yards.

Overlooking the sea is the Harbour and Colliery Office, and in front of this is John Tweed's bronze statue of Charles Stewart Vane-Tempest Stewart, sixth Marquess of Londonderry, who died in 1915. It portrays him in the robes of the Garter, his left hand on a sword and his right holding a scroll setting out some of his high offices, such as Viceroy of Ireland and Postmaster General.

At the bottom of the pleasant wooded dene leading to Dalton-le-Dale are the ivy-covered ruins of Dawdon Hall, where Sir Jordan de Dalden founded a chantry in 1325. The present Hall, with its crow-stepped gabled roof, is a farmhouse, formed from a Jacobean mansion built by the Collingwoods.

Sedgefield. A small town on a low gravel hill above the main road from Stockton to Durham, it boasts one of the finest churches in the whole county. It stands on the east side of the green, a spacious 13th century building with an imposing tower added in the 15th century by Robert Rodes, the wealthy merchant who gave Newcastle its noble cathedral tower. Ninety feet high, it is crowned by eight-sided turrets with battlements and pinnacles, and from it the curfew is still sounded every night, at eight in the winter and nine in the summer.

The nave and aisles date from about 1245, the arcades being particularly fine work of this period; the interior of the church is greatly enhanced by their tall clustered columns, their beautifully moulded arches, and their capitals are adorned with carved foliage, human heads, angels, and strange beasts. The chancel and transepts were built about 1290.

The east window with its fine flowing tracery is a notable feature of the chancel; but its chief attraction is the Restoration woodwork, which is indeed the glory of the church. The splendid oak panelling has cherub heads peeping out of a wealth of tracery, and two fierce human heads glowering at each other over garlands of fruit upon the cornice; the stalls have traceried canopies and bench-ends and poppy-heads with carved foliage; and the magnificent screen has seven open bays crowned by lovely and elaborate Gothic canopies rising in diminishing tiers to the top of the chancel arch. More fine wood-carving is to be seen in the 18th century organ case, with cherub heads supporting the pipes.

Two stone effigies, two brasses, and a font complete the catalogue of this church's ancient possessions. The font has a 15th century base and shaft of Frosterley marble supporting an elaborate 18th century bowl of grey Italian marble adorned with coats-of-arms.

The effigies, lying worn and mutilated in two pointed recesses in the south transept, represent an unknown 14th century knight and lady. In the floor in front of these figures is a little 600-year-old brass of a kneeling lady; the other brass, on the wall of the north aisle, portrays two skeletons in shrouds.

A bygone glory of Sedgefield is Hardwick Hall. A magnificent avenue of sycamores leads to the house and in the surrounding 300 acre park are fragments of some of the 18th century ornamental buildings for which it was once famed. On high ground facing the Hall is a graceful eight-sided domed temple with a square colonnade, set up in 1754. Not far off are the remains of a banqueting house designed by James Paine, the architect of Richmond Bridge in Surrey; most of the stone front remains with two pedimented windows flanking a round-headed doorway. There is also an imitation castle gateway, and a little ruined church built of stone from the ruins of Guisborough Priory in Yorkshire.

Sedgefield is one of the few places in England where the ancient Shrove Tuesday football game is still played. The teams play on the spacious green, the alleying places or goals being a quarter of a mile apart. If the ball is not alleyed by six in the evening it becomes the property of the sexton.

Shadforth. This is a quiet village in the valley of the Shadforth Beck, with white and grey houses lining a long narrow green, and a 19th century church on rising ground on the opposite side of the stream. In the south wall of the church is a modern window with a figure of St Cuthbert, to whom the church is dedicated.

A mile upstream from the village is the great gaunt ruin of Ludworth Tower, the most southerly of existing pele towers. A watchtower and refuge against the Scots, it formed part of a larger house built by Sir Thomas Holden in 1422. The west wall remains to a height of about 35 feet, and there are traces of fireplaces, three windows, a winding staircase, and a vaulted basement. Beside the ruins the tiny beck goes trickling by at the bottom of a great grassy ravine.

Sherburn House. On a steep rise above Sherburn Brook in this township, about a mile from the eastern outskirts of Durham, stands Sherburn Hospital, founded by Bishop Pudsey in 1181 for 65 lepers. The little battlemented gateway with its pointed ribbed vaulting is a relic of the original building, and another fragment of it survives in the chapel; most of the rest was destroyed by the Scots about 1300. In 1429, leprosy having almost died out in this country, the institution was converted into almshouses by Bishop Langley, though the funds still provide for the maintenance of two lepers elsewhere.

137

On the left of an attractive quadrangle with smooth lawns shaded by fine old trees, are long, low, creeper-covered almshouses built about 1760, and on the right is the master's dignified house, fronted by a fine pair of clipped yews. In front is the great gabled 19th century hospital block, and beside this is the chapel rebuilt after a fire in the Victorian Era but still keeping the core of Pudsey's original tower, with an upper stage beautifully arcaded. In the sanctuary is a 17th century oak armchair with flowers and foliage carved on its panelled back.

A short distance away, astride the little stream on the road to Durham, is a narrow mediaeval bridge with a single round arch. Beside it is a modern concrete bridge.

Shildon. This scattered industrial town to the south-east of Bishop Auckland has an important place in the history of railways. From Shildon started the first steam train in the world carrying passengers as well as goods. At Shildon were made many of the first locomotives for the historic Stockton and Darlington line, and later for the pioneer railroads of America. It is still one of the leading places in the world for the manufacture of railway-wagons.

Though Shildon is largely a product of the Industrial Revolution, the district has a place in earlier history. The part of the town known as East Thickley was the birthplace of Robert Lilburne, who played a prominent part in the Civil War. He was a Major-General in Cromwell's army, and proved himself an able commander; he was also one of the men who signed the death warrant of Charles I, and after the Restoration was banished to the island of St Nicholas, near Plymouth. His brother John rose to be a lieutenant-colonel in the Parliamentary Army, and afterwards became leader of the revolutionary party, the Levellers, which opposed Cromwell's assumption of supreme power.

A little to the south of East Thickley is Middridge Grange, a farm with a very different history. During the Civil War it was the home of Colonel Anthony Byerley, who commanded a regiment in support of the king and garrisoned his house with them. They built up a fine reputation for their never-say-die spirit, earning themselves the title of Byerley's Bulldogs.

But the really great man of Shildon was neither Cavalier nor Roundhead. He was the locomotive engineer and Methodist preacher Timothy Hackworth, who was buried in 1850 in the church-yard of the spacious 19th century church of St John, at the top of the sloping main street.

In Timothy Hackworth is centred all the pride which the people of Shildon have in the part played by their town in the development of railways. He is sometimes called the Father of Locomotives, and he was certainly one of the first in the field; moreover, his *Royal George*, built in 1827, was the first effectively to demonstrate the locomotive's superiority over all other available methods of traction.

Timothy Hackworth and George Stephenson were closely associated all their lives and were great friends. They were boys together, Hackworth being five years the younger, in the Northumberland colliery village of Wylam.

In 1810 Hackworth was working as a foreman at Wylam Colliery, and it is on record that as early as 1811 he and his friend William Hedley, a colliery viewer, co-operated there in the building of locomotives which were variously known as "Timothy's Dillies" and "Puffing Billies". (Stephenson did not build his first engine till 1814.)

The Stockton and Darlington Railway, the world's first passenger railway, had as its first engine *Locomotion*. This engine (now on Darlington Station) was built at Stephenson's Works, and Hackworth, as their manager, had an active part in its construction. Hackworth then became anxious to develop his own ideas, and took premises at Newcastle to set up business for himself; but Stephenson persuaded him to become locomotive engineer to the Stockton and Darlington Railway.

In 1840 Hackworth became proprietor of the Soho Engine Works at Shildon, and here, until his death on July 7, 1850, he continued to work and experiment—a happy, God-fearing man esteemed by all his fellows.

His memory is still venerated in Shildon today. In the town's fine park is a bronze statue of him—a bareheaded, frock-coated man holding a roll of plans. He looks over the wide sloping lawn and avenue of trees towards the railway-wagon works and the marshalling yards, with their many miles of sidings, and on the grass beside him is an original rail of the Stockton and Darlington Railway, the iron chairs resting on square blocks of stone instead of wooden sleepers. Close by is a little drinking fountain which has an iron canopy bearing medallions of Hackworth's *Royal George*.

The *Royal George* appears again on the bronze plaque fixed to Soho House, where Hackworth lived from 1833 to 1850. Nearly opposite Soho House is a long stone building with a chimney at one end, now used as a gymnasium. It is all that remains of the original

Soho works, which were established in 1827 and were the first in the world specially built to make railway locomotives. This was the principal locomotive factory in England until the Darlington works were opened in 1863.

A brass plate on the wall of the railway buildings beside the Masons Arms crossing recalls one of the greatest days in the history of railways. The inscription reads *From Shildon near this site the Stockton and Darlington Railway Company on the 27th of September 1825 ran the first passenger train drawn by a steam engine.*

On this historic occasion the train started at the Brusselton incline, and on arrival at Shildon was attached to a locomotive brought from Newcastle by road. George Stephenson drove it, and behind him were six wagons loaded with coal and flour, a passenger coach carrying directors and friends, 21 wagons filled with more passengers, and then six further wagons of coal. Altogether the locomotive hauled 450 passengers and a load of coal and merchandise which together must have weighed nearly 90 tons; but it reached Darlington, nearly nine miles away, almost two hours later.

At Darlington the last six wagons of coal were unhitched and the train went on its way to Stockton, 12 miles away, preceded by a man on horseback. It arrived there in three hours and seven minutes with about 600 passengers in or clinging to the wagons. Its arrival, we are assured, "excited deep interest and admiration".

Shincliffe. It stands at the foot of wooded hills only a mile from Durham, and the central tower of the cathedral can be seen rising majestically above the trees.

The way to it from the city is through a deep cutting, and down the hill, passing the University Sports centre on the left and the County Agricultural College on the right. Beyond is the bridge over the Wear, set up in 1825.

Shincliffe's quiet village street veers away from the modern main road from Durham to Stockton-on-Tees, and here, behind the houses, stands the church, with a stone spire of 1870.

Three of the windows are filled with fine modern glass. One was inserted in 1950 to mark the 100th anniversary of the church's rebuilding, and portrays St Cuthbert standing on a limpet-encrusted rock, feeding the seagulls. The second window, set up after the Second World War, depicts David grasping the hand of Jonathan ("the Lord be between me and thee"). The third is *in memory of Frederick Sidney Dennett, MA, head master Durham Cathedral Choristers' School 1914–1929, rector of Shincliffe 1929–1938.* It portrays St Aidan with two little boys—the future saints Cedd and Chad—in front of him, learning to read and write.

Between Shincliffe and a farmhouse called Old Durham are gravel workings where an important archaeological discovery was made in 1940. Foundations were revealed of a small bath-house which must have stood close to a Romano-British farmstead or villa, the first to be identified in County Durham. In 1948 two circular threshing-floors were found 40 yards from the bath-house.

Hitherto it had been supposed that the county was entirely a military area, but it is now known that it must have formed a food-growing civil zone in at least part of the Roman period. Pottery found on the site indicates reconstruction of a native farm at a time when the frontier was being pushed northward from the Tyne and Solway to the Forth and Clyde. The villa was probably burned down during the Pictish and Saxon raids of 367, and sometime in the 13th century its ruins seem to have served as a shelter or as a source of building stone.

Shotley Bridge. This is a large residential district on the outskirts of Consett, with a bridge crossing the Derwent into Northumberland. The river roars over the rocks beneath overhanging beeches, and below the bridge flows past a tall stone mill.

Cutlers' Hall, a stone house on the hill leading to Consett, is a link with some German sword-makers from Solingen who settled here about the year 1690 to escape religious persecution. It was built by William Oley, descendant of one of the original settlers, in 1787.

Perhaps the prettiest corner here is the cricket ground, bounded by the rushing river and a magnificent belt of trees. Here are two low stone buildings which belonged to Shotley Spa; its waters, reputed to be a cure for scrofula, still trickle into a round stone basin. In the year Queen Victoria came to the throne the grounds were laid out by a local Quaker named Jonathan Richardson, and the place became a fashionable resort. Charles Dickens visited the spa in 1839.

Sockburn. It is Durham's farthest point south, set in a long narrow loop of the Tees jutting into Yorkshire, seven miles south-east of Darlington. A quiet secluded little corner of the county it is, shared by three picturesque neighbours—a Hall rebuilt in 1837 in Elizabethan style, an ancient ruined church, and an 18th century farmhouse which has links with the poet Wordsworth.

It also has a legend. In the middle of the field below the Hall is a big fragment of limestone marking the traditional burial-place of the Sockburn Worm, "a dragon or fiery flying serpent" said to have been slain at this spot by the lord of the manor, Sir John Conyers, using the Conyers falchion, or broadsword, which is now in the Cathedral Library at Durham.

An avenue of tall lime trees leads to Sockburn Hall and the ancient church in its garden. The ruins consist of the chancel's 13th century east wall (with three lancet windows), the chancel arch, and two pointed Transitional arches of the south arcade. There is also an ivy-mantled 14th century chapel which was restored and reroofed in 1900 and contains several mediaeval relics.

Lying in this chapel is a 13th century stone effigy of a cross-legged warrior. He wears chain mail and flowing surcoat, his right hand grasps the hilt of his sheathed sword, and at his feet is a lion fighting a dragon.

A remarkable collection of fragments of pre-Conquest crosses and grave-covers found in the churchyard are displayed on the floor of the chapel. The most splendid fragment is a shaft some seven feet high, carved with chain ornament, and panels showing a deer and a hound. A gravestone lying on edge shows on both sides a man among animals, one group savage and the other quiet; it is possibly intended for Daniel in the lion's den. There are also four stones of the type known as hogback, one of them having two worn figures of bears biting at the ends.

Not far from the Hall stands Sockburn Farm, an 18th century house of brick with two low flanking wings and tall chimneys. It was here that William Wordsworth and his sister Dorothy stayed on their return from Germany, in the spring of 1799, as guests of their kinsmen the Hutchinsons, and here the poet fell in love with Mary Hutchinson.

Here also Coleridge, on a brief visit in October of the same year, set his affections on Mary's sister, Sara Hutchinson. Together they visited the church and examined the figure of the armoured knight:

> *She leant against the armed man*
> *The statue of the armed knight!*
> *She stood and listened to my lay*
> *Amid the lingering light.*

But it was a hopeless love, for Coleridge was already married. Discreetly he confided his feelings about Sara to his private diary, and then left Sockburn, never to return.

Meanwhile his friend Wordsworth was working on *The Prelude* and finishing *The Poet's Epitaph*. In December 1799 he and his sister left

Sockburn for Dove Cottage at Grasmere, where three years later his beloved Mary was to join him as his wife.

South Shields. This important industrial centre, seaport, and holiday resort is spread out at the county's northernmost point, between the North Sea and the last three or four miles of the River Tyne.

Evidence of the town's antiquity is to be found on the hill called The Lawe, overlooking the mouth of the Tyne. Here the Romans built a fort, probably called Arbeia, as a supply base for the garrison of Hadrian's Wall and for troops operating to the north of it; the rampart had the usual rounded corners and enclosed an area 205 yards by 120. Much of the site is now built over, but foundations of some of the earlier buildings—headquarters, granaries, barracks, and workshops—are to be seen in a little square called Roman Remains Park.

Excavations have been carried out here in recent years, and many of the objects unearthed (together with earlier finds) are finely displayed in a nearby museum which was opened in 1953. More relics are to be seen in the Museum of Antiquities at Newcastle University.

Outstanding among the exhibits here is a carved Roman tombstone with a figure of a woman seated in a wickerwork chair with her jewel box and sewing basket at her side; it is inscribed in Latin "To the divine shades of Regina of the Catuallaunian tribe, a freedwoman, and the wife of Barates the Palmyrene. She lived 30 years."

Another fine monument, called the Victor Stone, portrays a man banqueting in paradise. It bears a Latin inscription: "To the divine shades of Victor. He was by race a Moor, he lived 20 years, and was the freedman of Numerianus, a horseman of the first wing of Asturians, who most affectionately followed his former servant to the grave."

Also of considerable interest is a Roman sword, dating from about AD 200, and discovered in 1875, still in its wooden scabbard. It has a pattern-welded blade with inlaid decoration in gold bronze—an eagle on one side, and the figure of the war-god Mars on the other.

Among the smaller exhibits from the Roman fort are fragments of mortars for grinding food, tiles bearing a dog's footprints and the nails of a Roman soldier's boot, bone pins used by the women in dressing their hair, ivory needles, seal-boxes, fragments of glass vessels and ornamental pottery, coins, surgical instruments, and a little wolf's head carved in jet.

It is always fascinating to watch ships sailing to and fro on the busy tide of commerce, and there are few better vantage points for this than the South Pier of Tyne Harbour, a mile-long stone jetty stretching out to sea from the north-eastern tip of South Shields. Standing out prominently on the headland across the harbour can be seen the lofty ruins of Tynemouth Priory.

Near the pier are the North and South Marine Parks, affording fine coastal views as far as Souter Point, about four miles to the south. Smooth clean sands extend southward for a mile to Trow Point, and then comes a fine stretch of rocks past Frenchman's Bay to Marsden Bay.

Marsden Rock, on the southern edge of the borough, is a huge and striking mass 90 yards from the shore, with a lofty arch through which boats can pass at high tide. The neighbouring Marine Grotto has been adapted from some caves hollowed out of the cliff about 1830 and is used as a restaurant; it is approached by a lift from the coastal road above. On the cliffs are colonies of kittiwakes, oblivious of holiday crowds; the fulmar petrel also breeds here.

The clock tower prominent near the entrance to the pier is a memorial to William Wouldhave and Henry Greathead, the two South Shields men who share chief credit for the first practical lifeboat. On its walls are medallion portraits of the two pioneers, together with spirited reliefs of a lifeboat approaching a wreck in a stormy sea. Under a canopy beside the tower is a lifeboat which was launched in 1833 and saved over 1000 lives, and nearby is an anchor which is thought to have been dropped from one of the routed galleons of the Spanish Armada; it was hauled up by a North Sea trawler in 1920.

The story of the South Shields lifeboat dates back to 1789. In that year the *Adventure* of Newcastle grounded on the Herd Sands, at the mouth of the River Tyne, and was battered to fragments by the breakers. Thousands of people stood on the shore and helplessly watched the crew go to their death, for no known boat could have lived in such a sea, and to have launched one would only have added to the tragedy.

Following this disaster, the Tyne Lifeboat Society was founded in 1790, the first lifeboat service in the world. A prize was offered for a boat which could go to sea in a storm and rescue men from a fate such as had overtaken the crew of the *Adventure*; and among many competitors was William Wouldhave, clerk of the parish church of St Hilda, South Shields. He had no practical knowledge of boat-building, but he had sound ideas, and he claimed that his model would "neither sink, nor go to pieces, nor lie bottom up". Wouldhave's original model is in the town's museum, together with a painting by Ralph Hedley showing him working on it by candlelight.

Henry Greathead, a Yorkshireman who had set up in business as a boat-builder in South Shields, was shown Wouldhave's model and suggested that the keel should be curved, instead of straight; and he then got to work and built the lifeboat. It cost £149 13s 9d and it was paid for by the Committee of the Coal Trade in Newcastle.

It is only fair to state that a London coach-builder named Lionel Lukin invented and patented a lifeboat in 1785. But it had grave structural weaknesses and was soon forgotten. The Wouldhave lifeboat was quite unlike Lukin's. It was 30 feet long and 10 feet wide, lined inside and out with cork, and propelled by 10 oars. Although of very light draught it carried 20 people, and though of course far from perfect it was responsible for saving hundreds of lives.

Henry Greathead died in 1816, William Wouldhave five years later; South Shields still honours the memory of both.

From the lifeboat memorial, Ocean Road and King Street run westward in a straight line to a marketplace which occupies an area of about two acres. It is presided over by the Old Town Hall, a domed 18th century structure on pillars, which in 1910 was superseded by the more spacious and imposing building (with a clock tower 154 feet high), in Westoe Road, half a mile away.

On the south side of the marketplace, possibly on the site of a religious house founded by St Hilda in AD 648, stands St Hilda's Church—the oldest in the town, though it was rebuilt in 1810. At its eastern end is an apse adorned with striking reliefs of the Ascension.

The oldest feature is a 17th century font (a round bowl on a twisted stem) which was designed by Robert Trollope, the builder of Newcastle Guildhall. The most remarkable feature, suspended in the centre of the nave, is a little gilded model of an early lifeboat, with 10 men at the oars; it was made by one of Greathead's apprentices.

In the garden at the front of the church stands a weatherworn headstone on which another lifeboat is carved in relief; it commemorates the worthy William Wouldhave, clerk of this church, and categorically proclaims him "inventor of the invaluable blessing to mankind, the lifeboat".

The one other building which no visitor to South Shields should miss is the Public Library and Museum in Ocean Road.

In the entrance hall of the building are some delightful water-colours of South Shields and the River Tyne and surrounding country; on the staircase is a white marble bust of one of the town's distinguished sons—Sir Charles Mark Palmer, the Jarrow ship-builder, who in 1822 was born in King Street, quite close to where the library now stands.

A notable exhibit in the main gallery of the museum is a bronze statuette by Bertram Pegram of a wounded soldier riding a donkey, supported by Private John Simpson Kirkpatrick of the Australian Medical Corps, who was born in South Shields. For over five weeks during the Gallipoli campaign, Kirkpatrick and his donkey were almost hourly engaged in bringing in the wounded, often during heavy rifle and machine-gun fire. On the 19th of May 1915, Kirk-patrick himself was killed after making four journeys down Shrapnel Gulley, the deadliest part of the peninsula.

Staindrop. The fortunes of this little town with single wide street and pleasant green have for centuries been linked with the neighbour-ing castle. In his *Rokeby*, Sir Walter Scott refers to

> *Staindrop who from her silver bowers*
> *Salutes proud Raby's battled towers*

and certainly **Raby Castle** in its magnificent park is the glory of the place; indeed, it is one of the finest castles in all England.

The first known mention of Raby was in the reign of King Canute (1016–35), who called himself Emperor of the North. Then merely a small property, it was given by him to Durham Priory after his bare-foot pilgrimage from Garmondsway, near Trimdon. In the 12th century Raby came into the possession of the Nevilles, the great family of Norman descent which for the next 400 years was to make and unmake kings and help to shape the course of English history.

The great days of Raby date from the time of Ralph Neville, the hero of Neville's Cross, and his son John, some time High Admiral of England. They were overlords here for more than half of the 14th century, and in that time fortified and generally improved Raby, making it a supreme example of a feudal stronghold. To them is largely due the strength and magnificence which impelled Leland, writing in the 16th century, to describe Raby as "the largest castel of loggings in all the north country"; to those proud Nevilles, father and son, is due the rugged grandeur which despite inevitable alterations through the years Raby still displays in this 20th century.

The Nevilles held sway at Raby until 1569, when the failure of the Rising in the North led to their disgrace. Raby was then forfeited to the Crown, and in Crown possession it remained until 1626, when

Sir Henry Vane purchased it, together with Barnard Castle, for the sum of £18,000.

Sir Henry Vane was principal Secretary of State to Charles I, but he afterwards espoused the Parliamentary cause and twice in his lifetime Raby was besieged by Royalist forces. His eldest son, Sir Henry Vane the Younger, who inherited Raby Castle, was a lifelong champion of Parliament's rights and a close friend of Cromwell, Pym, and Hampden. It was to him that Milton addressed the sonnet beginning

Vane, young in years, but in sage counsel old.

Fearless, upright, and wise, he strenuously opposed the execution of Charles I; nevertheless, he met a like fate soon after the Restoration, being, as Charles II said, "too dangerous a man to let live".

To the illustrious Vane family Raby Castle still belongs, being now the seat of Lord Barnard, so it can be seen that the history of Raby is largely the story of two great families. Raby Castle is as closely linked with the names of Neville and Vane as Alnwick with Percy, or Arundel with Howard.

A visit to Raby Castle is a memorable experience. The park, exclusive of its many plantations, covers 270 acres. Two little lakes on the south side of the castle together cover an area of nine acres. Two herds of deer roam at will, adding grace to their sylvan setting.

The drive winds through the park, past many noble trees planted 200 years ago, and reaches the castle gatehouse—an impressive sight with its portcullis grooves, massive door, and the two little flanking towers which were added late in the 18th century by Henry Vane, second Earl of Darlington.

Passing through the gatehouse, which once guarded a drawbridge, the visitor finds himself within the two-acre area originally enclosed by the moat. This space, now a wide terrace surrounding the castle, affords a fine view of the park, the boundary wall having been reduced in height from 30 to three feet. Soaring above are the plain strong walls of the castle, punctuated here and there by towers which once looked impregnable.

Clifford's Tower, behind the gatehouse, is the largest; it is 80 feet high, has walls 10 feet thick, and retains some of its original windows and loopholes. To the left, in front of the Inner Keep, is the Kitchen Tower, original save for its modernised windows; it contains a 14th century kitchen 37 feet high, with a vaulted chamber below. An unusual feature is a passage in the thickness of the wall, linking the five windows. Next, beyond a short curtain wall, is the tower called

Mount Raskelf (after one of the Neville manors in Yorkshire) with four turrets on the roof and a low 18th century wall in front. This is at the north-east angle of the castle.

Beyond, in the centre of the east wing, is the Chapel Tower, containing a modernised 14th century chapel with some old trefoil-headed blind arches along the west wall which are now filled with modern paintings of members of the Neville family. Beside the south windows are original sculptured heads of John, Lord Neville—one of the builders of Raby—and his first wife, Maud Percy.

At the south-east corner of Raby Castle is Bulmer's Tower, a five-sided structure which is named after a Norman knight, Geoffrey de Bulmer, and is thought to be the oldest part of Raby. The upper part of this tower, which once stood detached from the rest of the building, is 14th century work.

The south side of Raby, between Bulmer's Tower and Joan's Tower (at the south-west corner), comprises 19th century buildings containing various living-rooms, including the dining-room, octagonal drawing-room, and great library, all reached from the inner court.

Joan's Tower, much modernised, is named after Joan Beaufort, John of Gaunt's daughter, who married Ralph Neville, Earl of Westmorland, and had 21 children. (The youngest was the Rose of Raby, mother of Edward IV and Richard III.) Along the battlemented wall of the terrace on its western side are 22 little cannon, together with a Russian howitzer captured in the Crimea.

The outstanding feature of the west front of Raby Castle is the stately Neville Gateway in the centre, the main entrance to the inner court. This has two flanking towers set obliquely to command a wide field of fire, and through it runs a vaulted passage—70 feet long and with a fine old door bearing the marks of heavy blows—which leads to the inner court.

In the north-east corner of this court is the mediaeval keep, still with the original iron gratings to the windows; it has a flight of stone stairs leading to an austere chamber called the Rose of Raby Room, with thick walls, floor, and roof, all of stone.

On the north side of the courtyard is the Lower, or Entrance Hall, with the Barons' Hall above it. The Lower Hall is thought to have been built by Ralph, Lord Neville, who died in 1367, and its original roof-line can be seen 10 feet above the upper windows. Ralph's son John built the Barons' Hall above, with its long double lancet windows, but in the 19th century architect William Burn made a new sloping roof and added new battlements to conceal it. Iron link-extinguishers brought from London stand beside the great arched entrance, which was made about the year 1800 so that carriages might drive right through the hall and emerge on the other side of the castle—a unique arrangement.

At the same time the ceiling was raised 10 feet, imitation vaulting being added, and the two rows of eight-sided stone pillars running down the middle of the hall were encased in imitation marble.

The main staircase of oak ascends to the vast Barons' Hall, 44 yards long, which was entirely reconstructed in 1845 and contains furniture of that date. Here in mediaeval times assembled the doughty warriors who owed allegiance to the Lords of Raby—

> *Seven hundred knights, retainers all*
> *Of Neville, at their master's call*

according to Wordsworth, in *The White Doe of Rylstone*. For here on November 13, 1569, was planned the insurrection which proved so fatal to the fortunes of the Nevilles—the Rising in the North, which was intended to restore the former religion and to put Mary Queen of Scots on the throne of England.

From the windows of the Barons' Hall are fine views of the park, and round the walls is an inspiring array of family portraits by such masters as Sir Peter Lely, Sir Godfrey Kneller, Allan Ramsay, Sir Joshua Reynolds, and John Hoppner. Of outstanding interest are Lely portraits of Christopher Vane, first Lord Barnard, and his wife Elizabeth, a couple alleged to have been so annoyed at their eldest son's marriage that they stripped the castle of furniture, lead, and glass, took off the doors, pulled up the floors, cut down the timber in the park, and destroyed all the deer. This Lady Barnard, widely known as the Old Hell Cat, died in 1725, but legend has it that she still haunts the ramparts at night, knitting with red-hot needles.

Many other family portraits and Old Masters, together with works of art of various kinds, are on the grand staircase and in the great oak-panelled library, as well as other rooms, which are shown to visitors. The treasures of Raby Castle are as magnificent as their setting.

At a little distance from the castle are 10 acres of gardens enclosed by mellow walls. The wrought-iron garden gate was designed by a celebrated architect, James Gibbs, and was originally in Shipbourne Church, near the Kent home of Sir Henry Vane. In a greenhouse against the wall of the south terrace is a huge fig tree which was brought from Italy about 1786 and still bears good crops.

Many of the owners of Raby Castle lie buried in the stately church of Staindrop, which is among the most interesting in the whole county. The oldest part of the building is the nave, which has 12th century Norman arcades crowned by a clerestory and dark oak roof of the 15th century. Above its eastern arches are traces of two windows which belonged to a Saxon church on the site, and to the left of the chancel arch is a Saxon sundial.

The tower is 13th century work, with a 15th century belfry which replaced a spire. The south aisle and vaulted porch date from about 1350, and the north aisle from about 1365. The chancel was rebuilt early in the 15th century and contains three magnificent sedilia of the period, but the little vestry on its northern side, once used as the town lock-up, is a 13th century building. A winding staircase with several steps made from mediaeval gravestones leads from this vestry to a priest's chamber which has a slanting opening to give a view of the altar.

In the chancel is some woodwork of outstanding interest. The massive oak altar-table was made in the reign of Charles I and is thought to have been a gift from the elder Sir Henry Vane; the handsome screen of dark oak is the only pre-Reformation chancel screen in County Durham; and there are also 24 handsomely carved stalls and desks of dark oak which were made for a college of priests founded here about 1400 by Ralph Neville, first Earl of Westmorland.

At the west end of the north aisle is a huge, ironbound 14th century chest which is thought to be another relic of the college which stood on the north side of the church but was demolished in 1548. Under the tower is a late 15th century font of Teesdale marble bearing the arms of Neville on a brass shield fastened to one of its eight sides.

In addition to architectural features and fittings of rare interest, Staindrop Church can boast an array of monuments which are among the finest in County Durham. Most of them commemorate lords and ladies who lived at Raby Castle. The oldest, in a recess in the south aisle, is thought to represent Elizabeth Fitzmeldred, who died about 1260; beside her is a little stone figure of a child. In a neighbouring recess lies a stone figure of a woman in a wimple and long robe with a little dog near her feet; this is believed to be the monument of Euphemia Clavering, mother of Ralph Neville, first Baron Neville, the victor of Neville's Cross and the builder of the south aisle of the church.

At the south-west corner of the nave is a thin battered figure of another lady of the Neville family; it rests on four lions, and there is another at her feet. Close to this, at the west end of the south aisle, is a battered, once magnificent alabaster altar tomb believed to have been made by the craftsman who fashioned the tomb of Henry IV at Canterbury. The sides have traceried panels alternately provided with canopied niches for statues, and lying on top is a figure of Ralph Neville, first Earl of Westmorland, who died in 1425. He wears armour, SS collar, and a richly embroidered sword-belt. Beside him lie his two wives in coronets and close-fitting dresses with flowing skirts. The first was Margaret, eldest daughter of Hugh, Earl of Stafford; the second was Joan Beaufort, daughter of John II of Gaunt.

This Ralph Neville, grandfather of Warwick the King-maker, was born in 1364. At 19 he was joint Governor of Carlisle, and was appointed to receive the ransom of the King of Scots. In 1397 he was made the first Earl of Westmorland, and Governor of the Tower of London. He afterwards joined the Lancastrians and helped to put Henry IV on the throne, and as a reward was made a Knight of the Garter and Earl Marshal of England.

Next to Ralph Neville's tomb is the remarkable oak monument of Henry, fifth Earl of Westmorland, who died in 1564. The Earl is portrayed in armour (note the heads of men carved on the knee-pieces) with his feet on a greyhound. On either side of him lie his first two wives, Anne and Jane, with long chains hanging from their waists and their feet projecting from elaborately fringed petticoats and resting on little pet dogs. In niches round the sides of the tomb kneel figures of seven children, each with its name carved above. Over the door nearby is a white marble bust of John Lee, an 18th century Attorney-general, sculptured by Joseph Nollekens.

Other notable monuments commemorate members of the Vane family who succeeded the Nevilles at Raby. On the wall at the west end of the north aisle reclines a white marble figure of Henry, second Earl of Darlington, who made extensive alterations to Raby Castle and also planted most of the woods now surrounding it. He was a well-known agriculturalist, and developed the famous breed of Durham Shorthorns. Carved on the sarcophagus beneath his figure is a relief of Raby Castle, where he died in 1792.

Close by are other family memorials, the most notable being a splendid white marble altar tomb with a sleeping robed figure by Westmacott of William Henry Vane, first Duke of Cleveland (d. 1842), keen sportsman and enlightened politician.

Stanhope. This pleasant old town, called the Capital of Weardale, is set amid miles of moorland at the spot where the Stanhope Burn meets the Wear and overlooked by long lines of terraced hillside where valuable limestone has long been quarried.

There is a delightful shady walk beside the Wear, and stepping-stones cross the river to Unthank Hall, a 17th century farmhouse with rugged stone walls and tall square chimneys. From this point the riverside road leads a little way upstream to an early 15th century bridge with a single arch, widened in 1792. Here the river, narrow and deep, rushes between mossy walls of rock.

Leading up Stanhope Dene at the west of the town is a path constructed during the Durham coal strike of 1891. It winds up through a glorious wooded gorge for more than a mile till it reaches the ravine of the Heathery Burn, a tiny tributary of the Stanhope stream. Here are traces of the famous Heathery Burn Cave, scene of one of the most important Bronze Age discoveries ever made in this country.

The cave was in the side of the ravine, but in 1843 its entrance was destroyed in making a tramway for a limestone quarry. On that occasion eight bronze rings were found, and discoveries were continually made until the abandonment of the quarry in 1872. By that time there had come to light a wonderful group of bronze objects, now preserved as the Heathery Burn collection in the British Museum. This collection represents the complete equipment of a Late Bronze Age family which had taken refuge in this cave and been overwhelmed by flooding; and it dates from a time when the age had reached its peak in Britain—about 1150-800 BC.

Among the more outstanding finds were six bronze cylinders with an internal diameter of four inches, for it is thought that if they were not merely armlets they were probably nave-bands of a four-wheeled vehicle, the earliest evidence of a wheeled cart in the country. Other interesting specimens are well-made spearheads, tanged and socketed knives, and at least 19 socketed axes. A bronze mould for making the axes, together with tongs, shows that metal was worked in the cave by smiths using Weardale copper ore. A gold armlet, a gold ring, bracelets and pins of bronze, and necklaces of teeth and shells were for the adornment of women; a razor, gouges, and chisels were used by the men. A big bronze cauldron with two handles had a deposit of carbon showing that it had been used for cooking; broken crockery and bones of beef, mutton, and game were also found.

Other traces of early human occupation in these parts have been found in Linnkirk Cave, in a fine gorge just to the east of the town.

Back in the centre of the town is the marketplace with dignified cross on four old stone steps. On the south side of the marketplace is the battlemented wall of Stanhope Castle, built in 1798 on the site of a mediaeval castle, and now a reform school for boys.

On the south side of the main street, behind a fine row of tall lime trees, another high stone wall half-conceals Stanhope Rectory, rebuilt in 1821 on the site of a manse which was the home of some distinguished men. Cuthbert Tunstall, rector here from 1508 to 1520, was scholar, statesman, and friend of Erasmus: in 1522 he became Bishop of London and in 1530 was translated to Durham. Isaac Basire, made rector in 1648, traveller, linguist, and scholar, was chaplain to Charles I and Charles II. Joseph Butler was rector here for 13 years prior to becoming Bishop of Bristol in 1738, and while living here planned his famous *Analogy of Religion*.

Stanhope's church, standing on a slope above the marketplace, dates from about 1200. Two heads smile down on the congregation from the chancel arch, and hanging on the north wall of the chancel are two black oak plaques with magnificent Flemish carvings of Christ and Peter walking on the water, and Adam and Eve standing beside the Tree of Life. Near them is a splendid little French painting of Christ and St Veronica.

In the west window is some mediaeval glass dating from the 14th to the 16th century. There are five faintly-drawn figures of prophets in white and gold, together with the heads of a female saint, an angel, and a cherub. The big middle medallion shows a bishop with mitre and crozier, and amid the colourful patchwork in the top light is the head of a bearded man.

By the wide tower arch stands a disused old font, and outside are several other ancient relics worthy of note—mediaeval grave-covers and a stone coffin by the porch, a sundial of 1727 on the south aisle wall, and a gargoyle nearby with the head of a fox.

Preserved in the vestry is a Roman altar found in 1747 on Bollihope Common, about four miles south of the town. It bears a Latin inscription meaning:

Sacred to the Unconquered Silvanus. Caius Tetius Micianus, prefect of the Sebosian wing, on account of a boar of enormous size which was captured, which many of his predecessors were unable to take, gladly placed this altar, discharging his vow.

Silvanus was the god of the woods, worshipped by hunters.

Near the churchyard gate is a remarkable fossilised tree stump. Found high on the moors near Edmundbyers Cross, it is said to be 250 million years old.

153

Stanley. It is a plain industrial town, sprawling across a breezy hillside in north-west Durham. The tower of its 19th century church, capped by a spire, is a landmark for miles around, and the church-yard affords an extensive view over the northern part of the county.

At the entrance to the East Stanley cemetery a monument in pink and grey granite recalls one of the most tragic disasters in Durham mining history. It is inscribed "In memory of the 168 men and lads who lost their lives in the West Stanley Colliery Explosion on February 16th 1909".

Sunderland. The biggest town and chief port of County Durham, this is also one of the greatest shipbuilding and shiprepairing centres in the world. On coal and ships were Sunderland's fortunes founded, but unlike some of our big towns, it is not entirely a product of the Industrial Age; indeed, its history dates from Saxon times, when it was known as Wearmouth.

At Monkwearmouth, the part of the town north of the Wear, Benedict Biscop founded the monastery which, together with the one at Jarrow, was to be the home of the saintly historian, Bede. That was in AD 674.

The territory on the south side of the Wear has had a continuous existence as a port for at least 10 centuries, and for eight of them has been called Sunderland—the part sundered from the monastic lands by the river, according to the most plausible explanation of the name.

In 1897 Monkwearmouth became part of Sunderland, and more recently the boundaries have been extended further north to include the attractive seaside resort of Roker and Seaburn, only a few minutes' ride from the heart of the town.

Evidence of Sunderland's antiquity must be sought in the parish churches of St Peter's at Monkwearmouth, and St Michael's, Bishopwearmouth, and also in the town's splendid Art Gallery and Museum. For the rest it is a great industrial town and seaport, with a harbour affording 125 acres of safe anchorages, docks capable of accommodating the biggest cargo-vessels, and shipbuilding yards with an outstanding production record. The characteristic sights and sounds and smells of Sunderland are those associated with ships and coal and timber, as well as others inseparable from marine engineering and a host of modern industries.

The old parish church of Bishopwearmouth—St Michael's—stands in a green garden at the top of Sunderland's busy High Street. Because of mining subsidence, it was largely rebuilt in 1934–35 to the design of W. D. Caröe, and is a handsome structure although, except for the four massive round arches of the west tower, little of the mediaeval church is visible.

On the south side of the church lies the battered stone figure of a knight—Sir Thomas Middleton of Silksworth, who died about 1400; and on the south wall is a brass commemorating the church's most distinguished parson—William Paley. He was rector here from 1796 until his death in 1805, and during this time wrote his *Natural Theology*. The memorial pays ponderous tribute to one who

devoted his singular gifts of masculine thought and transparent language to the investigation of the principles of human duty, the elucidation of the witness of nature to nature's God, and the confirmation by new and powerful arguments of the wavering faith of a doubting age.

An entry in the register for 1665 says that Jenny Reed of Bellingham in Kent brought the Plague from London by ship, and that 30 Sunderland people died of it in three months. Another entry, dated May 29, 1841, records the marriage of Robert Surtees, the sporting novelist, to Elizabeth Fenwick of Bishopwearmouth.

Two other famous men in Sunderland's story are commemorated in Mowbray Park, which affords a fine view of the town—of the towers of its churches and public buildings, of the tall cranes at the mouth of the river, and of the grey North Sea beyond.

Prominent here is a colossal bronze statue (by William Behnes) of Sir Henry Havelock, the Indian Mutiny hero, who was born at Ford Hall, Bishopwearmouth, in April 1795. On the top of a grassy mound not far off is a monument to another hero of the town. It is a little bronze statue of a barefooted boy nailing up a flag (with the butt of a pistol for a hammer) and it commemorates

Jack Crawford, the sailor who so heroically nailed Admiral Duncan's flag to the main-top-gallant-mast of HMS Venerable *in the Battle of Camperdown in October 1797.*

HMS *Venerable* being the Admiral's ship, it was the particular mark of the enemy, and her colours had been shot away several times, at length crashing down with part of the mast. It was then that Jack ran aloft under heavy fire and performed his great deed.

Jack Crawford was born in Sunderland in 1775, and died there 56 years later, a victim of cholera brought to the town on a ship from Riga in October 1831. A big silver medal given to him by the people of Sunderland, and worn by him at Nelson's funeral, is in the town's museum.

Reminders of many other chapters in Sunderland's story are to be seen in the Central Library, Museum and Art Gallery beside Mowbray Park.

In the entrance hall is a bronze relief of Sir Joseph Wilson Swan, inventor of the electric incandescent lamp and a pioneer in the science of photography, who was born in Sunderland in October 1828. Upstairs are the vacuum pump and other apparatus which he used in his experiments.

To the left of the stairs is a bronze inscription commemorating the first stage appearance of Sir Henry Irving—at Sunderland on September 29, 1856.

Old Sunderland is portrayed in many of the landscapes in the gallery, and relics of the town's past are finely displayed in the museum.

The collection of Sunderland glass and pottery is notable. Much of the ware is decorated with mottoes, verses, and views. Beautifully engraved glass goblets show fully-rigged ships sailing under the old bridge, and there are painted glass rolling-pins which sailors took home to their sweethearts.

The Sunderland Company of Glassmakers began operations on the Southwick bank of the Wear in 1698, and the town still has its artists in glass. A notable example of their skill is the intricately fashioned model of the civic coat-of-arms, made in 1966, and displayed in the entrance hall.

A splendid display of natural history exhibits completes the rich and varied collection which this Museum and Art Gallery offers.

Not the least of Sunderland's great sights is Wearmouth Bridge, which carries the main coastal road across the river to Monkwearmouth, and affords fine views of the big ships tied up at the wharves below, with a forest of cranes in the background. Opened in 1929, it is notable for its great steel arch with a span of 375 feet. On the parapet is a bronze plate with a medallion picture of the former bridge (opened in 1796) and an inscription to the memory of its builder, Rowland Burdon, MP.

On the north side of the bridge, spread out for two or three miles along the Wear, is Monkwearmouth. This old part of Sunderland, almost completely rebuilt in recent years, preserves in its midst a church (St Peter's) which is a precious link with Saxon England.

It is possible that an early Irish–Saxon monastery stood on the site where St Peter's, Monkwearmouth, now stands, but the first stone building was set up by Benedict Biscop about AD 674. In that year Ecgfrid, King of Northumbria, granted land for the purpose, and Bede tells us that the church was quickly built by Benedict "after the manner of the Romans in which he ever took delight". Benedict brought masons from Gaul, and with them came glaziers; indeed this is believed to have been the first church in England to have glass in its windows.

Benedict was a Northumbrian noble who, tired of worldly ways, made several pilgrimages to Rome, and finally returned home determined to promote Christianity in his own land. It was the books which he brought back from his travels that enabled Bede to pursue his studies at Monkwearmouth and Jarrow. Eight years after founding the monastery here at Monkwearmouth he established another at Jarrow, and by the year 715 these two houses had 600 monks.

Towards the end of the 9th century the Danish pirates Hubba and Hingmar destroyed Monkwearmouth, and if it ever recovered from this onslaught it must have suffered again under the Conqueror. But in 1076 it was rebuilt by Aldwin of Winchcomb, and until the Dissolution was dependent on Durham. During this period it was governed by a resident official known as the Master of Wearmouth.

The only part of Monkwearmouth Monastery still remaining is the Church of St Peter, and the only relics of its Saxon days are to be found at the west end, although restoration has made even this work difficult to date.

The long and narrow nave was rebuilt in the middle of the Victorian era; the north aisle, transept, and porch are 19th century additions; three windows in the north aisle are filled with beautiful 20th century glass—(more work by Leonard C. Evetts)—representing Benedict Biscop, Abbot Ceolfrid, and St Hilda; and the chancel is chiefly 14th century work, with modern windows. But the lower west wall of the nave and part of the tower may belong to the very church built by Benedict and known to Bede. (An interesting panel of modern glass in the east window shows Benedict superintending the building of this tower.)

The lower stage of the tower, with four round-headed doorways, forms a porch, and if not the original work of Benedict, must certainly have been built by the middle of the 8th century. It is thrilling to stand here and reflect that you are in Saxon England, on the very spot where the Saxon founder of Monkwearmouth and Jarrow once stood—perhaps Bede himself—13 centuries ago. The two pairs of short round pillars which support the arch of the western doorway are the only shafts still remaining in their original position in any early Saxon church, and the plain barrel-vaulted roof of the porch is said to be the only example of Saxon vaulting above ground in England. The long flat stones which form the lower parts of the sides of the western doorway still bear carvings of entwined serpents, and set in the wall a few feet above the arch is a frieze of worn stone panels with faint carvings of various animals.

Above the porch is a room lit by a round-headed window with cable-moulding on its inner splays which is said to be 7th century work. Over this window can be seen a triangle of darker masonry with traces of a Saxon carving of the Crucifixion.

The whole of the tower above this may well have been added when the monastery was re-established after the Norman Conquest, though some authorities hold it to be 10th century work. On each side except the east is a belfry window of two lights separated by a round shaft and framed in strapwork.

It is also thought that the west wall of the nave may be Biscop's work. High up can be seen two narrow round-headed windows, and set into the wall beside them are four baluster shafts like those in the porch: they were turned round and reset in 1866.

Preserved under glass in the north transept is a fine collection of carved stonework which also belonged to the Saxon church. Two of the stones have carvings of two lions in bold relief some 18 inches long; they formed supports for the abbot's stall and the presbyters' bench which ran round the east end of the church until its destruction by the Danes. On another stone is carved a fearsome dragon, and there is also part of a 9th century cross with a damaged panel of two warriors in combat. One of the oldest fragments is a corner of a 7th century grave-cover with a beautiful interlacing pattern almost identical with the ornament on the Lindisfarne Gospels.

Two other interesting links with the past are contained in frames near the chancel arch. One is the head of an angel on a fragment of a mediaeval fresco which was taken down from the north wall in 1873. The other is a facsimile from an illuminated manuscript, an illustrated Bible made in Wearmouth Monastery about AD 700 and taken to the Pope by Abbot Ceolfrid in AD 716. Its origin was only discovered in 1887.

On the floor near the pulpit lies a worn stone figure of a priest, and lying at the back of the nave are two mediaeval grave-covers with carved crosses and swords. On a panelled altar tomb under a canopy in the chancel lies a legless armoured figure which is believed to be the memorial of William, Lord Hylton (d. 1435), the builder of **Hylton Castle**, three miles to the west of this church.

Hylton Castle as we see it today is a blackened stone tower, three storeys high, with four turrets capped by overwhelming battlements supported on worn corbels. Among the many heraldic shields carved on the tower is one bearing the Washington coat-of-arms, the three stars and two bars, known heraldically as "Gules, two bars, and in chief three mullets silver". They were borne by the Washingtons of the neighbouring village of Washington and, according to tradition, were later adapted by George Washington for the Stars and Stripes. This shield, some 500 years old, is the oldest known stone carving of the Washington arms.

Close to the castle are the outer walls and the traceried east and west windows of the chapel, with the ruins of two remarkable five-sided transepts which once had two tiers of round-headed windows.

North of Monkwearmouth stretch the pleasant parks and promenades and beaches of Roker and Seaburn, popular with holiday-makers. One of the parks has a lovely rocky ravine running down to the sea under a high bridge. Another, Roker Cliff Park, consists of 12 breezy acres of lawn on top of the cliff overlooking the low Holey Rocks. It forms a fine promenade, a quarter-of-a-mile long, with views of Sunderland Harbour to the south and Whitburn Bay to the north.

In a little garden enclosure beside the coastal road skirting Roker Cliff Park is a grey cross, 24 feet high, which was unveiled in 1904 by the Archbishop of York as a national memorial to the Venerable Bede, the saintly scholar who was born between Wear and Tyne in 673 and died at Jarrow on Ascension Day 735. Designed by Charles Clement Hodges of Hexham and carved by W. Milburn of York, it is composed of three stones, weighing $11\frac{1}{2}$ tons, which were hewn from Lord Armstrong's estate at Rothbury in Northumberland.

Carved in relief on the cross are graphic scenes from Bede's life. One shows him, a small boy, arriving at the gate of Jarrow Monastery; others depict him writing his *Historia Ecclesiastica*, and on his death-bed, translating St John's Gospel. On another side of the cross is an ascending vine with reliefs of Bede's contemporaries—the weak King Ceolwulf to whom the history was dedicated, John the Arch-chanter, who taught Bede singing, Trumbert of Lastingham, who taught him Latin and Divinity, and his chief teacher Benedict Biscop, the builder of the monasteries of Monkwearmouth and Jarrow where Bede spent nearly all his days in devotion and studies.

Roker also has in St Andrew's a 20th century church of considerable interest. Completed in 1907, it is an imposing structure in local grey stone, with a massive east tower. The spacious interior is notable for its great nave arches and for the artistic richness of its furnishings.

The dedication stone lettered by Eric Gill, the huge stone font carved by Randall Wells, Ernest Gimson's ebony lectern, inlaid with pearl, and his altar cross, candlesticks, and processional cross in polished wrought iron are all examples of fine craftsmanship.

A mural painting of the Creation, by McDonald Gill, covers the walls and ceiling of the chancel. The reredos is a tapestry designed by Sir Edward Burne-Jones and woven by William Morris and Company; it has for its theme the Adoration of the Wise Men. The east window, a composition in warm colours by H. A. Payne, represents the Ascension.

Sunderland Bridge. Like its more famous namesake, 15 miles to the north-east, it has some important bridges over the Wear. One is a mediaeval stone bridge of four round arches which was partly rebuilt in 1769, and widened in 1822 after a mail-coach accident in which two passengers were thrown over the parapet and killed. The bridge is still used, but a modern steel bridge now carries the Great North Road across the river a little further downstream.

Above the old bridge, where the river runs slowly beneath overhanging trees, is a lofty brick railway viaduct carrying the main Edinburgh–London line; it is almost exactly 250 miles from King's Cross. Below the bridges the Wear is joined by the Browney, a dark stream flowing from the moors near Satley.

The village is pleasantly situated along a quiet turning off the busy main road, but its church, a 19th century building in Norman and Gothic style, is perched above the stream of traffic at the corner. Its ancient forerunner, a primitive little Norman building with an empty bellcote, stands, forlorn and unused, near Croxdale Hall, about half-a-mile to the east. Over its round-headed south doorway is a tympanum with a much-worn carving of the Tree of Life.

Croxdale Hall is a plain but imposing stone house with a wide and beautiful view to the south-east and a densely wooded dell on the north. For centuries it was the home of the Salvin family, who worshipped in the Roman Catholic chapel adjoining the house but were buried in the little Norman church nearby.

Tanfield. This tiny village round a green has a 700-year-old church with an inscription (under a sundial) stating that it was rebuilt and enlarged in 1749. Further extension and restoration took place in the 19th century.

A noteworthy relic is a marble slab in the chancel floor, dated 1628, and bearing this epitaph:

> *Under this hard marble lies closed in clay*
> *The corpse of that worthy Sir William Wray.*
> *He sent five babes to glory, his way to prepare,*
> *And two sons and two daughters of virtues rare.*

At the east end of the south aisle is a white marble wall monument with a cloaked figure of John Eden (of Beamish Hall) mourning over a sarcophagus bearing a medallion relief of his beloved sister, Dorothea Methold, who died in 1857.

Close to the village is a remarkable antiquity called the Causey Arch. Built about 1727, and probably the oldest surviving railway bridge in the world, it is scheduled as an ancient monument of national importance. Constructed of stone, it has a span of 35 yards, and once carried two railway tracks of timber, each four feet wide. The wagonway of which it formed part was laid down by the group of coal-owners called the Grand Allies; it carried coal for the five or six miles from Tanfield to the Tyne.

Thorpe Thewles. Four miles north-west of Stockton it lies, a little village astride the main road to Durham. Close by, in a finely wooded park adorned with several lakes, is Wynyard Hall, a seat of the Marquis of Londonderry. A classical building with a balustraded roof and a noble portico on Corinthian columns, it was built by Sir Matthew Wyatt, in place of the mansion which was destroyed by fire in 1841, soon after its completion. Among its outstanding features are a sculpture gallery 120 feet long, and a private chapel added in 1880.

Soaring finely above the trees at the highest point of the park is a 127-feet-high obelisk set up to commemorate the Duke of Wellington's visit in 1827 to the third Marquis of Londonderry, who had fought with him in the Peninsular War.

In the middle of the village is a little church built in 1887. The altar stone of Tees marble, together with an ancient stone coffin in the churchyard, came from the ruined church of Thomas à Becket which stands in the fields about two miles to the north.

Some of St Thomas's Norman walls remain, with a few lancet windows and a pointed south doorway. In the south-west angle of the nave is an arched brick recess which formed the fireplace of the

161

18th century pew of Wynyard Hall, and close to it are the ruins of the 14th century chapel called the Fulthorpe Porch. Here stood the coped stone coffin of Roger de Fulthorpe which is now in the graveyard of the new church.

Tow Law. This breezy little hilltop town with wide views lies close to the eastern edge of the moors, 10 miles north-west of Bishop Auckland. Its vicar from 1888 to 1934 was Thomas Espin, author and editor of several astronomical works, who built an observatory in the vicarage garden. A stone cross near the church door marks his last resting-place.

The 19th century church where he preached for so many years has a chancel screen with an astonishing collection of ferns, cones, nutshells, and acorns which he collected on his extensive travels throughout Europe. It also has a fine window in his memory, portraying St James holding a staff and St Philip with a basket of loaves and fishes; above is the starlit sky, inscribed: *They shall shine as the stars for ever and ever.*

Also depicted in attractive modern glass are the northern saints, Oswald, Cuthbert, and Aidan.

Trimdon. In the centre of its big village green stands a roughly-built church with a heavily-buttressed bell turret. It has been considerably altered and restored through the centuries, and the chief token of its antiquity is a Norman chancel arch, its curve flattened with the burden of time, its pillars bowed with age.

In the village cemetery is a reminder of the perils which miners face every day. It is a tall stone monument "set up in memory of the 74 men and boys who lost their lives by the explosion at Trimdon Grange Colliery, Thursday, February 16, 1882 . . . 44 of whom are here interred." The remarkable reliefs round the base symbolise the grim story.

About two miles to the west is the isolated hamlet of Garmondsway, the "place called via Garmundi". According to tradition King Canute and his retinue walked barefooted and bareheaded from here to Durham, a distance of seven miles, to do penance at the shrine of St Cuthbert.

Ushaw. The name of this district is known far and wide, for in its midst, on a hill 600 feet high, stands the Roman Catholic College of St Cuthbert.

Ushaw College, famed among Catholics all over the world, is the successor of the college which was founded by Cardinal Allen at Douai in 1568 and destroyed during the French Revolution. For a few years the professors and students carried on their work at Crook Hall, near Lanchester; then, in 1808, they moved to this spacious new college. It has since been enlarged, and now there are usually some 350 pupils in residence, most of them training for the Roman Catholic priesthood.

The college stands on a terrace commanding wide views and is itself an imposing sight. Members of the public can obtain permission to visit it, and they are well rewarded, for the buildings contain a wealth of fine pictures and precious manuscripts, as well as many sacred relics; one of the greatest treasures preserved here is the famous ring of St Cuthbert—a gold ring set with a big sapphire—which was taken from the coffin of St Cuthbert in 1540.

The main buildings surround a big quadrangle, chief among them being the Chapel of St Cuthbert, the library, and the big refectory, with the massive tables and benches designed by Augustus Pugin. There are also five smaller chapels or oratories, attached to long cloisters.

The Chapel of St Cuthbert, which dates from 1884, has a beautiful east window portraying scenes in the life of this beloved saint, with many blue-clad figures making up a harmonious colour-scheme. On the north side of the choir is another notable window, glowing with figures of St Thomas of Canterbury, the Blessed Cuthbert Maine, St John Fisher, and St Thomas More.

The library, 120 feet long and containing upwards of 40,000 books in its tall carved oak cases, is famed for its theological collection. Among its treasures are several early illuminated manuscripts; a 14th century missal which belonged to James Coldwell, Bishop of Norwich and Secretary of State to Edward IV; the handsome and striking Bobbingworth Psalter of the 15th century which belonged to the Walsingham family; and no fewer than 130 books printed before 1500.

Also preserved here is the library of John Lingard, the historian. A student of Douai College, and one who narrowly escaped death when it was wrecked by the revolutionaries, Lingard later served Ushaw College with distinction both as professor and vice-president. In 1811 he retired to the village of Hornby, near Lancaster, and there spent the last 40 years of his life compiling and revising his *Antiquities of the Anglo-Saxon Church* and his monumental *History of England*, the only work of its kind written by a Roman Catholic. He died in 1851, and was buried here at Ushaw; a Latin inscription on a wall above his grave in the cloister pays tribute to his memory.

John Lingard's correspondence is preserved in the archives here, together with letters of Cardinals Wiseman and Manning, charters of King John and Hugh Pudsey, Bishop of Durham, documents dealing with the Earls of Derwentwater, and an original manuscript of the poet Francis Thompson, who was a pupil here.

At the eastern end of the college buildings are large three-sided stone alleys where games called Keeping-up and Trap are played with balls and wooden battledores made on the premises. These games are excellent practice for the more popular Ushaw game of Cat, which is played between the football and cricket seasons, from the Feast of St Cuthbert until the end of May.

Nearby is the remarkable-looking College Farm, a building with grey stone walls and slated roofs which was erected in 1851 from the design of Joseph Hansom, inventor of the hansom cab. The central block is an enormous gabled barn.

Washington. This industrial township halfway between Gateshead and Sunderland has a proud place in the annals of the family which gave America its first President; as the nucleus of an ambitious new town for 70,000 people it has an important place in the future of the region.

Washington, Durham County, was many centuries old when Washington, District of Columbia, was founded; and there were men bearing the name of Washington (in varied spellings) living here in Norman times—they were lords of the manor here from 1183 to 1376. The old village, in fact, has the distinction of having cradled the Washington family, which in course of time spread to many other parts of England, including Sulgrave in Northamptonshire, and thence to America. Here lived the remote ancestors of George Washington; they were English squires, and their coat-of-arms of three mullets and two bars (in unheraldic terms, three stars and two stripes) may well have been the origin of the American national flag.

Here, to this day, stands the Old Hall, which embodies the remains of their manor house; and here too stands a church on the site of the house of prayer in which they worshipped.

The Washington family story goes back to the year 1183, when William de Hertburn exchanged his manor with the Bishop of Durham for that of Wessynton, or Wassynton, or Wassington—the name had many spellings. He paid a rent of £4 a year and the service of attending the bishop's Great Hunt with two greyhounds. He assumed the local name, William de Wessyngton, and it occurs as a witness to Durham charters.

The family remained here until 1376, when the manor was sold to the Blakyston family; the deed of sale (with a wax seal bearing the three stars and two stripes) is preserved in Durham Cathedral Library. After this the family records show that they were living in various other counties—in Westmorland, Yorkshire, Warwickshire, and Northamptonshire; and it was from Sulgrave in Northampton-shire that the American President's great grandfather, John Washington, emigrated to America in company with his brother Lawrence.

Washington Manor passed through various hands, and in 1610 reverted to the See of Durham. It was then acquired by Bishop James, a man described by a contemporary as a little inclined to hoard his money, but otherwise as kindly and quiet a bishop as ever lived.

It was Bishop James who rebuilt the manor house—the gabled Old Hall which is still standing and incorporates some early masonry belonging to the house in which the Washingtons lived—a pillar and two stone arches built into a wall, the jamb of a newel stair, and a blocked window. It now houses a small museum and a community centre.

Surrounded by fine trees to the north of the Old Hall is the spacious 19th century successor of the Norman church known to the Washington family. It was rebuilt in 1833, the rector then being Henry Perceval, son of the Prime Minister who was assassinated in the lobby of the House of Commons by a crazy bankrupt named Bellingham.

The only relic of the ancient church is a Norman font with a shallow round bowl. Generations of Washingtons must have been baptised in it, and now the Stars and Stripes hangs on the wall above.

In the south wall of the church are three windows worthy of attention. One commemorates Frederick Hill, "headmaster of Biddick School 1926–1949, historian of Washington and an active promoter of Anglo-American friendship". Another marks the site of the mediaeval porch belonging to the Lords of the Manor of Washington. In the south chapel is a window portraying David and Ruth; it commemorates Robert Lee—not the American general, but a man who served this village for 42 years as schoolmaster, and this church for 56 years as organist and choirmaster.

A Washington village boy who grew up to win a small measure of fame was John Brand, antiquarian and topographer. Son of the parish clerk, he was born here in 1744, and after being a pupil and usher at Newcastle Grammar School eventually became a parson in

M

the City of London and chaplain to the Duke of Northumberland. His best-known work is *Observations on Popular Antiquities*, but he is also remembered for his *History of Newcastle* in two volumes.

Distinction in far wider fields was to be won by a girl who was born in Washington in 1868. Her name was Gertrude Bell, daughter of Sir Thomas Bell, the iron-master, and a grand-daughter of the famous metallurgist, Sir Isaac Lowthian Bell.

She was one of the most extraordinary women of her time; before she was 20, she obtained a first class in modern history at Oxford, and later performed astonishing mountaineering feats in the Alps.

In 1913, after several adventurous journeys in Syria and Palestine she set out from Damascus to reach the hidden heart of Arabia. She travelled some 550 miles across the deserts to Hail, in the centre of northern Arabia. There the local tribesmen forbade her to go farther south, because they were on bad terms with their southern neighbours.

She then turned north and went on 450 miles or more to Baghdad, making friends everywhere with the nomad Arabs, and completing one of the greatest journeys ever carried out by a lone woman explorer.

During the First World War Gertrude Bell's knowledge of the tribesmen of northern Arabia made her invaluable as an Intelligence officer, and she acquitted herself with honours.

But it was after the war that the power of her personality helped to shape events in the Middle East. She went to Mesopotamia as the Secretary of the British Commissioner, but in reality she was Britain's representative in dealing with the Arabs, who knew and trusted her.

The future of Mesopotamia was then being considered, and Gertrude Bell insisted that it must become an independent state. It was largely due to her advice and influence that the Emir Feisal became King of Iraq.

Her mission accomplished, she remained in the country to which she had devoted herself. Its antiquities had always been one of her greatest interests and she was instrumental in the founding of a national museum in Baghdad in 1923, three years before her death.

In Baghdad this remarkable Englishwoman died, and there in the British cemetery she lies.

West Rainton. Lying four miles north-east of Durham, near the busy main road to Sunderland, this township has a 19th century church with two remarkable features. One is the spire which soars to a height of 130 feet and is visible for many miles around; the other is a tablet recording the gift of the tower and spire by Sir George

Elliot, MP, in 1877. The inscription also states that the tablet is a portion of a block of granite obtained by Sir George Elliot in 1876 from the Great Pyramid of Ghizeh by permission of Ismail Pasha, Khedive of Egypt.

A similar link with the Pharaohs is to be seen in Penshaw church.

Westerton. A tiny village on a hill above the main road between Bishop Auckland and Spennymoor, it has a reminder of the 18th century astronomer, Thomas Wright, who was born in 1711 at Byers Green, two miles away. Known as Westerton Folly, it is a round stone observatory tower which he built, and it has a wonderful all-round view which embraces Durham Cathedral and the Penshaw monument. On its wall is a tablet set up by the University of Durham in 1950 to commemorate his treatise, *Theory of the Universe*, published 200 years earlier.

Thomas Wright's father, a carpenter, sent his boy to school at Bishop Auckland. The lad used to steal away from his playmates, and he would later be found studying a book in a hedge, or perhaps on a haystack. When barely 10 he was apprenticed to a clockmaker, and studied astronomy in his spare time; but he quarrelled with his master and ran away.

Thomas's father had opposed his mathematical bent, but offered to make a sailor of him, and accordingly, in 1730, the young man made a trial trip from Sunderland to Amsterdam; but he did not take kindly to the sea, and on returning home decided to open a mathematical school at Sunderland. After various vicissitudes he finally settled down and became a fashionable teacher of mathematics and astronomy.

In 1750 he produced his *Original Theory or New Hypothesis of the Universe*, illustrated by a number of plates, a work which secured for him an honoured place in the history of astronomy.

Thomas Wright died on February 22, 1786, and was buried in the churchyard of St Andrew's Church at Bishop Auckland.

Whickham. It stands on high land overlooking the broad valley of the Tyne about three miles west of Gateshead, and it boasts some pleasant corners as well as fine views. The lion and the unicorn guard the entrance to King George's Field, and beside this recreation ground is a delightful 13-acre park, The Chase, with fine trees and lawns and flower beds.

Standing back from the main street, above the large open space called Church Green, is the ancient house of prayer. It was restored in 1862 by Anthony Salvin but still retains some Norman work, as well as a low 13th century tower. The porch has a sundial dated 1651, and let into its west wall are two big fragments of mediaeval tombstones, each with a finely carved cross.

The interior is unusual, for it has two 19th century arcades on the north, and a Transitional south arcade with four round arches on round pillars. The dignified chancel arch with cushion capitals is Norman work, and another legacy from the church's early years is the round font. In the sanctuary are two 17th century armchairs of plain black oak.

Two memorials pay tribute to a parson and organist who between them gave 120 years of devoted service to this church. One is a brass (near the organ) commemorating William Willis, who entered into rest in July 1924, having served here as "organist and rector's warden for upwards of 70 years". The other is a marble inscription (in the chancel) to his friend Henry Byne Carr, rector of this parish for 50 years, 1846–96; it reads:

Under him and largely through his devoted work and liberality this old parish church was restored, churches built at Marley Hill and Dunston, and lastly at Swalwell; the church green saved to the village, the church schools restored and maintained, and anxious times of cholera and destitution overcome.

Canon Carr's predecessor here was Henry George Liddell, grandfather of the little girls for whom Lewis Carroll wrote *Alice in Wonderland.*

In the churchyard are two other memorials of particular interest. One is a canopied statue of a sturdy bearded man with his right elbow resting on a pillar, and an inscription recording that *in this sacred spot commanding a full view of that noble river, the well-loved scene of former triumphs, rest the mortal remains of Henry (Harry) Clasper, the accomplished oarsman and boatbuilder, of Derwenthaugh, who died July 12th 1870 aged 58.*

The other monument, a stone cross at the west end of the churchyard, commemorates one who was more widely known. It was set up in memory of William Shield, musician and composer, who was born at neighbouring Swalwell in 1748 and was buried in Westminster Abbey in 1829. He was the son of a local boatbuilder, and while apprenticed at his father's trade used to play the violin at evening concerts. When his apprenticeship was ended he decided to make music his profession and became leader of the Spa Orchestra at Scarborough through the influence of his actor friend John Cunningham, some of whose poems he set to music. At the request of the Bishop of Durham he provided a composition for the consecration of St John's Church at Sunderland in 1769.

For 18 years William Shield was first viola at the Italian Opera in London, and was also composer to Covent Garden Theatre. When Haydn visited London, in 1791, he was constantly in his company and he never tired of telling people that he had learned more in four days from the Austrian composer than he had ever learned elsewhere in four years. In 1817 he became Master of the King's Musick.

Stretching along the right bank of the Derwent about two miles south-west of Whickham is **Gibside**, once one of the most splendid estates in the North of England, and still beautiful, though the days of its glory are departed.

The house was built by William Blakiston early in the 17th century, but 100 years later the property came by marriage to the wealthy Bowes family of Streatlam, and it was George Bowes, MP, who laid out the grounds and made Gibside a show place.

In 1767 George Bowes's only daughter, Mary, married John Lyon, ninth Earl of Strathmore, thus founding the famous Bowes-Lyon family to which Her Majesty the Queen Mother belongs. Nine years later the Earl died suddenly and his widow married a notorious adventurer, Andrew Robinson Stoney, who, having dissipated much of her fortune, was imprisoned for threatening her life.

In 1806 the front of the Jacobean mansion was rebuilt by the tenth Earl of Strathmore, a grandson of George Bowes, MP, and father of the John Bowes who founded the Bowes Museum at Barnard Castle. But gradually it fell into disuse, and in 1920 it was dismantled, some of the fittings going to Glamis Castle.

Now it is all rather forlorn. The long battlemented front of the house, with its staring glassless windows, is relieved by a projecting porch bearing the royal arms and the date 1625. The dignified stables, the classical ruined orangery, and the banqueting house, all 18th century additions, stand as reminders of the vanished magnificence of yesteryear, as does the Column of British Liberty, the most striking landmark on the estate. This Doric pillar, 140 feet high, which was begun in 1750 and took seven years to build, is surmounted by a symbolic 12-foot statue, carved on the spot by Christopher Richardson of Doncaster.

From this column an avenue of trees with a wide grass terrace runs for nearly a mile to the domed chapel of grey Streatlam stone, a masterpiece by James Paine which was begun in 1760 and remained unfinished for over 40 years. Now it is a National Trust property, and occasional services are held here in a setting which is surely unique in this country.

Built somewhat on the lines of a Greek temple, it has a portico with four round pillars on a balustraded balcony, and fine draped urns perched on the parapet above.

Round-headed windows of plain glass shed light on a strange interior. In the centre, railed off, stands the altar; behind it is an imposing three-decker pulpit with an umbrella-shaped and urn-capped sounding-board; and in the four corners of the chapel are big box pews.

In the circular crypt below the chapel are a dozen niches. In one of them is the coffin of George Bowes, founder of the estate, moved from Whickham Church in 1812. The tenth Earl of Strathmore and his wife, afterwards Lady Hutt, also lie here, but the body of their son John Bowes, together with that of his French wife, was moved to Barnard Castle in 1929.

Whitburn. This is an attractive village on the most pleasant part of the Durham coast, between Sunderland and South Shields, and is graced by a well-kept green with a stately avenue of sycamores.

In a quiet, well-shaded corner is an ancient church with a tall and well-proportioned tower capped by a short lead-covered spire. It is a landmark for mariners.

Though much restored in Victorian times, the church still displays its early 13th century origin. Its fine nave arcades, with round pillars and pointed arches, are of this period, and so, too, is the tower arch. Another ancient feature is a curious window known as the Vesica Piscis; it is shaped like a cross-section of a fish, an early Christian symbol. In the 15th century upper stage of the tower are two remarkable pre-Reformation bells with Latin inscriptions and little reliefs of the Madonna and Child and the Martyrdom of St Andrew.

On a panelled altar tomb by the door lies the figure of Michael Mathew, who died in 1689—a corpulent old gentleman wearing a periwig, a neckcloth with square ends, a coat with big buttoned skirts and wide sleeves, rolled breeches, and square-toed shoes with a skull between them. On the sides of the tomb are kneeling figures of two women, with four chubby boys dressed exactly like their father.

Outside the south door is a mediaeval stone coffin which was found during the 19th century restoration of the church; and built into the exterior of the west wall are three mediaeval grave-covers with floriated crosses. Against the wall is the big gravestone of rector Thomas Baker, who died in 1866 after ministering here for nearly 56 years.

Whitworth. It is a quiet place, only a mile or so from the busy industrial town of Spennymoor, which lies halfway between Bishop Auckland and Durham. On coal and iron was Spennymoor founded; that was in the middle of the 19th century: today its mines and foundries have been replaced by modern factories for a wide range of electrical and engineering industries.

Whitworth, by contrast, has its roots in Norman England, the manor being mentioned in the Boldon Book of 1183.

Whitworth Hall was rebuilt last century, but for more than 300 years it has been the home of the Shafto family, and one of its proudest possessions is a Reynolds portrait of the handsome, yellow-haired Robert Shafto, man of fashion and MP for County Durham, who died in 1797. His name lives in the famous north-country ballad of unrequited love:

> *Bobby Shafto's gone to sea,*
> *Silver buckles on his knee;*
> *He'll come back and marry me,*
> *Bonnie Bobby Shafto.*

The tune is a traditional air of the Northumbrian bagpipes, and was originally called *Brave Willy Forster*. It was elaborated into *Bobby Shafto* by Peacock about the year 1800.

Whitworth Church, originally Norman but completely rebuilt in the 19th century, stands in the grounds of the Hall, surrounded by lofty trees. A notable possession is the fine 17th century oak armchair in the chancel, with a carving of a man's head peeping from foliage on the back. On the south side of the nave are three windows commemorating Catherine Duncombe Shafto, who died in 1872 at the age of 101 and was buried in the family vault in the churchyard.

A curious feature to be seen in the churchyard is the modern stone bench against the west wall of the church. On the bench, protected by a modern canopy, lie two 13th century stone effigies. One is a figure of a cross-legged knight in armour, with a big shield on his left arm and a sword in his right hand; his feet rest on a writhing human figure, with a hound lying near the left leg. The figure is thought to represent Thomas de Acle, who died about 1290, and the figure of the lady in loose gown and cloak beside him is presumably a memorial of his wife.

Near the south wall of the church is a headstone with three sleeping cherubs carved above an hourglass and crossbones, symbols of mortality. It marks the grave of three young brothers, sons of John Wilkinson of Old Park, who all died within a month of each other in 1727.

A distinguished 19th century vicar of Whitworth was Robert Gray, who in 1847 became the first Bishop of Cape Town and was later Metropolitan of South Africa.

Winston. An attractive little village on a hill overlooking the Tees, it has a fine stone bridge which was built in 1763 to facilitate the carrying of coal from County Durham into Yorkshire. Its single arch, spanning 37 yards and said to have been the longest single span in Europe at that time, withstood the terrible Tees flood of 1771.

The bridge forms a feature of the magnificent view from the churchyard, where the river can be heard roaring over rocks at the bottom of the richly-wooded valley.

The church has a little 19th century turret with a conspicuous spire, but much of the building dates from the 13th century, and the walls of the broad chancel contain Roman stones from the fort at Piercebridge. In the porch is part of the head of a Saxon cross carved with a pellet pattern and a little praying figure.

A well-preserved relic is the font—dating from about 1300—with a pair of fighting dragons carved on its bowl. (There are also dragons carved on the ends of the old choir-stalls.) By the font rests a worn 13th century grave-cover with birds perching on a floral cross.

One of the boys baptised at this font in 1750 grew up to win a measure of fame as a map-maker. His name was Aaron Arrowsmith. He learned mathematics from William Emerson, the eccentric genius of Hurworth, and then, having been robbed of his inheritance by his stepfather, set off for London at the age of 20. A man of astonishing industry, he made many fine large-scale maps of various parts of the world, including work for the East India and Hudson's Bay companies. He died in London in 1823.

Witton Gilbert. This village on the main road from Durham to Lanchester has a little Norman church at the end of a lane. It dates from about 1150, and although rebuilt in 1863 still displays some of the original work. In the south walls are two round-headed windows and a blocked Norman doorway; the tall chancel arch contains the original Norman stones, and the plain old font still stands on its massive Norman base.

Built into the wall over the west window of the north aisle is a much weathered carving of a hand raised in blessing; it is thought to have been one of the arms of the churchyard cross. On the south wall of the sanctuary is a marble inscription to Richard Richardson, who preached from this church's panelled Jacobean pulpit every Sunday for 59 years—from 1780 until his death in 1839.

North of the church is a farmhouse, Witton Hall, which contains fragments of a little leper hospital founded about the same time as the church. High up in a wall are the tops of two lancet windows.

From the churchyard there is a pleasant view down the Browney valley towards the scant remains of Bearpark, summer retreat of the priors of Durham from the 13th century to the Reformation; beyond rise the towers of Durham Cathedral.

Half-hidden by the trees on the side of Coalpark Gill, just over a mile north-west of Witton Gilbert, are the lofty ruins of Langley Old Hall, an early Tudor mansion built by Henry Scrope, seventh Baron of Bolton. The buildings once stood foursquare round a courtyard, but only fragments of the east and west wings remain. The east wing consists of the ruins of the great hall; the west wing is represented by two ruined walls with empty doorways, glassless windows, and traces of a newel stair high up at the corner. Beside the west wing is a length of the moat (now usually dry) which guarded the house in the days of its splendour.

Witton le Wear. It is pleasantly situated on a wooded hill above the Wear, and from its graceful two-arched bridge, built after the flood of 1778, there is a fine view of Witton Castle across the river; the battlemented walls and turrets of grey stone rise majestically among the trees in the lovely park.

Originally a manor house, Witton Castle was fortified by Sir Ralph Eure as long ago as 1410, and despite all the changes wrought through the centuries it still keeps its mediaeval aspect. The chief features are an ancient keep and a big, square courtyard with two fortified gateways and three angle towers.

The interior of the castle displays a wealth of fine furniture and paintings; among several portraits of members of the Lambton family, the most notable is Sir Thomas Lawrence's famous picture of the first Earl of Durham's only son, *The Red Boy*.

Standing on the bank above the village green is a church which dates from Norman days but has been almost completely rebuilt. Its oldest feature is an arcade with three pointed arches on round pillars; this contains the original masonry, replaced stone by stone.

Among other relics preserved from the earlier building are a 17th century helm over the vestry door, a carved 17th century chair in the north aisle, and two mediaeval gravestones built into the walls of the porch. On the south wall of the nave is a white marble monument to John Farrer, who died in 1808 after long and devoted service in this village as parson and schoolmaster, callings symbolised by the shepherd's crook and cane carved above the inscription.

On the south side of the sanctuary is a window with figures of St Peter and St Paul commemorating James Hodgson, vicar here from 1878 to 1921. Below are two smaller panels showing the white-haired vicar and his wife Ann kneeling in prayer, and, in the background, his church before it was rebuilt.

On the south side of the churchyard is the shaft of an ancient cross, capped by a sundial.

Wolsingham. A small but busy steel-manufacturing town, it stands at the junction of the Wear and the Waskerley Beck. A big iron bridge of 1893 is astride the river, and two single-arched stone bridges of the early 19th century span the beck.

Two miles up the beck in a delightful setting is Tunstall Reservoir: it is a mile long, covers 60 acres, and holds 520 million gallons of water. Lower down the beck is a farm called Baal Hill House, which in earlier times was the lodge of the local bailiff of the bishops of Durham; it has a barrel-vaulted basement which was part of a pele tower.

As the beck enters the town it passes a field, called Chapel Walls, containing grassy banks marking the site of the bishops' hunting lodge which was destroyed by the Scots in 1316; and also, possibly, of a hermitage of Saint Godric, the founder of Finchale Priory, near Durham.

On a bank above the road to Lanchester is Redgate Cross, reached by a flight of stone steps. The inscription tells a tale of the bad old days of religious intolerance:

Near this spot Venerable John Duckett was arrested. He was afterwards tried at Sunderland and taken to Tyburn where he was executed for being a priest Sep. 7th 1644.

From this fine viewpoint the visitor can look down on the little town, spread out below with the river winding its way through. Mile upon mile of Weardale can be seen from here in a great panorama which stretches away until the trees and the fields are lost in the bare brown expanse of distant hills.

Wolsingham's church was almost completely rebuilt in the middle of the 19th century, but the tall, heavily-buttressed tower has retained its Norman lowest stage, and two hideous old corbel heads adorn its modern arch. In the sanctuary are two old armchairs of carved oak. A white marble monument in the north aisle pays tribute to Peter Ionn, who died in 1821 having served as curate and master of the grammar school for 38 years. It was set up by his scholars and records their *grateful remembrance of his care in teaching them the principles of useful knowledge, and in training them up in the paths of religion and virtue.* Above the inscription is a relief showing a pile of school books, a globe, and some quill pens.

APPENDIX

Places of interest open to the public

(* Indicates National Trust Property)
(† Indicates property in care of the Ministry of Public Buildings and Works)

Barnard Castle: The Bowes Museum
Bishop Auckland: Auckland Castle Deer House
Durham: Durham Castle
Finchale Priory: †Finchale Priory
Gibside: *Gibside Chapel
Staindrop: Raby Castle
Sunderland: †Hylton Castle
Washington: *Washington Old Hall
Witton-le-Wear: Witton Castle

DURHAM TOWNS AND VILLAGES

In this key to our map of County Durham are all the towns and villages treated in this book.

Stockton - Billingham
LIBRARY
Technical College